American Poetry
and
Japanese Culture

American Poetry
and
Japanese Culture

American Poetry
and
Japanese Culture

Sanehide Kodama

ARCHON BOOKS
1984

This publication has been supported by the national endowment
for the humanities.

*The paper in this book meets the guidelines for performance and
durability of the Committee on Production Guidelines for Book
Longevity of the Council on Library Resources.*

Library of Congress Cataloging in Publication Data

Kodama, Sanehide, 1932–
American poetry and Japanese culture.

Bibliography: p.
Includes index.
1. American poetry—Japanese influences. 2. Japan in
literature. 3. United States—Relations—Japan.
4. Japan—Relations—United States. 5. American poetry—
History and criticism. 6. Japan—Civilization. I. Title.
PS159.J3K6 1984   811'.009'3252   84-10966
ISBN 0-208-02030-6

Contents

Acknowledgments

Grateful acknowledgment is made to the following for permission to reprint material.

The Beinecke Rare Book and Manuscript Library, Yale University, for Ernest Fenollosa manuscript material in the Collection of American Literature: "Saibi," "To Kinryo Ho-odai," "Chokanko," "Kojo-gin," and "Jiju Gishun-en"; and the manuscript material of Richard Wright's twenty haiku: "Standing in the field," "With a twitching nose," "The dog's violent sneeze," "An empty sickbed," "I would like a bell," "From across the lake," "The spring lingers on," "A freezing morning," "A soft wind at dawn," "A leaf chases," "Having appointed," "In the afterglow," "Enough of dawn," "Coming from the woods," "I am nobody," "The crow flew so fast," "Out of winter mist," "A sick cat," "Glittering with frost," and "Keep straight down." Reprinted by permission.

Jack Cain for "empty elevator" from *The Haiku Anthology*, ed. Cor van den Heuvel. Copyright © 1974 by Anchor Press / Doubleday. Reprinted by permission.

City Lights Books for selections from *Howl and Other Poems* by Allen Ginsberg. Copyright © 1956, 1959 by Allen Ginsberg. Reprinted by permission of City Lights Books.

Copper Canyon Press for selections from *The Silver Swan* by Kenneth Rexroth. Copyright © 1976 by Kenneth Rexroth. Reprinted by permission.

Bernard Lionel Einbond for "the white of her neck" from *The Coming Indoors and Other Poems* by Bernard Lionel Einbond. Copyright © 1979 by Charles E. Tuttle Company. Reprinted by permission.

Faber and Faber, Ltd. for two excerpts from *After Strange Gods: A Primer of Modern Heresy* by T. S. Eliot. Copyright © 1934 by T. S. Eliot; excerpts from "The Waste Land" from *Collected Poems 1909–1962* by T. S. Eliot; selections from *Personae (1926)* by Ezra Pound. Copyright © 1926 by Ezra Pound. Used by permission of New Directions Publishing Corp. and Faber and Faber, Ltd.; selections from *The Cantos of Ezra Pound*. Copyright © 1934 by Ezra Pound. Reprinted by permission of New Directions Publishing Corp. and Faber and Faber, Ltd.; selections from *Letters of Ezra Pound*, ed. D. D. Paige. Copyright © 1934 by Ezra Pound. Reprinted by permission of New Directions Publishing Corp. and Faber and Faber, Ltd.; selections from *Literary Essays of Ezra Pound*, ed. T. S. Eliot. Copyright © 1935 by Ezra Pound. Reprinted by permission of New Directions Publishing Corp. and Faber and Faber, Ltd.; selections from Ezra Pound's *Selected Prose, 1909–1965*, ed. William Cookson. Copyright © 1973 by the Estate of Ezra Pound. Reprinted by permission of New Directions Publishing Corp. and Faber and Faber, Ltd.; selections from *Gaudier-Bzreska: A Memoir* by Ezra Pound. Copyright © 1970 by the Estate of Ezra Pound. Reprinted by permission of New Directions Publishing Corp. and Faber and Faber, Ltd.

Larry Gates for "At the river bend" from *The Haiku Anthology*, ed. Cor van den Heuvel. Copyright © 1974 by Anchor Press / Doubleday. Reprinted by permission.

Grey Fox Press for "Grain elevators" by Albert Saijo; "Lonely grain elevators" by Lew Welch; and "Grain elevators" by Jack Kerouac, from *Trip Trap: Haiku along the Road from San Francisco to New York, 1959* by Jack Kerouac, Albert Saijo, and Lew Welch. Copyright © 1973. Reprinted by permission.

Grove Press, Inc. for "My Mother's Ghost" and "On the Fifteenth Floor" by Allen Ginsberg from *Journals: Early Fifties and Early Sixties*, ed. Gordon Ball. Copyright © 1977 by Allen Ginsberg. Reprinted by permission.

J. W. Hacket for "time after time" from *The Zen Haiku and Other Zen Poems of J. W. Hacket*. Copyright © 1983 by Japan Publications, Inc. (Distribution in USA by Kodansha International / Harper and Row, New York). Reprinted by permission.

Harcourt Brace Jovanovich for "Window" from *Chicago Poems* by Carl Sandburg. Copyright © 1916 by Holt, Rinehart, and Winston, Inc; renewed 1944 by Carl Sandburg; "Fog" from *Chicago Poems* by Carl Sandburg. Copyright © 1916 by Holt, Rinehart, and Winston,

Inc; renewed 1944 by Carl Sandburg; excerpts from "The Waste Land" from *Collected Poems, 1909–1962* by T. S. Eliot. Copyright © 1936 by Harcourt Brace Jovanovich; renewed 1963, 1964 by T. S. Eliot. Reprinted by permission.

Harper and Row, Publishers, Inc. for eleven haikus from *The Richard Wright Reader*, ed. Ellen Wright and Michel Fabre. Copyright © 1978 by Ellen Wright and Michel Fabre. Reprinted by permission of Harper and Row, Publishers, Inc.

Houghton Library, Harvard University for excerpts of letters of Hilda Doolittle, Charles A. Longfellow, Henry Wadsworth Longfellow, Amy Lowell, and Percival Lowell. Reprinted by permission.

Houghton Mifflin Co. for excerpts from *The Complete Poetical Works of Amy Lowell* by Amy Lowell. Copyright © 1955 by Houghton Mifflin Co. Reprinted by permission.

Scott Johnson for copies of Gary Snyder's letters. Used by permission. Etheridge Knight for "In the August Grass" from *The Norton Anthology of Modern Poetry*, ed. Richard Ellman and Robert O'Clair. Copyright © 1973 by W. W. Norton and Co. Reprinted by permission.

Alfred A. Knopf, Inc. for two lines of "Thirteen Ways of Looking at a Blackbird" from *The Collected Poems of Wallace Stevens* by Wallace Stevens. Copyright © 1954 by Alfred A. Knopf, Inc. Reprinted by permission.

Little, Brown and Co. for excerpts from *Franny and Zooey* by Jerome David Salinger. Copyright © 1961 by J. D. Salinger. Reprinted by permission.

Michael McClintock for "Glimmering morning," "the first melt," and "Dead Cat" from *The Haiku Anthology*, ed. Cor van den Heuval. Copyright © 1974 by Anchor Press / Doubleday. Reprinted by permission.

Bradford Morrow for selections from *The Phoenix and the Tortoise, One Hundred Poems from the Japanese, Beyond the Mountains, The Heart's Garden / Garden's Heart, The Collected Shorter Poems of Kenneth Rexroth, One Hundred More Poems from the Japanese, New Poems, On Flower Wreath Hill,* and *Morning Star.* Copyright © 1951, 1964, 1966, 1968, 1974, 1976, and 1979 by Kenneth Rexroth. Used by permission of Bradford Morrow for The Kenneth Rexroth Trust.

National Park Service, Longfellow National Historic Sites for excerpts from manuscript letters of Charles A. Longfellow and photograph of a room in Longfellow's house. Used by permission.

New Directions Publishing Corp. for "Oread" by Hilda Doolittle from *Collected Poems 1925*. Copyright © 1925, 1953 by Norman Holmes Pearson; selections from *Personae (1926)* by Ezra Pound. Copyright © 1926 by Ezra Pound. Used by permission of New Directions Publishing Corp. and Faber and Faber, Ltd.; selections from *The Cantos of Ezra Pound*. Copyright © 1934 by Ezra Pound. Used by permission of New Directions Publishing Corp. and Faber and Faber, Ltd.; selections from *Letters of Ezra Pound*, ed. D. D. Paige. Copyright © 1934 by Ezra Pound. Used by permission of New Directions Publishing Corp. and Faber and Faber, Ltd.; selections from *Literary Essays of Ezra Pound*, ed. T. S. Eliot. Copyright © 1935 by Ezra Pound. Used by permission of New Directions Publishing Corp. and Faber and Faber, Ltd.; selections from Ezra Pound's *Selected Prose, 1909–1965*, ed. William Cookson. Copyright © 1973 by the Estate of Ezra Pound. Used by permission of New Directions Publishing Corp. and Faber and Faber, Ltd.; selections from *The Classical Noh Theater of Japan* by Ernest Fenollosa and Ezra Pound. Copyright © 1959 by New Directions Publishing Corp.; interviews in *New Directions 17*. Copyright © 1957 by New Directions Publishing Corp.; selections from *Gaudier-Brzeskia: A Memoir* by Ezra Pound. Copyright © 1970 by the Estate of Ezra Pound. Used by permission of New Directions Publishing Corp. and Faber and Faber, Ltd.; selections from *Collected Longer Poems of Kenneth Rexroth* by Kenneth Rexroth. Copyright © 1944 by Kenneth Rexroth; selections from *The Morning Star* by Kenneth Rexroth. Copyright © 1979 by Kenneth Rexroth; selections from *One Hundred More Poems from the Japanese* by Kenneth Rexroth. Copyright © 1974, 1976 by Kenneth Rexroth; selections from *One Hundred Poems from the Japanese* by Kenneth Rexroth. Copyright © 1955 by Kenneth Rexroth; selections from *New Poems* by Kenneth Rexroth. Copyright © 1974 by Kenneth Rexroth; selections from *Beyond the Mountains* by Kenneth Rexroth. Copyright © 1951 by Kenneth Rexroth; selection from "Marriage" by William Carlos Williams from *New Directions 16*. Copyright © 1957 by New Directions Publishing Corp; selections from *Collected Shorter Poems* by Kenneth Rexroth. Copyright © 1940, 1949, 1952, 1962, 1963, 1966 by Kenneth Rexroth; selections from *Regarding Wave* by Gary Snyder. Copyright © 1967, 1968, 1969, and 1970 by Gary Snyder; selections from *Back Country* by Gary Snyder. Copyright © 1957, 1958, 1959, 1960, 1961, 1962, 1963, 1964, 1965, 1966, 1967, and 1968 by Gary Snyder; selections from *Turtle Island* by Gary Snyder. Copyright ©

1969, 1971, 1972, 1973, and 1974 by Gary Snyder. Used by permission.

Marjory Pratt for "Not a breath of air" from *The Haiku Anthology*, ed. Cor van den Heuvel. Copyright © 1974 by Anchor Press / Doubleday. Used by permission.

Gary Snyder for selections from his poems, essays, interviews, and letter. Used by permission.

Robert Spiess for "Bluejays in the pines" from *The Haiku Anthology*, ed. Cor van den Heuvel. Copyright © 1974 by Anchor Press / Doubleday. Used by permission.

State University of New York Press for "Shadow," "The Guarded Wound," "Anguish," "November Night," "Roma Eterna," "Triad," "Moon-Shadow," and "Epigram"; and a selection from "Birth Moment," from *The Complete Poems and Collected Letters of Adelaide Crapsey*, ed. Susan Sutton Smith. Copyright © 1977. Used by permission.

Viking Press for selections from *Writers at Work: The Paris Interviews, Second Series*, ed. George Plimpton. Copyright © 1963 by The Paris Review, Inc. Reprinted by permission of Viking Penguin, Inc.

Nicholas Virgilio for "Deep in rank grass" from *The Haiku Anthology*, ed. Cor van den Heuvel. Copyright © 1974 by Anchor Press / Doubleday. Used by permission.

Richard Wilbur for passages of "Thyme Flowering among Rocks" from *Walking to Sleep: New Poems and Translations* by Richard Wilbur. Copyright © 1971 by Richard Wilbur. Used by permission.

Mrs. Yvor Winters for excerpts from "The Magpie's Shadow" from *Collected Poems of Yvor Winters* by Yvor Winters. Copyright © 1978 by Yvor Winters. Used by permission.

Mrs. Ellen Wright for twenty haiku by Richard Wright from the manuscript material in the Collection of American Literature, Beinecke Rare Books and Manuscript Library, Yale University. Used by permission.

Introduction

In 1860 Walt Whitman wrote "A Broadway Pageant" on the occasion of a New York parade in which American citizens marched with the Japanese "two-sworded" envoys who visited the United States for the ratification of a treaty, and he saw in it the symbolic fusion of East and West. Whitman advised the "Libertad" to "bend your proud neck" to "the nobles of Niphon," for the procession seemed to him to foreshadow the possible influence on America of the East, whose philosophy was, he thought, both fresh and "venerable," inclusive and transcendental, reconciling contradictions; Whitman himself later incorporated these ideas into his idea of "religious democracy."

As Whitman foresaw, recent American poets have shown increasing interest in Japan and its culture. This book traces historically how American poets have encountered Japan and have been inspired by Japanese subjects, forms, attitudes, and values since the time of Whitman and Longfellow, through the period of Pound, Amy Lowell, and the imagists, down to Kenneth Rexroth and Gary Snyder.

Not only poets but also novelists and playwrights in America have been interested in Japan since the middle of the last century, and especially in the present one. The last two are not much discussed here, not because they are unworthy of critical attention, but because the poets have absorbed what they have considered valuable for their art from Japan from a more purely aesthetic point of view. They have filtered, transformed, and assimilated what they thought was the best into their art, and by so doing they have enriched their own cultural tradition. Though Japan observed by American poets may not represent the whole image of Japan in America, it certainly represents the best part of it.

In 1877 Henry Wadsworth Longfellow wrote about the Imari

pottery and the subtle Japanese beauty of its design in his "Keramos." His son Charles had been in Japan, sending him letters and packages of curios. Longellow tried to "reproduce" in his poem various Japanese images, and, inspired by these "counterparts" of natural objects in Japan, he was led to meditate upon the aesthetic relation of his "art" to "nature."

In the midst of the vogue of Japonisme in the early twentieth century, Ezra Pound wrote some "*hokku*-like poems," such as "In a Station of the Metro." Amy Lowell wrote a number of short imagistic poems like Pound's, and so did John Gould Fletcher, Richard Aldington, H. D., and other imagist poets. They were all influenced by haiku and Pound's "theory of superposition." Another less-known but important "unconscious imagist" poet, Adelaide Crapsey, wrote a number of jewel-like five-line poems which she called the "cinquains." She had been inspired by the French translations of the Japanese *tanka*, which also comprises five lines.

Luckier still than other imagists was Ezra Pound, who obtained Ernest Fenollosa's manuscript notebooks containing rough English translations of Nō plays and Chinese poetry as well as essays on Chinese ideograms. Pound "retranslated" from the notebook, for instance, a Chinese poem by Rihaku, "The River-Merchant's Wife: A Letter." But the portrait of the young, tender, and innocent river-merchant's wife is more like the image of an idealized Japanese woman of American Japonisme than a T'ang period Chinese woman.

The whole legacy of the imagist movement would have been a skeleton of poetic theories if the imagists had worked without the knowledge of Japanese haiku, tanka, and ukiyoe. Imagist poetry depended much on these forms in tone, technique, and imagery. And, thanks to the vogue of Japonisme, the translations of haiku and tanka were more immediately and tangibly appreciated by the imagists, and they could develop their kind of sensibility from what they found in the subtlety and refinement of Japanese culture. It is not too bold to state that the imagist movement itself might not have existed if there had been no vogue of Japonisme around the turn of the century.

Chapter 1 discusses these poets in relation to their historical background. Later, post-World War II poets are also discussed briefly so as to provide an overview of the entire book. In writing the chapter, I am much indebted to Earl Miner's *The Japanese Tradition in British and American Literature*. It deals with a broader subject than this book, including fiction, drama, and fine art in America and Great Britain, and it is certainly a valuable book, giving an overall view. But, with some exceptions, it does not offer much discussion of individual American poets, and it was published in 1958. Since then the beats and others have written much poetry displaying obvious Japanese influence. Research material referred to here has also become available since then.

In Chapter 2 and in the following chapters I consider those American poets most indebted to Japan: Amy Lowell in Chapter 2, Ezra Pound in Chapter 3, Kenneth Rexroth in Chapter 4, and Gary Snyder in Chapter 5. Other poets discussed in the book include Carl Sandburg, T. S. Eliot, Wallace Stevens, Yvor Winters, Richard Wright, Richard Wilbur, and Allen Ginsberg. In these chapters I try to trace the process of absorption and re-creation of Japanese values by the poets in their poems.

Certainly Japanese literature is more indebted to America than American literature is to Japan. Practically all the major American poets, writers, and philosophers have been translated into Japanese. Sōseki Natsume is indebted to Whitman, Poe, and William James, as well as to Shakespeare, Shelley, and Jane Austen. Junzaburo Nishiwaki echoes Pound, Eliot, and other modernists as well as Laforgue, Baudelaire, and Mallarmé. Kenzaburo Ōe owes much to William Faulkner as well as to Franz Kafka and Jean-Paul Sartre. Some remarkable studies of the influence of writing from foreign cultures on Japanese literature recently have been done by Japanese comparatists. But the Japanese influences on foreign literature have not been much investigated either in Japan or abroad.

I chose this subject and dared to write a book in English largely upon the encouragement of two respected American scholars now deceased: the late Prof. C. L. Barber, whose inspiring course in modern American poetry I took while a student at Amherst College, and the late Prof. Norman Holmes Pearson, with whom I worked at Yale University as a visiting fellow. I have been encouraged to write a book on this subject also by some other scholars whom I met in Japan and in the United States; among them are Prof. Sidney Ahlstrohm of Yale University, Prof. Sacvan Bercovitch, Prof. Rikutaro Fukuda, and Prof. Muneharu Kitagaki. I will be delighted if the book pleases some of them as well as others who are interested in the subject.

In preparing the book I consulted the unpublished letters of Amy Lowell, and the books she owned, bequeathed to Harvard University and now catalogued in its Houghton Library; the unpublished letters of Charles A. Longfellow at Longfellow National Historic Site, Cambridge; Ernest Fenollosa's manuscript notebooks at the Beinecke Rare Book and Manuscript Library, Yale University; and the unpublished poems of Richard Wright at the same library. I would like to thank those at these institutions, who have given me permission to publish some quotations from their holdings. I am grateful to the Fulbright Commission, the American Council of Learned Societies, and Doshisha Women's College for financial assistance that enabled me to read these materials. I would like to thank Princess Mary de Rachewiltz, who arranged for me to meet her father, Ezra Pound, in Rapallo, Italy, and Paris, and who gave me the photographic copies of the Japanese manuscript paintings and poems that are the sources of his "Canto 49." I would also like to thank Kenneth Rexroth, who patiently answered many of my questions and gave me suggestions; Mr. Megumi Nakamura, who helped me check reference material; and the late Prof. Kōjiro Yoshikawa, who helped me interpret Chinese poetry. Special thanks must go to Prof. Richard Bedford of Doshisha Women's College, Profs. Toshio Kimura, Nobunao Matsuyama, B. D. Tucker, and Philip Williams of Doshisha University, and Prof. Earl Miner of Princeton University, who kindly read through my typescript and gave me valuable suggestions. But I am of course responsible for whatever errors remain in the book.

The Chinese names are romanized in Chinese sounds, transliterated in Wade system. The Japanese is romanized as in Kenkyūsha's *New Japanese-English Dictionary*. When necessary, the Japanese pronunciation is added to the Chinese sound in parentheses, for instance, Chang-an (Chōan). It is necessary when Fenollosa and Pound transliterate the Chinese in Japanese sound. When the Chinese name romanized in Japanese sound is quoted, the Chinese sound is added to the Japanese sound in brackets, for instance, "Anrokusan [An Lu-shan]."

The Japanese personal names are romanized in two ways. For those who flourished before Meiji Restoration (1868), the family names are written first, and then the given name, as they are written traditionally in Japan. For instance, Matsuo Bashō and Minamoto no Morotada. But for those who enjoyed life after the Restoration, the given names are written before the family names in the Western way. For instance, Sōseki Natsume and Yasunari Kawabata.

Some parts of the following chapters have been published before:

Chapter 1 is based on my lecture, "When American Writers Look at Japan," at the annual meeting of the Comparative Literature Association of Japan, June 9, 1979. The section on *Cathay* in Chapter 3 was published in *Paideuma*, vol. 11, no. 2 (Fall 1982), originally written in Japanese. The section on "The Seven Lakes Canto" in the same chapter appeared in *Paideuma*, vol. 6, no. 2 (Fall 1977), as "The Eight Scenes of Sho-sho." The chapter on Rexroth is the abridged translation of my essay, "Kenneth Rexroth and Classical Japanese Literature," written in Japanese, appearing in *Annual Report of Studies*, vols. 29 and 30 (Doshisha Women's College), and *Asphodel*, no. 20 (English Literature Association of Doshisha Women's College). With some additions, a part of that essay appeared in *For Rexroth: Ark 14* (New York: The Ark, 1980) as "Kenneth Rexroth and Japan: A Homage from the Far East." I take this opportunity to thank the publishers for permitting me to print these portions here. All other parts of the book are published here for the first time.

Recently Japanese economic and technological development has attracted attention of critics of various countries throughout the world. Jean-Jacques Servan-Schreiber wrote in his *Le Defi Mondial* (1980) that Japan has become a remarkable country which the "genie" of the West has created. This "strange" nation, according to him, is "the greatest technological country," at the forefront of technological development. In his *Japan As No. 1* (1979), Ezra Vogel analyzed Japanese forms of human relationships and their peculiar way of collecting information, and added to the book the subtitle "Lessons for America." (The book is actually more filled with lessons for Japan.) But the point I would like to make is that, though the economists and engineers may only now be looking for models in Japan, the American poets have been absorbing Japanese values for a long time. I will be delighted if this book interests those people who are concerned with the total relationship between the United States and Japan.

I

General Observations

Historical Background

Some Americans knew about Japan from very early times. Before the Revolutionary War, the majority of Americans accepted their status as English subjects, and therefore assumed quite naturally that English history and culture were a part of their own.[1] The knowledge of the Far East that the English and other European people had, however limited it might have been, was also shared with Americans.

Through Marco Polo and other travelers to the Orient, through St. Francis Xavier and other Spanish missionaries, through Captain John Saris, and William Adams and Richard Cocks of the East India Company in Japan, and later through Dutch merchants and sailors, some information on Japan reached the British Isles,[2] accumulating steadily if in fragments. According to Saburō Minagawa, fifteen Japanese men were in London in 1613.[3] One of the non-conformist groups of Puritans, who stayed in Amsterdam and Leyden for twelve years before sailing on the *Mayflower* in 1620, had contacts with British merchants and Dutch voyagers who "made them faire offers aboute going with them."[4] It is hard to imagine that they did not hear anything about Japan there, at least indirectly, through the Dutch sailors returning from the Far East. The early settlers in Massachusetts Bay Colony seem to have shared the myth about "the riches" of the East, as is evident from a reference in Anne Bradstreet's poem "To My Dear and Loving Husband."

> I prize thy love more than whole mines of gold,
> Or all the riches that the East doth hold.

It may show that "the Tenth Muse" and her contemporary colonists might also have shared the widespread legend about Japan being filled with gold, which originated from Marco Polo's account on "Zipangu" where, as he describes it, "they have gold in greatest abundance."[5]

Those who went to America later also must have been interested in voyaging, and some of them read Richard Hakluyt and Samuel Purchas's *Hakluytus Posthumus, or Purchas His Pilgrimes* (1625), containing more realistic narratives of voyages to China and Japan. They might have read Engelbert Kaempfer's *The History of Japan*, which was published in London in 1727. But more popular was *Gulliver's Travels*, published a year before, in which Jonathan Swift, with knowledge derived from William Adams and William Dampier (1652–1725), as well as from Kaempfer, sent his protagonist to "Yedo" and "Nangasac" in Japan toward the end of his third voyage.[6] We may say quite safely that some Americans knew of Japan even before they went to America. But all of their knowledge of the East came indirectly, through the European continent and England, reaching them, as it were, westbound.

Soon after the Revolutionary War, American shipowners began trading with China, using remodeled privateering boats and later clippers, some of them sailing around Cape Horn.[7] In this way Americans began to acquire a first-hand knowledge of the Far East. They were to rediscover Japan from the opposite side of the globe, the information reaching them, as it were, eastbound.

The first American vessels visited Japan in 1791, sixty-two years before the Perry expedition. On their way back from China to the States, with iron, copper, and skins on board, the *Lady Washington* and the *Grace* dropped in at Kashinoura of Ōshima at the southern tip of Kii Peninsula "under stress of wind and wave."[8] Captain John Kendrick of the former ship tried to get in touch with the Japanese. When the news reached the local government that "the Red Hairs from a land called America" were there with huge ships, some samurai were dispatched to drive them off. But by the time they arrived at the shore, the ships were gone, having been supplied with fuel and fresh water.[9]

With the discovery of profitable whaling waters near Japan, more American boats sailed around the Ogasawara Islands and even off Rikuchu shores, via Honolulu as well as by way of the North Pacific route. A whaling boat at that time might kill about 500 whales during a year's cruise. But such boats also saved many lives of shipwrecked Japanese sailors and fishermen. In 1813, Junkichi of Owari and two other sailors were shipwrecked, and were rescued by an English ship near California after fifteen months on the Pacific. In 1832, when Otokichi, Kyukichi, and Iwakichi drifted on the *Hojunmaru* from Owari into the Pacific, they arrived at the Oregon coast fourteen months later without encountering an American boat on the sea.[10] During the 1840s more American whaling ships sailed in Japanese waters and saved Japanese lives. When Denzo of Nishihama and four other fishermen of Tosa were shipwrecked and living in a cave on Torishima in 1841, they were discovered and rescued by the *John Howland*, an American whaler, and brought to Hawaii. Among them was Manjiro of Nakahama, later known as "John Mung," who then was taken to Captain William Whitfield's home at Fairhaven, Massachusetts, to be educated.[11]

In the same year, Herman Melville was on the Pacific, on board the *Acushnet*.[12] Ten years later he published his *Moby-Dick* (1851), describing the Japanese islands floating like Milky Ways on "this serene Pacific."

> It [the Pacific] rolls the mid-most waters of the world the Indian Ocean and Atlantic being but its arms. The same waves wash the moles of the new-built Californian towns, but yesterday planted by the recentest race of men, and lave the faded but still gorgeous skirts of Asiatic lands, older than Abraham; while all between float Milky-Ways of coral isles, and low-lying, endless, unknown Archipelagoes, and impenetrable Japans. (Chapter 111)

Beautiful views of Japanese coastlines probably were witnessed from many American ships at the time. After 1814 and the Treaty of Ghent, the abolition of privateering and the general disappearance of pirates made it possible for American ships to sail around the world more safely, visiting the mountainous islands of Japan.[13] But Japan was also a dangerous and "impenetrable" country; if any foreigner except a Dutchman landed there, he was supposed to be sentenced to death. The shipwrecked Americans who drifted to the Japanese shores, however, were usually questioned, tried, and sent to Nagasaki by *kago* (palanquins, the best vehicles of transportation then). They then sailed to the South Seas on Dutch boats, and could return eventually to the United States. But strangely, a little before Perry, some American ships were semi-officially chartered by the Dutch and were permitted to sail for trade into Nagasaki harbor with Dutch flags on their masts. Thus the

Americans had a greater opportunity to know Japan than did either the British or the French; they were able to press Japan to open its ports to them, and to treat the shipwrecked better.

After several attempts, the United States government finally "determined to send the *Mississippi* and *Susquehannah* and several frigates and sloops-of-war" to Japan. On January 28, 1852, a Mr. Giddings spoke in Congress:

> The reason for the uncommon energy displayed at our Navy Yards is that our government thinks it proper to send a large force to Japan, to back up our demands on the Emperor for the return of our seamen, and perhaps for the opening of more of his ports for our commerce. Last July, the Sasquehannah [*sic*], a steam frigate, was sent out to Japan, with Commodore Aulick, who bore a letter to the Emperor from our President Fillmore, proposing amity and Commerce, and to send back, at our expense, the Japanese seamen who were rescued from shipwreck by our vessels. . . .

The talk was "attentively listened to in the House," according to the *New York Times* reporter. On April 12, 1852, "sundry documents relating to the Japanese expedition were sent in to the Senate," among which was the letter of President Millard Fillmore to the emperor of Japan. The *New York Times* gives "an interesting extract from the letter."

> I send you by this letter an envoy of my own appointment, an officer of high rank in his country, who is no missionary of religion. He goes by my command to bear to you my greeting and good wishes, and to promote friendship and commerce between the two countries.
>
> You know that the United States of America now extend from sea to sea; that the great countries of Oregon and California are parts of the United States; and that from these countries, which are rich in gold and silver and precious stones, our steamers can reach the shores of your happy land in less than twenty days.
>
> Many of our ships will now pass in every year, and perhaps in every week between California and China; these ships must pass along the coast of your Empire: storms and winds may

cause them to be wrecked on your shores, and we ask and expect from your friendship and your greatness, kindness for our men and protection for our property. We wish that our people may be permitted to trade with your people, but we shall not authorize to break any law of your Empire....[14]

What followed is well known: Commodore Perry's visit to Uraga in 1853 with the "black ships," followed by negotiations between Townsend Harris and Inoue Shinano no Kami and Iwase Higo no Kami, and the voyage of the Japanese envoys to the United States for ratification of the treaty in 1860.

Whitman, Longfellow, and Japan

When Chief Ambassador Shimmi Buzen no Kami and seventy-six members of the embassy[15] of "two-sworded" samurai arrived in San Francisco on March 29, 1860, the American people were ready to welcome them. Though this was a little before the Pony Express, the news spread quickly. Wherever they went—Panama, Washington, D.C., Philadelphia and New York—the newspapers wrote about them. The Japanese envoys were surprised at "teregarafu" (telegraph), twenty-one gun salutes, "burikki" (tin) roofs, "four or five storied brick" buildings, and the sudden visit of the mayor of San Francisco. One of the envoys wrote in his diary: "Mayor is the highest official of this city, but he visited us without a guide, without notice. It shows his friendliness but he lacks politeness."[16]

The U.S. government and the larger cities accommodated the envoys at their best hotels and held parties for them. People crowded around the hotels for their name cards, which the Japanese samurai wrote for them with *fude*, and for the coins with square holes that they tossed from the hotel windows. When they finally arrived in New York by boat from South Amboy, N.J., and paraded in barouches in Manhattan with eight thousand American soldiers on June 16, 1860, several hundred thousand people watched them. All the windows and rooftops on the streets were crowded with people. "The sidewalks were literally packed," according to a member of the embassy, and people "were sticking out thousands of Japanese and American flags from the windows."[17] According to another account," people crowded like clouds and haze."[18] According to a New York newspaper, one

Japanese in the procession "tied a handkerchief to the end of a stick, and gaily waved it to the ladies in return for their civilities." Some lay back "in their barouches and smoked."[19]

Among the crowd was Walt Whitman. He seems to have been observing the procession more soberly. He sent his poem on the event to the *New York Times*, which published it on June 27, 1860, with the title "The Errand Bearers." The poem later was included in the *Leaves of Grass* as "A Broadway Pageant."

> Over the Western sea hither from Niphon come,
> Courteous, the swart-cheek'd two-sworded envoys,
> Leaning back in their open barouches, bare-headed,
>   impassive,
> Ride to-day through Manhattan.

The term "Niphon," though often used in the newspapers of the day, is the corrupted form of "Nippon" or "Nihon," which means "Japan" in Japanese. "Two-sworded" means wearing two swords, one short and another long, on the left waist, as symbols of the samurai class in the Edo period. "Bare-headed" indicates *sakayaki*, the fashionable hairstyle of Japanese men from the sixteenth century till the Haircut Act (1871) at the Meiji Restoration: shaving the front hair above the forehead and tying the rest near the top of the head. They were "impassive" because the samurai, especially the high-ranking officers, assumed that it was vulgar to express their emotion on their faces. They must have looked sober. Whitman begins the poem rather excitedly, but it is a tone used for disguise. Soon he soberly suggests he saw something important in the occasion, that the procession they were watching was not a circus.

> Libertad! I do not know whether others behold
>   what I behold,
> In the procession along with the nobles of
>   Niphon, the errand-bearers.

What he "beheld" in the procession becomes clearer in the second and third sections of the poem, in which appear the kaleidoscopic images of "Polynesia," "brahmin," "Assyria," "the Hebrews," "the Altay mountains," "China," and "England." "Geography, the world," he exclaims, "is in it [i.e., in the parade]."

> The ring is circled, the journey is done,
> The box-lid is but perceptibly open'd nevertheless the
>   perfume pours copiously out of the whole box.

What Whitman beheld in the pageant was the encounter of the West with the East before people's eyes in America, and "bright" and "fragrant" prospects for cosmic fraternity and unity. What he beheld was exactly what he had prophesied in his earlier poems, the excited tone reflecting his joy in the discovery.

But in the pageant Whitman also "beheld" something more than the prospect of closer physical and spiritual contacts between East and West. To him, the Japanese envoys were also the "messengers" of the Eastern philosophies that had fascinated him. He felt that the Eastern philosophies, radically different from the rationalism of the previous century, would make the Americans realize the necessity of facing space, the "kosmos," which would enable them to see the transcendental nature of man in the vast and harmoniously ordered system of the universe. Like Emerson and Thoreau, who had been familiar with the *Bhagavad-Gita* (in Charles Wilkins' translation), Whitman also thought the Oriental ideas were, in that sense, the source of inspiration.

> The Originatress comes,
> The nest of languages, the bequeather of poems,
>   the race of eld,
> Florid with blood, pensive, rapt with musings,
>   hot with passion, . . .
> The race of Brahma comes.

Therefore, the Americans would have to bend their necks to "the venerable Asia."

> Young Libertad! With the venerable Asia, the all-mother,
> Be considerate with her now. . . .
> Bend your proud neck to the long off mother now sending
>   messages over the archipelagoes to you,
> Bend your proud neck low for once, young Libertad.

In the same manner and in the same spirit, Whitman celebrated the opening of the Suez Canal and the completion of the transcontinental railroad, both in 1869, in his "Passage to India." In contrast to Emily

Dickinson, who took an ambivalent attitude to the "docile and omnipotent" locomotive intruding into her quiet world of Amherst when she saw it "lap the Miles," Whitman welcomed the "Fierce-throated Beauty" which was now "tying the Eastern to the Western sea." He praised also the "procession of steamships" through the Suez Canal, which, with the Atlantic cable and the trans-continental railroad, would promise further and faster cross-cultural understanding and a harmonious world.

> For purpose vast, man's long probation filled,
> Thou rondure of the world at once accomplish'd.

But to Whitman the trains and ships also should be vehicles to search for unknown truths. Toward the end of the poem, Whitman shows his interest more in the voyage of the "soul." "Passage to more than India!" he cries, and like the religious prophet advises the readers to explore the spiritual realms of the universe.

> Sail forth—steer for the deep waters only,
> Reckless O soul, exploring, I with thee, and thou with me,
> For we are bound where mariner has not yet dared to go,
> And we will risk the ship, ourselves and all.

Both "A Broadway Pageant" and "Passage to India" reflect Whitman's optimistic expectation that the West's encounter with the East will bring about cooperation instead of conflict, inspiration instead of logic, and unity instead of fragments. But while Whitman actually saw the Japanese envoys on Broadway, he did not see the last spike driven into the tie at Promontory, Utah, or the Indians coming through the straits along "the level sand" stretching beyond Port Said. His confidence, or trust, in "the marriage of continents" in "Passage to India" is grounded in his transcendentalist belief that "the true son of God [i.e., the true poet] shall absolutely fuse them," but the belief is based on his own experience of having seen the alien people, particularly the Japanese envoys nine years before, enthusiastically welcomed by the Americans.

In his later years, with increasing knowledge of the East's "past"—"the flowing literatures, tremendous epics, religions, castes"—Whitman tended to feel that the Oriental inclusiveness and peace were congenial to his own ideal. He praises the East in his "Specimen Days" and recommends it to the poets of the day as the "womb" bearing the best subject for a poem.

The East—What a subject for a poem! Indeed, wherelse [*sic*] a more pregnant, more splendid one? Where one more idealistic-real, more subtle, more sensuous-delicate? The East, answering all lands, all ages, peoples, touching all senses, here, immediate, now—and so indescribably far off—[20]

The East, including Japan, is to him "realistic-ideal," "immediate" and "far off," "incalculably old" and yet "fresh as a rose." It is the "garden" of reconciliation of contradictions and of transcendental harmony, which is in essence the ideal of his democratic cosmopolitanism. This ideal was attained by his constant concern with the East; and is evident in his addition of "Yedo" to his earlier version of "Salut au Monde!" and his later changing of it to "Tokio" in the 1881 version of his *Leaves of Grass*.

In 1877, Henry Wadsworth Longfellow wrote "Keramos," which dealt with Japanese Imari pottery. One of his motives in composing the poem may have been his growing interest in Japan during the 1870s. His son Charles was sending letters and gifts to his family from Japan between 1871 and 1873. A pair of very large Imari vases is still in the Longfellow House in Cambridge, Mass.

Charles Appleton Longfellow, having roamed about Mexico, Europe, India, and the West, had sent his father a telegram on June 1, 1871, from San Francisco.

HAVE SUDDENLY DECIDED TO SAIL FOR JAPAN TODAY GOODBYE SEND LETTERS TO THE ORIENTAL BANK CORPORATION YOKOHAMA CAL[21]

Father Longfellow seems to have been more perplexed than pleased when he wrote his son:

We have been delighted to receive your letter from the Pacific steamer, and are now looking for tidings from Japan.... I am a little anxious about your money matter. Your balance in Bank, August 1, was $1916.37....

His attempt to bind his son with economic ties seems partly to reflect Longfellow's fear of his son's travels through a country little known to him. But by the time he received news from Yokohama and "Yedo," he had met a few Japanese in Cambridge, began to know more of the country and was more relaxed.

> We were all delighted with your journal of your journey through the interior of Niphon. It was read aloud in the Library, with Mr. Green among the audience. We take great interest in Yr. travels. . . . I had a visit also, not long ago from Anamori [Arinori] Mori the Japanese Ambassador, and we have in the Law School a very nice youth from Chicugo [Chikugo], Japan, by the name of Eneas Yamada. So we are pretty well informed about matters in that remote region.

The polyglot professor even learned some Japanese words. Jovially he wrote to "Charlie":

> Medeto! Which I understand is Japanese, "I wish you a happy New Year." Perhaps it should be written May-day-to; as that is the sound of the word, as it came from the beardless lips of Eneas Yamada this morning.

He had written to his son, "We begin to think that you are now sufficiently Japanned,"[22] but the father himself, too, seems to have been "Japanned." The son coaxed him, "P.S. Please don't forget the money."[23] And with the money he bought plenty of souvenirs, including pottery. From Nagasaki, which Charles Longfellow "fell in love" with, and where he stayed three weeks longer than he had planned, he wrote to his younger sister, Alice:

> This is a great place for vases and I have a pair in my eye that I think Uncle T. will like. So I shal[l] get them for him.[24]

Two days before he left Yokohama for Shanghai, he sent the last letter to his father from Japan. "I have at last made up my minde [sic] to tear myself away from Japan," he wrote. "It has been a hard struggle as the longer I stay, and more I know of the language, manner and customs, the better I like it." And Charles warned his father that he would receive eighteen packages of "curios" from Japan, at which he would "be rather astonished."[25]

We cannot tell from the correspondence whether the "vases" Charles Longfellow bought at Nagasaki included Imari products, nor whether the Imari vases at the Longfellow House now are the ones he sent home with eighteen packages of curios. But it is certain that Henry Wadsworth Longfellow was gradually "Japanned" during these years, and, by the time he wrote "Keramos" on May 7, 1877, he had substantial knowledge of Japanese, especially Imari, pottery.[26]

However, the poem he finally wrote was not solely about Imari pottery. The speaker in the poem, watching and listening to an American potter singing and turning the wheel, is "transported on wings of song" and imagines himself visiting various places famous for ceramics. He visits Delft in Holland, meets Bernard Palissy in France, and flies over to Faenza, Firenze, and Apulia in Italy. At the bazaars in Cairo, he is surprised at "the fabulous earthen jars / Huge as were those wherein the maid / Morgiana found the forty thieves" in the story of Ali Baba. In China he drops in at King-te-tching, "a burning town," and Nanjing with "the Tower of Porcelain." Toward the end of his journey, the speaker visits Japan.

> Cradled and rocked in Eastern seas,
> The islands of the Japanese
> Beneath me lie; o'er lake and plain
> The stork, the heron, and the crane
> Through the clear realms of azure drift,
> And on the hillside I can see
> The villages of Imari.

Through the "twisted columns of smoke" of "the villages of Imari,"[27] he sees the "lovely" jars with "the bright flowers," "ripple of waves," "Fujiyama's cone," and "the saffron dawn" painted on them. As the speaker realizes that these Japanese images are "the counterfeit and counterpart / Of Nature reproduced in Art," he is brought back from the daydream to the potter's shop in Massachusetts, and there he muses, wrapped in his "visions like the Seer." Art, he thinks, is the reproduction of nature, "chastened and softened and subdued/Into a more attractive grace, / And with human sense imbued." He goes on to write:

> He is the greatest artist, then,
> Whether of pencil or of pen,
> Who follows nature. . . .
> who sets his willing feet
> In nature's footprints, light and fleet,
> And follows fearless where she leads.

With an obviously Romantic glazing on Alexander Pope's dictum, Longfellow interprets nature not as a static and mechanical measure, but as something more organic and active, like a mysterious guide, inspiring the artist's imagination. It is significant to note that Longfellow tries to reproduce in his poem the subtle beauty of Japanese design, and that, stimulated by it, he is brought to meditate upon the nature of his art.

Although Whitman and Longfellow have different themes in their respective poems on Japanese subjects, they have something in common in their manner of describing Japan. They do not describe Japan per se, but describe it as an integral part of the world, with other places on the globe. They seem to be trying to allocate to Japan its proper place in the panorama of their new world maps. Longfellow is locating Japan in the world of ceramics. Whitman, who celebrates the "Errand Bearers" coming to New York from the "Western seas," located Japan to the east of all the countries of the world he can name east of the United States. Melville is depicting Japan in the same manner. He locates the Pacific in the center of the world, "the Indian Ocean and the Altantic being but its arms," and places the "impenetrable Japans" among the Pacific "Milky-Ways." American authors dealing with Japan in the later years do not do this.

Why do all three of these mid-nineteenth century American authors writing about Japan try to locate it on a world map? Of course they did not have the chance to acquire enough knowledge of Japan to write a whole work devoted to it. But it also may be true that it was a reflection of the ethos of the time in which they lived. With the increasing number of adventurous Americans sailing abroad and bringing back news from other countries of the world, the Americans—especially those on the East Coast in the mid-nineteenth century—began to turn their eyes outward, as well as to the west, and, as they came to global perspectives, they felt a kind of agoraphobic need for the fixed axes—the latitudes and longitudes. They were eager to compare and relate what they found with what they knew, and to bridge between the known and unknown, the old and new.

Many Americans of that period who went to Europe, for example, had a strange complex toward Europeans. Mark Twain was one of them, and Henry Adams, writing shortly after, another. They admired the advanced and refined civilization and culture in Europe; looking at American backwardness, which they had to admit, they had vague feelings of inferiority toward the Europeans. But, on the other hand, reflecting on the cleanliness and beauty of the New World, and their ideals of freedom, equality, and democracy, they looked down at corruption and Machiavellian maneuvering in European politics and foreign relations under the monarchs, and felt superior to the Europeans.[28]

In contrast to their "Oedipus complex" toward their European "father," the Americans sought the "mother" image in Asia. For Whitman, "the venerable Asia" is "the all-mother," "the long off mother," the "originatress" and the "bequeather" of old wisdom, to whom you must "bend your proud neck." For President Fillmore, Japan was the country from which, as quoted before, "we ask and expect ... kindness for our men and protection for our property." But at the same time Americans in general felt that America, as a rich and powerful modern nation, was superior to Japan. It extended "now ... from sea to sea," again according to Fillmore, "rich in gold and silver, and precious stones...." Whitman was more idealistically democratic. He thought the Americans should "salute" and approach all the peoples of the world, including "you Japanese man or woman," as "equals." The American success at creating an opening to Japan, while the European nations were still attempting it, could be attributed to such complex, and therefore flexible, attitudes toward Japan—the Americans' realism of power politics, their reverence for Japan as if toward mother, and the idealistic philosophy of equality, good will, fair play, and the absence of territorial ambitions behind their foreign policy. Later, during the 1870s, the Americans were to cooperate with the Meiji government in revising the "unequal treaties" between Japan and the Western powers, by sending such legal specialists as Henry W. Denison to Tokyo. It shows the Americans tried to heighten the relative position of Japan in the political and cultural constellation. The fact that the Americans were concerned with the Japanese and their own position in the world brings us back to the discussion on their eagerness to compare themselves with, and identify themselves in relation to, other peoples and places. This consciousness seems best illustrated in Whitman's well-known poem:

> A noiseless patient spider,
> I mark'd where on a little promontory it stood isolated,
> Mark'd how to explore the vacant vast surrounding,
> It launch'd forth filament, filament, filament, out of
>   itself,
> Ever unreeling them, ever tirelessly speeding them....

Like Whitman's spider weaving its net, the Americans, exploring "the vacant vast surrounding," wanted to see the "bridge you will need be form'd" and "the gossamer thread you fling catch somewhere."

This sentiment also underlies Richard Henry Dana's description of Japan in his journals, where he constantly compares Japan with other places in the world. Watching the scenes of Nagasaki he writes:

> Tuesd. Apr. 10. [1860] Beautiful morning, & nothing can be more lovely than the scene fr. the deck of our steamer. There are patches of granite rock, with evergreen shrubs & trees about them as on the coast off Beverly & Manchester, & patches of cultivated land.

Dana walks into a theater and listens to music.

> The singing, like that I have heard in the streets, is deeper toned than the Chinese.... The streets are wider than those of Chinese cities, full twice as wide, & well flagged with broad stones, and neater than the Chinese.

The comparisons, though not always effective, are abundant. To give a few more examples:

> The young girls, too, are pretty. Low broad foreheads, of the Greek type, thick black hair, white teeth & intelligent eyes are common.

> The yards are lined, & walks are lined with hedges, close cut as in England,—their own invention, centuries old.

> The Japanese language has more vowels than the Chinese. It has, occasionally, a little of the sound of the rougher Spanish. Instead of the Hwangs, Kongs, Chungs of China, they have Kanagáwa, Yokoháma, Yeddo, Meto &c., & the pretty salutation of *Ohio*, & the alingáto for thank you.[29]

A Japanese traveler would not write his account with such constant comparisons. Kafū Nagai in his *Amerika Monogatari* is more concerned with the people's way of living in each place he visits. But Dana, by comparing Japanese streets with Chinese, or Japanese yards with English, seems to be trying to relate Japan and its culture to what he already knew well.

It is reminiscent of Washington Irving's comment on Otokichi and another Japanese sailor who drifted onto Oregon's shore. When he received a letter from Nathaniel Wyeth, a Boston merchant and adventurer, he wrote a section, "Wreck of a Japanese Junk on the Northwest Coast," as an appendix to his *Adventure of Captain Bonneville, U.S.A.*

> The following extract of a letter which we received, lately, from Mr. Wyeth, may be interesting, as throwing some light upon the question as to the manner in which America has been peopled. "Are you aware of the fact that in the winter of 1833, a Japanese junk was wrecked on the north west coast, in the neighborhood of Queen Charlotte's Island; and all but two of the crew, then much reduced by starvation and disease, during a long drift across the Pacific, were killed by the natives? The two fell into the hands of the Hudson's Bay Company and were sent to England. I saw them, on my arrival at Vancouver, in 1834." [30]

Washington Irving also is relating the Japanese to what he already knew, the native Americans, and is explaining the Pacific Ocean as a corridor or "bridge" of the two races. By constantly comparing Japan with, and relating it to, what they already knew better, and by allocating Japan a place in the world map, the Americans, in their period of exploration and expansion, possibly were trying to make sure that their new knowledge of Japan would fix in their minds, and by so doing they might have been trying to reascertain their own identity.

The Turn of the Century: Japonisme

Toward the end of the nineteenth century, increasing numbers of Americans became interested in Japan and tried to explore and understand it more deeply and fully. As Pinkerton sings in *Madame Butterfly,*

> His life is not satisfied unless he makes the flowers of any nation his own treasure, [31]

the adventurous Americans were curious about, and eager to absorb, the cultures of other nations. They were particularly concerned with Japan during this period, probably because they thought it was the country they "rediscovered" west of the West, which, they learned, unexpectedly had an old, curiously sophisticated but highly and richly developed culture worth knowing. Between 1890 and 1910 Ernest Fenollosa, Percival Lowell, and John La Farge lectured and published on what they saw and thought in Japan; Lafcadio Hearn, Winnifred Babcock, Mary Fenollosa, and Frances Little wrote stories with Japanese characters in them; and David Belasco's *Madame Butterfly* was on the Broadway stage.

In Japan, however, during these years, people gradually turned away from America toward Europe. The Japanese government had sent a large party to America in 1872, with Tomomi Iwakura as chief ambassador. More than a hundred Americans were invited to Japan as teachers at various schools, such as Kaisei College in Tokyo, Ferris Seminary in Yokohama, Meishinkan in Fukui, and Doshisha in Kyoto. Ulysses S. Grant and his wife visited Japan in 1879, and were invited to dinner by Emperor Meiji. In 1887, at Rokumeikan, Premier Hirobumi Ito held a masquerade party, which he heard was in fashion in Philadelphia, disguising himself as a Venetian nobleman. But by 1890 the honeymoon was over. With the enactment of the Imperial Constitution (1889), and the wars with China (1894–95) and Russia (1904–05), Japanese passion toward the United States rapidly cooled off. The number of American teachers in Japan dropped. Increasing numbers of Japanese politicians became skeptical of American values, considering the ideas of the Founding Fathers as too revolutionary, and the practice of electing the president and governors by popular votes as too vulgar and dangerous.

Strangely enough, however, many Americans writing on Japan during this period continued to admire it. It may have something to do with the general sentiment of the Americans of the time. If there was a period in American history that may be called imperialistic, it was this time. Though the so-called yellow journalism was partly responsible, with the Spanish-American War (1898) and the acquiring of Cuba, Guam, and the Philippines, the majority of Americans were pleased to imagine the Stars and Stripes waving on Pacific islands, with which they might have felt paternal sympathy. Lafcadio Hearn, as is well known, wrote a number of stories about Japanese legends and customs, charming many American and British readers. Percival Lowell, whose *Soul of the Far East* (1887) had inspired Hearn to visit Japan, introduced readers to its beauties throughout the book, maintaining that the essential quality of Japanese culture was Oriental "impersonality." Lowell also published *Noto* (1891), a journal of his journey to "the remote corner of Japan," and *Occult Japan* (1895), on the Shinto religion. Ernest Fenollosa took lessons in painting from the Kano School masters, in the Nō play from Minoru Umewaka, and in Chinese history and poetry from Kainan Mori in Tokyo; he lectured in the States on the beauties of ukiyoe (wood-block prints), on Japanese and Chinese paintings, on Chinese ideograms, and poetry, and on his view of the art of Japan. But what matters most here are the imaginative works of literature on Japan, which reflect the period of the popularization of Japan's "exoticism."[32]

Though *Madame Butterfly* is better known as an opera by Giacomo Puccini (1904), its libretto was based on the successful play by David Belasco with the same title, first staged in 1900 at the Square Theater in New York. The play, however, had been based on a longer novel written by a Philadelphia lawyer, John Luther Long (1861–1927), published in 1897. Long had heard the story from his sister, Mrs. Irwin Correl, who had been living in Tokyo, Yokohama, and Nagasaki as the wife of a missionary since 1886. She heard the story from a Japanese peddler.

In David Belasco's version, Butterfly, a young Japanese woman, is presented with cherry blossoms at her home on a hill, overlooking the harbor. She is dressed in a kimono, waiting for her husband, Pinkerton. He has been at sea for $2\frac{1}{2}$ years. Before he left her, he had promised her that he would come back to her when the robins nested. (Actually there are no robins in Japan!) A robin flies over the hill, but does not nest. Nakodo calls on her, and introduces her to a rich, middle-aged man, Yamadori, urging her to remarry. But Butterfly declines saying, "I'm marry to Lef-ten-ant B. F. Pik-ker-ton." (Her English sounds like pidgin, rather than "Japanese English.") Only two dollars remain of the money he has left for her. Then suddenly she hears the sound of the cannon from a ship anchoring at the harbor; she sees with her telescope that it is Pinkerton's ship. Pinkerton, however, has been married to an American girl. When he comes up the hill with his friend, he hears Butterfly singing a lullaby to his baby. Unable to bear his emotion, he leaves the place, giving some money for her to his friend, who explains the situation to Butterfly. She almost falls into a swoon just as Kate, Pinkerton's new wife, climbs up the hill. She meets Butterfly and makes an offer to adopt the baby. The heroine now understands what she should do, and quietly tells Kate to come back in fifteen minutes, giving his money to her. When Kate comes with Pinkerton, Butterfly is lying on the bloody floor. Waving the American flag in the hands of the baby, she says, "Too bad those robins didn' nes' again,"[33] and dies. Though unnatural to Japanese readers, and also to American readers now, Pinkerton's suffering, Kate's generosity, and particularly Madame Butterfly's love and self-sacrifice might have appealed to the contemporary American audience, as the approving criticisms of the time indicate.

In John Luther Long's less popular version, however, there is a scene in which Butterfly's relatives have a talk with Pinkerton after their marriage. They mildly insist that, though they all believe in Buddhism and worship their ancestors, perhaps Pinkerton should be added to their family records, since Butterfly not only is his but also belongs to the whole family. However, he rejects the proposal. He even criticizes them as "back numbers," and Butterfly is "solemnly disowned."[34] This part is totally omitted in Belasco's version.

Beside the indirect causes of Butterfly's suicide—her naiveté, her financial distress, and her rejection of a second marriage—Long seems to emphasize also her isolation, her being cut off from her relatives. But Belasco's version emphasizes her innocence and tender love for Pinkerton. Believing in his promise that he would come back, Butterfly says to Nakodo, "I am jus' waitin'—sometimes cryin', sometimes watchin', but always waitin'."[35]

Belasco seems to be trying to describe the Japanese woman as patient, beautiful, innocent, gentle, and obedient. As a number of short stories and novels, as well as plays and operas, were written about Japan in this period, the country, and especially its women, gradually were described as more beautiful than they were. As they were popularized, they were more "beautified," idealized and stereotyped. When compared with the caricatures like coquettish Yum-Yum, who was in love with Prince Nanki-Poo in the British play by Sir W. S. Gilbert, *Mikado, or the Town of Titipu* (1885), it is clear that the Americans developed their own image of Japan and Japanese women during this period. The British image of Japan then was still old-fashioned and was more a product of fancy, with its stress on "sweetness and light," than a result of liberal thinking.

A Japanese Nightingale by Winnifred Babcock also presents a beautiful, young, innocent, and gentle Japanese girl. The author was born in Nagasaki in 1879 and grew up in Japan, so her description is more realistic and natural than Belasco's. But she was educated in Canada, wrote essays and stories mostly in Jamaica and New York for American readers, and her image of Japan was distinctively American. Her pseudonym, Onoto Watanna, looks like, but is quite unlike, Japanese. But it is surprising to note that she published so many novels on Japan: *The Old Jinrikisha* (1895), *Miss Nume of Japan* (1899), *A Japanese Nightingale* (1901), *Wooing of Wisteria* (1902), *Daughter of Nijo* (1904), *A Japanese Blossom* (1906), and *Tama* (1910).

A Japanese Nightingale is set in Tokyo in the middle of the Meiji years. Jack Bigelow visits Japan after graduating from an American college. One day he is invited to a moon-watching party and is introduced to Yuki, a geisha with blue eyes. She is pretty in her kimono and very intelligent; she sings and dances gracefully, and is popular among the American guests. Shortly after, she visits him with a *nakodo* (go-between), asking him, "Please marry me." Astounded, Jack replies he only could be her friend, but soon finds himself falling in love with her. Though reluctant now, she is persuaded to get married by the nakodo's arrangement. The subtle changes of feelings between the two are exquisitely described in the manner of Jane Austen. After marriage, Jack loves her even more. Yuki seems to love him also, sometimes singing and beating drums for him, but occasionally she weeps mysteriously, and wants money.

As their life continues, she begins to weep even more often. He gives her more money but she refuses it. Then Taro Burton, one of Jack's college friends, comes back to Yokohama. Jack picks up Taro at the pier and takes him home to show him his new wife. When Taro and Yuki meet, they look shocked. After a moment of silence, Taro exclaims, "She is my sister! Oh my God!" Yuki flies out never to return.

Jack and Taro visit the latter's mother, now living alone, her British husband having died. She is delighted at her son's return, but is surprised at her daughter's disappearance. While Taro was abroad, Yuki became a geisha, and was sending her earnings to him. It was just when Taro asked for more money for his return voyage that Yuki decided to get "married" to Jack.

On hearing the story, Taro stands up, faints, hits his head, and dies. Jack desperately searches for Yuki all over Japan, till finally he is informed by the police of Yuki's departure for America, and he prepares to return to there. Except for the last parts, which are like a sightseeing guide the novel is well written. Considering that it was written only forty years after the treaty ratifications, Babcock's understanding of Japan is amazingly deep.

It is also surprising that many other novels like this were written about the time of the Russo-Japanese War. Frances Little, who visited Japan in 1902 as a kindergarten teacher at Hiroshima, wrote *The Lady and Sada San* (1912) and *The House of the Misty Star* (1914). Mary Fenollosa, who came to Japan with her husband, wrote *The Breath of the Gods* (1905), *The Dragon Painter* (1906), and other novels. It is ironic that at the same time Japan was beginning to become militaristic, Japanese women were popular in America. Yuki is as beautiful, gentle, and innocent as Madame Butterfly. She also sacrifices herself at the critical moment. In *The Dragon Painter* by Mary Fenollosa, a novel dealing with the problem of succession in a Japanese painter's family, Umeko, his only daughter, hides herself in a nunnery—also at the critical moment.

Japanese women are described as sitting gently on *tatami* (mats), surrounded by *fusuma* (paper-covered sliding doors), wearing kimonos, seldom going outdoors. Japanese men are courteous but haughty and obstinate, as Taro, Yamadori, and the painter Kano, or mean and vulgar like the nakoda. The people are portrayed as lovers of beauty, enjoying cherry blossoms in the spring and the moon in the fall. Such images as cherry blossoms, chrysanthemums, cranes, lotus flowers, swords, dragons, and Fuji are scattered around. If they take a trip, they go to Nikko, Kamakura, or Hakone. The stereotyped and "beautified" image of Japan seems to have been molded and popularized during this period of *Madame Butterfly* and *A Japanese Nightingale*. The more popularized, the image of Japan became, the more stereotyped it grew, and this image was to remain solidly inbedded in American minds for more than a half century.

Behind the popularity of Japan in literature, as well as in arts and architecture in America, were the Centennial Exhibition in Philadelphia, and the World's Fair at Chicago in 1893, where thousands of Americans crowded to see the Japanese pavilions. Also there were Japan's unexpected but overwhelming victories over imperial Russia on the continent and on the sea of Japan. Japanese popularity may have something to do with the backlash of feminism. It may also have something to do with Europeans' interest in Japan; Paul Gauguin went to Tahiti in 1890, and other French impressionist painters were influenced by ukiyoe. *Madame Chrysantheme* (1888) by Pierre Loti, and essays by English writers such as Robert Louis Stevenson's "Yoshida Tora-Jiro" and "Chushingura" and Rudyard Kipling's *From Sea to Sea*, in which he writes about his visits to Nikko, Kamakura, Kioto, and Kobe, helped to popularize Japan. But European and British images of Japan were somewhat different from American. Pierre Loti, for instance, looked down on the women of Nagasaki. Besides their colonialism, the Europeans had a consciousness that they were at the center of world civilization, while the majority of American writers, sharing the idea of the equality of all men, held a more sympathetic attitude toward the Japanese. Such writings on Japan by ardent Japanese as *The Intercourse between the United States and Japan: An Historical Sketch* (1891) and *Bushido, The Soul of Japan* (1900) by Inazo Nitobe, and *The Awakening of Japan* (1904) and *The Book of Tea* (1906) by Kakuzo Okakura, might have played important roles. The activities of Baron Kentaro Kaneko and Jo Niishima might have as well. But during the vogue of Japonisme in literature, American readers also bought many dime novels.

When there was no radio or films, one of the major American pastimes was reading books. From the middle of the nineteenth century, a number of railroad novels were written in England, and a number of dime novels in America. Among the dime novels were Western stories that had similar plots. The hero is usually sincere, sturdy, and good at gunplay. The heroine is young, pretty, and religious. The woods and lakes are tableaux like those in the *Leather-Stocking Tales*. With popularization via the dime novels, the West was beautifully described but simplified and stereotyped.[36] The literature of Japonisme can be understood as an extension of the stereotypes of dime novels.

Certainly the Wild West and Japan are different in many aspects. The former was pioneer country, with prairies, gold mines, Indians, and rogues, full of dangers. Japan in the Edo period, on the contrary, was a land of peaceful and densely populated islands over the ocean with a relatively mature civilization. But to many Americans, mostly on the East Coast, the West and Japan may have looked quite similar: both were lying invitingly somewhere far in the west, full of attractions. But the trip there was quite dangerous. This consciousness, mixed with a sense of "manifest destiny" and a feeling of finding a new neighbor, might have had something to do with the fact that Japan, like the West, was popularized, stereotyped, and idealized by the American writers of the time.

In Search of Japanese Values

As Americans began to come into direct contact with Japan and experience that culture firsthand in the latter half of the nineteenth century, such American writers as Melville and poets such as Whitman and Longfellow, who wrote about Japan, tried to allocate it a proper place in world culture. Toward the turn of the century, travelers to Japan, mostly from the Boston area, began writing books about their experiences. As things Japanese were imported and more books about Japan were written, Japan gradually was popularized and stereotyped in American novels and plays in the early twentieth century.

Then came the third response. While Japonisme was still in vogue, American poets were introduced to classical Japanese poetry, particularly to the English and French translations of haiku, tanka, and Nō plays, and they created highly artistic poetry by imbuing their work with a touch of Japan. The kind of sensibility, subtlety, intensity, and suggestiveness characteristic of Japanese poetry became a part of the common property of that generation of poets, including Amy Lowell, Adelaide Crapsey, Ezra Pound, Carl Sandburg, John Gould Fletcher, William Carlos Williams, H. D., Witter Bynner, Conrad Aiken, T. S. Eliot, Yvor Winters, and others.

Amy Lowell, a professed imagist, was an ardent admirer of Japanese art since her adolescence, when she received letters and gifts from Japan from her brother Percival. She wrote a number of haikulike poems, often inspired by ukiyoe. Adelaide Crapsey, "an unconscious imagist," also was one of those who admired Japanese poetry. Japanese tanka, particularly in English and French translations in five lines, inspired her to create the new and delicate poetical form that she called cinquain.

Ezra Pound, as discussed in the beginning of Chapter 3, formed a literary principle from haiku, which he called "the theory of superposition." That is, he declared that, when two images are superposed, they reflect each other like two sets of mirrors, and each becomes a metaphor of the other, mutually interpreting and complementing the meaning, fusing themselves into a one-image poem. After Pound applied his principle to a two-line poem, "In a Station of the Metro," he tried a longer one of several lines.[37] He than tried still longer one-image poems with more lines superposed on more lines, even in translations from Fenollosa's notebooks, such as "The River Song," which greatly resemble the basic structure of the *Cantos*.

Of course, the *Cantos* cannot be explained only in terms of disassembled images and the theory of superposition. The ideas of collage, periplum, fugue, Odyssean voyage, Fenollosa's Chinese characters, Nō plays, pragmatism, a Dantesque conception of time, and the "idea in action" are all dissolved into the thought that went into the structure of the *Cantos*. But it is important to note that not only the poets but the painters, composers and experimental filmmakers after Pound inherited and developed the idea of superpository theory to create the whole body of a particular type of avant-garde art. Gaudier-Brzeska, the sculptor, George Antheil, the composer, and John Blackage, the experimental filmmaker, were some of those who were inspired by Pound's ideas.

William Carlos Williams earlier wrote a number of short poems, some of which echo the haiku. A representative example may be a humorous four-line poem:

> So different, this man
> And this woman:
> A stream flowing
> in a field.

Though the poem does not keep to the authentic syllable count, it is written in the form of superposition. It might even be said that Williams' *Paterson* is a longer superpository poem in the same sense that Pound's *Cantos* is.

Carl Sandburg's *Chicago Poems* includes eleven short poems in the section called "Handfuls," in which Sandburg is trying to capture a Japanese note by his own devices. Though not fully, "Flux" resembles what Pound calls the form of superposition, in which two images are juxtaposed in four lines. But his three-line poem, "Window," is probably closer to the imagists' notion of haiku.

> Night from a railroad car window
> Is a great, dark, soft thing
> Broken across with slashes of light.

His better-known "Fog" in the same section may be attributed to Sandburg's acquaintance with Japanese wood-block prints as well as to the haiku.

> The fog comes
> on little cat feet.

> It sits looking
> over harbor and city
> on silent haunches
> and then moves on.

He has been familiar with some ukiyoe printers, and later writes "Old Hokusai Print," and other poems with admiration to the old painter. But the description of the feline fog in the poem reminds us of "The Love Song of J. Alfred Prufrock," though the similarity may be accidental.

T. S. Eliot, who spent several years in Harvard Yard, where "of course [Japanese poetry] was all in the air,"[38] as Conrad Aiken recollected, produces the same effect as the superpository form in *The Waste Land* by quoting from, alluding to, or parodying a passage in classical literature and forcing it to reflect upon the previous passage.

> The river's tent is broken: the last fingers of leaf
> Clutch and sink into the wet bank. The wind
> Crosses the brown land, unheard. The nymphs are departed.
> Sweet Thames, run softly till I end my song.

Or

> "That corpse you planted last year in your garden,
> "Has it begun to sprout? Will it bloom this year?
> "Or has the sudden frost disturbed its bed?
> "Oh keep the Dog far hence, that's friend to men,
> "Or with his nails he'll dig it up again!
> "You! hypocrite lecteur!—mon semblable,—mon frère!"

Turning to Wallace Stevens, we find that some of his "Thirteen Ways of Looking at a Blackbird" resemble the "*hokku*-like poems" written by the imagists in London.

> The blackbird whirled in the autumn winds.
> It was a small part of the pantomime.

Impressionistic in essence, his poetry with Japanese elements reflects the French and imagist absorption of Japan.[39] Stevens seems less interested in the study of Japanese poetry than in imitating some impressionistic pieces done in Japanese fashion.

John Gould Fletcher's commitment to Japan, however, seems quite serious. We are told that his emphasis on "psychological suggestion" comes from his "analysis" of haiku and tanka.[40] His *Goblins and Pagodas* (1916) reflects the depth of his knowledge not only of Japanese poetry but of Japanese fine art and Buddhism. The main sources of his information are Percival Lowell, Lafcadio Hearn, Yone Noguchi, and Ernest Fenollosa. But his poetry often tends to be too explanatory and loquacious to be concisely poignant and suggestive. Compare his "Green Symphony" with H. D.'s "Oread" on the same subject.

> Trees splash the sky with their fingers,
> A restless green rout of stars.
>
> With whirling movement
> They swing their boughs
> About their stems:
> Planes on planes of light and shadow
> Pass among them,
> Opening fanlike to fall.
>
> The trees are like a sea;
> Tossing,
> Trembling,
> Roaring,
> Wallowing,
> Darting their long green flickering fronds up at the sky,
> Spotted with white blossom-spray.
>
> ("Green Symphony," II, 11.1-15)

> Whirl up, sea—
> whirl your pointed pines,
> splash your great pines
> on our rocks,
> hurl your green over us,
> cover us with your pools of fir.
>
> ("Oread")

In any event, thanks to the vogue of Japonisme, and to such writers as Lafcadio Hearn, the imagists could more immediately and tangibly appreciate the English and French translations of tanka and haiku. The same can be said of their contemporaries who, although not members of the imagist group, wrote occasional imagistic poems. Adelaide Crapsey, it might be noted, wrote most of her cinquains before the imagist movement was launched, quite unaware of their theories. The fact is that imagistic poetry could be written without knowledge of the imagist poetics, by modeling Japanese poetry. Certainly such imagist principles as exhibited in Pound's "A Few Don'ts by an Imagist" (1913) and in the manifesto in *Some Imagist Poets* (1916) were greatly helpful. But the whole legacy of the imagist movement might have been like a skeleton of poetic theories if the imagists had not known the Japanese art. It may not be too bold to state that the imagist movement itself might not have existed, or would have been quite different from what it was, if there had been no vogue of Japonisme or no translations of haiku or tanka around the turn of the century.

After World War I, as the Japanese empire was trying to expand to the south, the national interests of the United States and Japan became incompatible. But some Americans and Japanese were seriously concerned with "promoting mutual understanding" and tried to "learn" from each other. Theodore Roosevelt once wrote to his classmate at Harvard, Baron Kentaro Kaneko:

> It seems to me, my dear Baron, that Japan has much to teach the nations of the Occident, just as she has something to learn from them. . . . Certainly I myself hope that I have learned not a little from the fine Samurai spirit, and from the ways in which that spirit has been and is being transformed to meet the needs of modern life.[41]

However, Yvor Winters was another of those who "learned" from Japan. Some of his 28 short poems in "The Magpie's Shadow" (1922) are like Japanese poetry in their simplicity and concision.

Awakening
New snow, O pine of dawn!

The Hunter
Run! In the magpie's shadow.

Spring Rain
My doorframe smells of leaves.

A Deer
The tree rose in the dawn.

Awaiting Snow
The well of autumn—dry.

As he wrote later in the preface to his *Collected Poems*, Winters was "familiar with many translations from the poetry of the Japanese." But he was also familiar with that of the American Indians, by which he was probably more influenced.

> *The Immobile Wind* and nearly all of *The Magpie's Shadow* were written while I was at the sanatorium in Santa Fé. . . . There was no French influence on these poems, except as it might have filtered through the Imagists. I had been reading Bridges and Hardy, whom I admired but who did not influence me at this time, and Emily Dickinson and Adelaide Crapsey, who may have influenced me. I was familiar also with many translations from the poetry of the Japanese and of the American Indians; the Indians especially were an influence on *The Magpie's Shadow*.[42]

However, the achievement of utmost concentration and sharp concreteness also may have come from his knowledge of Japanese poetry as well as of the poetry of the imagists, Dickinson, and Crapsey. His way of classifying his poems by seasons—(1) In Winter; (2) in Spring; (3) In Summer and Autumn—certainly seems to echo the usual division of a collection of haiku by seasons.

After World War II, the new generation of American poets tried to search for something far deeper than exoticism, poetical form, or device; they tried to explore the values of Japanese spiritual life. The most influential of them was Kenneth Rexroth, who maintained an interest in Japanese culture when nearly all Americans had rejected it just before and during the war, and who reinterpreted it as a new source of values for the postwar generation. In the values underlying the world of classical Japanese poetry and Shingon Buddhism, he sensed the possibility that there might be a means to save modern civilization from destruction. In place of Western rationalism and individualism, he could find in Japanese works a new world view in which man and nature are in a coexistent, harmonious relationship. His philosophy emerges, like a lotus flower from the mud, in the mandala of his longer poems, such as *The Heart's Garden / The Garden's Heart* and "On Flower Wreath Hill."

A similar attitude can be seen in Gary Snyder, who is more concerned with ecology. Seeking new values in Zen Buddhism, as well as in the American Indian way of life, he weaves an ecological web for the world. A number of other beat and postbeat poets share the same attitudes as Rexroth and Snyder. Many of them have written their poetry while searching for fresh values and inspiring visions hidden among Japanese as well as Indian and Oriental cultures.

We have discussed briefly how American authors have looked at Japan, tentatively and arbitrarily dividing the history into three periods, before 1890, 1890 to 1910, and thereafter. These dates should be taken only as guideposts, for the tendencies of a period often linger into the following periods. For instance, although Adelaide Crapsey and Amy Lowell started to write their poetry seriously before 1910, they exhibited the tendencies of the second and third periods, as they searched for new forms for their poetry in Japanese culture.

In the following chapters, all the poets mentioned above will not be discussed in detail. Amy Lowell has been selected for further comment because she is one of the earliest among poets of her generation to show interest in Japanese art, and to try to re-create the Japanese sensibility in the haiku, done in her own way. Adelaide Crapsey deserves further attention because she was interested in the tanka. Ezra Pound is discussed because he kept his interest in Japan longer than other imagists by obtaining the notebooks of Ernest Fenollosa, and also because he has influenced tremendously a wide range of poets during a major part of this century. I have decided to treat the works of Rexroth because he not only was a bridge between the pre- and post-World War II generations of poets, but was an earnest and enthusiastic reinterpreter of Japanese values. Snyder has been taken up because he is one of those who represent the generation, antipodal in sensibility and mode of expression to the "modernist," metaphysical, academic poets, while retaining his interest in Japan, and especially in its religious values.

2

Amy Lowell
and
Adelaide Crapsey

Lowell and Japan

Although her first volume of poetry, *A Dome of Many-Coloured Glass*, published in 1912, was criticized sharply by the young modernists,[1] it exhibits some germs of the unique talents of Amy Lowell (1874–1925), which emerge more clearly in her maturer works: her susceptibility to the moments of beauty and her symphonic inclusiveness of the wide range of experiences. She was to write, on the one hand, short, compact, jewel-like, haikulike, imagistic poems, and, on the other, longer, often narrative, "polyphonic," Whitmanesque poems in loose forms, powerful rhythms, and sometimes with prophetic posture. "What is poetry?" she asks in a poem, "Fragment," in the first book of her poetry. It is, she writes:

> glass that's taught
> By patient labour any hue to take
> And glowing with a sumptuous splendor, make
> Beauty a thing of awe; where sunbeams caught,
> Transmuted fall in sheafs of rainbows fraught
> With storied meaning for religion's sake.

"By patient labour," she thinks the poet must train himself to be able to respond to a wide range of experiences. And poetry, she believes, is like a pane of multicolored stained glass, which constantly changes white "sunbeams" into "sheafs of rainbows." Obviously Amy Lowell is alluding to Shelley's lines in "Adonais," from which she took the title of her book of poems:

> Life, like a dome of many-coloured glass,
> Stains the white radiance of Eternity.[2]

Among her shorter poems in *A Dome of Many-Coloured Glass*, poems that are delicately "stained" by Keats and Shelley, with whom Amy Lowell was familiar through Leigh Hunt's *Imagination and Fancy* (1844),[3] there are two poems on Japanese subjects: "A Japanese Wood-Carving" and "A Coloured Print by Shōkei."

"A Japanese Wood-Carving" is a poem about a piece of sculpture made "of wood with colours dim," probably sent from Japan by her brother Percival, and hung "High up above the open, welcoming door" in the library of her house.

> An artist once, with patient, careful knife,
> Had fashioned it like to the untamed sea.
> Here waves uproar themselves, their tops blown back
> By the gay, sunny wind, which whips the blue
> And breaks it into gleams and sparks of light.
> Among the flashing waves are two white birds
> Which swoop, and soar, and scream for very joy
> At the wild sport.

She seems to be attempting to capture the peculiarly Japanese stylization of the waves when she describes their tops as "blown back." But they are depicted in brightly colorful images: "flashing" waves are breaking "into gleams and sparks of light." The "white birds" "swoop, and soar, and scream" in the sun above "the blue." The description of the scene is like any New England seashore, coupled with the "uncontrollable" images of Shelley's west wind and his "singing" and "soaring" skylark. The Japanese piece of wood itself, however, is neither bright nor screaming. As we are told, it is dark and silent, "with colours dim." The stained glass of Amy Lowell is so richly colorful that the originally "dim" Japanese wood carving seems suddenly to be "transmuted" into something American—bright and speedily moving. But she ends her poem with an air of perfect control.

> Hanging above the high, wide open door,
> It brings to us in quiet, fire lit room,
> The freedom of the earth's vast solitudes,
> Where heaping, sunny waves tumble and roll,
> And seabirds scream in wanton happiness.

We now realize the "Japanese wood carving" is a mystic doorway —higher than the actual door ("Hanging above the high, wide open door")—through which the speaker goes in and out. It is her imagination, which is the world of "the freedom of the earth's vast solitudes." It is, in other words, a poem about imagination, like Keats's "Ode on a Grecian Urn," in the sense that the speaker becomes involved in imagining by confronting the antique foreign piece. Keats's speaker seems to experience a far richer and more subtly moving "happy" world of the "cold pastoral," which is "for ever warm. . . . All breathing human passion far above." Lowell's speaker on the other hand, only wanders into a colorful and "delightful" world, which, however, is filled with exotic beauty.

"A Coloured Print by Shōkei,"[4] in the same book of poetry, is a tighter piece of work in four stanzas with softer rhymes. It begins with the description of a mountain path:

> It winds along the face of a cliff
>> This path which I long to explore,
> And over it dashes a waterfall,
>> And the air is full of the roar
> And the thunderous voice of waters which sweep
> In a silver torrent over some steep.

It brings the reader immediately into the scene of the picture. The path is again the path into the imagination, where, like Keats's "Nightingale," the speaker smells and hears and feels the surroundings, though later she will be brought back into reality.

> Oh! The dampness is very good to smell,
>> And the path is soft to tread,
> And beyond the fall it winds up and on,
>> While little streamlets thread
> Their own meandering way down the hill
> Each singing its own little song, until
>
> I forget that 'tis only a pictured path,
>> And I hear the water and wind,
> And look through the mist, and strain my eyes
>> To see what there is behind;
> For it must lead to a happy land,
> This little path by a waterfall spanned.

The poem is a pleasant piece of work, a beautiful revery. But the speaker does not have an intense emotional experience such as ecstasy before death, or pain in happiness. The speaker does not have the urgent desire, or even need, for escape from a painful life, as did Keats. The speaker is delighted to explore into "a happy-land," but seems just as happy to come back to the world of reality.

Both the Japanese picture and the wood carving are the subjects but not the essential themes of Amy Lowell's poems. They are, however, important vehicles through which she tries to communicate the richer exotic experience of her imagination. She seems to love them, and the world behind them. But ironically she seems uneasy about remaining there long. They are in a sense decorations in her poems, just like the Oriental objects in her Victorian-style rooms: not essential to her life, but without which her life is incomplete.

Lowell's interest in the Far East dates back to her girlhood. She was familiar with Japanese prints and haiku much earlier than Pound. Pound probably began to read Chinese poetry after he went to England in 1908. That year Ernest Fenollosa died in London; his widow gave Pound Fenollosa's notes on Nō plays and Chinese poetry in 1913. But Amy Lowell had been receiving letters and gifts from her brother Percival in Japan since 1883, when she was nine years old. Percival Lowell (1855–1916), nineteen years older than Amy, was an astronomer, best known as the discoverer of Pluto. But when young, he traveled around the world and spent most of his time between 1883 and 1893 in Japan, writing four books on the Far East.[5] On August 4, 1883, he wrote from Fukushima to his nine-year-old sister:

> Dear big Amy,
>
> So you want to have another letter from me, do you! Well imagine yourself in the middle of a big plain and a lot of great big baby carriages each drawn by a man. In one of these I ride and as you are not very large yet, though you will probably be gigantic by the time I get home, suppose you come & sit with me.

Amy seemed to like her brother, who teased her all the time but was kind to her. He continues:

> Unfortunately we are going very slowly, only walking along in fact, but if the men were running I think you would like it as I do.... At the next village the jinrikisha men, that is the name of the big baby carriage, said they could go no further

so we were obliged to get cows to carry our baggage and
we walked. . . . I send you [one word illegible].

Yr loving brother
Percival[6]

We cannot tell from the letter what he sent to his sister at that time.
But apparently from time to time Percival sent presents to her from
Japan, with which she decorated her large home, Sevenels, at Warren
and Heath streets in Brookline, Massachusetts. She was to inherit this
house years later.

During his stay in Japan, Percival Lowell was asked to be foreign
secretary and councillor to the special mission from Korea to the United
States, and he accepted after much hesitation. He went back temporarily
to the States in the fall of 1883, and visited Sevenels with his young
Japanese interpreter, Tsunejirō Miyaoka. They must have excited young
Amy with many stories about Japan during their sojourn of a few weeks.
Thirty-eight years later, she could still remember the delightful days.

I remember so well sitting in your lap and pulling your hair,
and being reprimanded by my mother for overfamiliarity. But
you were so good to me and played with me so delightfully,
how could I resist considering you a play-fellow of my own
age. I regret more than I can say that you did not find time to
come out here when you were in America.[7]

Miyaoka was by then a lawyer in Tokyo, and Amy, having trained
herself as an imagist, was an established poet with more than a half
dozen books of poetry published. She continues in the same nostalgic
tone.

My brother Lawrence told me that you wished to see the
"baby." Alas, I am afraid you would have found a great deal
of change in that individual, but certainly no lack of remem-
brance. I have often thought of my playmate of a few weeks
with regard and affection. Sturgis Bigelow has told me something about you, and makes me more than ever sorry that we
failed to meet.

In return for a "charming little book" from Miyaoka given her at
Christmas, she sent him a copy of her *Can Grande's Castle*. It contained,
as she wrote, "some reference to Japan, a Japan which I have never seen,

but which seems to be so intimately connected with all my childish memories." She is referring to her long poem, *Guns as Keys: And the Great Gate Swings.*

> I wrote the poem out of a sort of atavism and after much reading of Japanese literature, of which, it is needless to say, I am an ardent admirer. The prints and picture books like the little one which you have just given me, and which my brother Percival used to send across the Atlantic all through my childhood, made Japan so vivid to my imagination that I cannot realize that I have never been there. Certainly it imbued me with a love for the country and the people, which the games we used to have together strengthened so much that I shall always feel a bond drawing me to your country. . . .

From her long letter to her old "play-fellow," one can feel how much she loved and admired Japan and its art and how large a part of her heart it occupied for a long time.[8] *Guns as Keys: And the Great Gate Swings,* which H. D. read "with great pleasure,"[9] is a long poem on the 1853 expedition to Japan by Commodore Matthew Calbraith Perry. The story is written in "polyphonic prose," interspersed with short lyrics on old Japanese life. "Polyphonic prose," according to Amy Lowell, is "the freest, the most elastic, of all forms." It has "fundamental principles, and the chief of these is an insistence on the absolute adequacy of the manner of a passage to the thought it embodies." Another principle of "polyphonic prose" is the use of what she calls "return." By "return" she means simply "the recurrence of a dominant thought or image, coming in irregularly and in varying words, but still giving the spherical effect." She continues:

> It will be seen, therefore, that "polyphonic prose" is, in a sense, an orchestral form. Its tone is not merely single and melodic as is that of *vers libre,* for instance, but contrapuntal and various.[10]

"The spherical effect" reminds us of the music of the spheres, and "contrapuntal" its microcosmic version, the fugue. And the fugal structure is what Ezra Pound was trying to incorporate into his *Cantos* at the time. "Polyphonic prose" is Lowell's departure from imagism, just as the search for structure in a "longer one-image poem" is the farewell to imagism for Pound.

In *Guns as Keys* the short imagistic lyrics on Japanese subjects are not mere decorations. These haikulike lyrics on various aspects of old Japanese life are functionally placed as counterparts to the prosaic story of Perry's voyage on the warships. The Eastern and Western themes are ingeniously juxtaposed, balanced, and harmonized, just like two themes in a fugue.

In part 1, the voyage from the East Coast of "the paddle wheel steam frigate, *Mississippi*, of the United States Navy" is told in prosaic form. Then there is a short lyric depicting peaceful life in Mishima, Japan. Commodore Perry's voyage across the Atlantic to Madeira is described, again in prose. Then a short lyric on Tora-no-mon. The voyage down the west coast of Africa is told in prose, followed by a short lyric on *Oiran*. Thus the four warships move eastward through the Cape, and the Indian Ocean, to Singapore and Canton, while the quite life continues in Japan. Tension is increasingly heightened as the ships approach Japan.

> The figure-head of the *Mississippi* should be a beneficent angel.
> With her guns to persuade, she should lay the foundation of
> such a market on the shores of Japan. "We will do what we
> can," writes the Commodore, in his cabin.
>   Outside the drapery shop of Taketani Sabai,
>   Strips of dyed cloth are hanging to dry.
>   Fine Arimitsu cloth,
>   Fine blue and white cloth,
>   Falling from a high staging,
>   Falling like a falling water
>   Sliding over a high cliff. . . .

The scenes of the short lyrics—of Sanno quarter, of Asakusa with ladies coming to see peonies, of a daimyo's procession, of geisha, of the River Tenryu—eleven in all, unrelated to one another, are taken from scenes of Edo period wood-block prints, probably sent by Percival Lowell. The source of inspiration of the lyric on *Oiran* is probably one of the scenes of Matsubaya by Utamaro or Eisui. The Occidental and the Oriental themes are set in juxtaposition. They are contrasted and paralleled like two themes in polyphonic music, and then brought to a crescendo.

Naturally, there is an ambivalent attitude toward the expedition in the poem. The narrator of the multivoiced polyphonic prose poses both as an excited American patriot and as a Japanophile and prophetic critic.

> These monkey-men have got to trade, Uncle Sam has laid his plans with care, see those black guns sizzling there.... Commerce-raiding a nation; pulling apart the curtains of a temple and calling it a trade. Magnificent mission! Every shop-till in every bye-street will bless you. Force the shut gate with the muzzles of your black cannon. Then wait—wait for fifty years—and see who has conquered.

Ironic tone is obvious here. Amy Lowell's familiarity with, and her love of, Japanese art has enabled her to have a double vision.

In part 2, the arrival of the four ships at Uraga and its immediate effects on the "Land of Great Peace" are described.

> Cannon! Cannon! from one of the "black ships." Thirteen thudding explosions, thirteen red dragon tongues, thirteen clouds of smoke like the breath of the mountain gods. Thirteen hammer strokes shaking the Great Gate, and the seams in the metal widen. Open Sesame, shotless guns; and "the Only, High, Grand and Mighty, Inviolable Mysteriousness, Chief Barbarian" reveals himself, and steps into his barge.

Here again one can see the double vision. Commodore Perry's landing is described from American and Japanese points of view. And the two are curiously interfused, showing again the ambivalent attitudes of the narrator to the expedition.

The poem ends with the same suspending chords. The postlude is composed of three short pieces, each representing a scene some years after the Perry expedition. The first of them is a poem about a deserted castle moat in Japan with lotus flowers under the pale moon.

> In the Castle moat, lotus flowers are blooming,
> They shine with the light of an early moon
> Brightening above the Castle towers.

The image may have been suggested by such pictures as John La Farge's sketches of Japan in his *Artist's Letters from Japan*, a copy of which Amy Lowell owned. One of the illustrations is a picture of an old castle moat with lotus leaves spreading all over and seven lotus flowers blooming.

In the background are stone walls, a gate, a tower, trees, and mountains. La Farge makes a comment on his own sketch during his trip to Tokyo from Yokohama.

> The landscape is lovely, and we saw the shapes we know so well in the prints—the curious shapes of the Japanese pines; little temples on the hillside; and rice-fields with their network of causeways, occasionally a horse or a peasant threading them. The land is cultivated like a garden, the lotus leaves fill the ditches, and one or two pink flowers are just out.[11]

One cannot be sure whether he meant by "ditches" the castle moats. But when he sketched the moat, La Farge probably was unaware that the moats had become shallower after the Restoration in 1868, one of the causes of which had been Perry's visit to Japan. Amy Lowell's poem on the castle moat with lotus flowers is therefore appropriate in suggesting the change of scenes in Japan after the opening of the "Great Gate."

The second poem in the postlude, "1903, Japan," is about a Japanese youth who killed himself. Before he threw himself from "the high cliffs of the Kegon waterfall," he carved on the tree trunk:

> How mightily and steadily go Heaven and Earth! How infinite the duration of Past and Present! Try to measure this vastness with five feet. A word explains the Truth of the whole universe—*unknowable*. To cure my agony I have decided to die. . . .

The model for the youth is a student of philosophy at Tokyo High School, Misao Fujimura. But the direct source of the passage is Seichi Naruse's essay, "Young Japan," in *The Seven Arts*.[12] Discussing the consequences of the uncertain values in the early Meiji period, Naruse shows the event as symbolic of the time.

> To the older generation this suicide was not a call but rather a sudden peal of thunder. To kill oneself because of a philosophical dilemma or a view of life was beyond the reach of their imagination. . . . It was pointed out that western culture was poisonous and that there was need of returning to the ancient Japan. But the outcry was too feeble to turn back the

powerful trend of the times. The suicide was only too symbolic of the state of the Japanese youth. The heavy flood of European culture was too overwhelming.

Overwhelming confusion of ideas in the flood of Western civilization into Japan led to the realization of a person's limitedness against the whole of human knowledge and the further vastness of the universe. Pessimism emerging from a sense of failure in the search for the truth led to the conclusion that the truth was "unknowable." "Death was exalted" by the young Japanese, and the Kegon became "a popular sanctuary." To Amy Lowell this was one of the most tragic results of Perry's visit to Japan fifty years before.

The last piece of the postlude, "1903 America," is about the memorial exhibition of the paintings of Whistler, who was fascinated by Japanese art. "All day long the throng of people is so great that one can scarcely see them," she writes. "Debits—credits? Flux and flow through a wide gateway. Occident—Orient—after fifty years."

A deep sense of irony seems to underlie the entire poem. It becomes more obvious toward the end. The main purpose of the expedition was to open commerce between the United States and Japan, but its effects are more strongly felt in the fields of arts and philosophy. "Uncle Sam has laid his plans with care," but the unexpected results are there— suicide and Whistler and revolution. This sense of irony is a reflection of the complex feeling of Amy Lowell toward the expedition. In the preface to *Can Grande's Castle*, she writes:

> I have tried to give a picture of two races at a moment when they were brought in contact for the first time. Which of them has gained most by this meeting, it would be difficult to say.[14]

On the one hand the opening of the "Great Gate" is a welcome event for her. As a citizen of the United States who spent her girlhood in the age of expansion and imperialism, she was delighted at imagining American flags waving in the Pacific, as were many other Americans. As a Lowell she was for the expansion of commerce. As a close friend of Augustus Belmont, a grandson of Comdr. Joseph Matthew Perry, she shared with him some family sentiments toward the great achievement of the naval officer.

Above all the opening of the "gate" had enabled her to encounter

Japanese art, which she so loved and admired. But on the other hand the opening was not a totally welcome event for her. The Japanese people whom she loved were thrown into confusion. They began to underestimate their traditional beauty. But because of her complex feelings, because of her deeper knowledge of the two countries, she was able to realize that to evaluate the international encounter only in terms of gain or loss was of dubious value. Because of her dual vision, she was able to suggest that commerical relation between the countries inevitably would alter their entire relationship, which she said the two peoples should accept and be prepared for by having pluralistic viewpoints and with a hope that the opening of the gate is not like opening "Pandora's box."[15]

Guns as Keys as a whole is a powerful poem. But taken individually some of the short lyrics on the Japanese scenes in the "polyphonic prose" lack intensity. They are descriptive and explanatory, compared with the still shorter lyrical poems on Japanese subjects collected in *Pictures of the Floating World* (1919). "I have endeavoured only to keep the brevity and suggestion of the *hokku*," she writes in her preface.[16] Certainly the brevity and suggestion of the haiku is there. But the chief sources of these poems seem to be elsewhere. The title of the book, which is a literal translation of ukiyoe, popularly known as wood-block prints, suggests that Amy Lowell has tried to re-create the beauty of ukiyoe in the poems. Certainly she has achieved in these poems the kind of intensity that ukiyoe gives to the viewer. Ukiyo, with a heavy Buddhist connotation, means "this temporal world," as opposed to paradise. The ukiyoe painters' consciousness of the limitedness of this "floating" world seems to have led them to catch the moments of fragile beauty, often with exaggeration, comparable to the baroque sensibility.

Some poems in the section "Lacquer Prints," in *Pictures of the Floating World* are Amy Lowell's own arrangements of the Japanese legends from her readings. "Document" is an episode about Katsushika Hokusai (1760–1849) in his later years. "The Emperor's Garden" is a variation of the legend about Ashikaga Yoshimitsu (1358–1404), who was a shogun, not an emperor.[17] "Disillusion" is about a Japanese scholar who killed himself by jumping into the crater of a volcano.

Some other poems in "Lacquer Prints" are free adaptations of classical Japanese poems. The source of "From China" is a tanka by Abe no Nakamaro (701–70) who died in the foreign land. "Temple

Ceremony" is almost a literal translation of a tanka of Sōjō Henjō (815–95), who was a courtier before he became a Buddhist priest in his later years.[18] The sources of the two poems based on the tanka, "From China" and "Temple Ceremony," possibly could be William N. Porter's translations of *Hyakunin Isshu, A Hundred Verses from Old Japan* (1910).

But most of the rest of the poems in "Lacquer Prints" are Amy Lowell's attempts to re-create the beauty of ukiyoe. The title itself of "One of the 'Hundred Views of Fuji' by Hokusai" suggests that the four-line poem was inspired by one of Hokusai's *Fugaku Hyakkei*, a collection of wood-block prints with one hundred views of Mount Fuji:

> Being thirsty,
> I filled a cup with water,
> and behold! Fuji-yama lay upon the water
> Like a dropped leaf!

Hazel Durnell thinks that Lowell was inspired to write this poem by "The Surface of the Water at Misaka, Kai Province," in which "Fuji is mirrored upside down in the water of Lake Kawaguchi." But the real source is elsewhere. Among the books Amy Lowell bequeathed to Harvard University in 1926 was *One Hundred Views of Fuji*. And one of the pictures in the book, "Haichū no Fuji" (Fuji in a Cup of Sake), shows a man sitting and holding a small cup, in which is reflected Mount Fuji dancing like a dropped leaf.[19] The man in the picture is pointing humorously to the cup of sake for the viewer to see the small and deformed top of the sacred mountain. This is more likely the source of inspiration for the poem. There are some differences, however, between the Hokusai print and Lowell's poem. The cup is obviously filled with sake in the picture, for *hai* in "Haichū no Fuji" means "a cup for sake." But in the poem the man fills the cup "with water." It might be that Amy Lowell neglected the title of the picture in Japanese and Chinese ideograms, or it might be that she could not read the ideograms. Yet the humor in the Hokusai print is successfully re-created dramatically in Lowell's short poem.

The source of inspiration of another poem is also ukiyoe, in another book that Amy Lowell bequeathed to Harvard University: "Five Nightingales and Pale Red Plum," in *Kachōgaden*. The rice paper used for the prints in the volume is creamy white.

Desolation

Under the plum-blossoms are nightingales;
But the sea is hidden in an egg-white mist,
And they are silent.[20]

Amy Lowell had written poems on Japanese art since "A Coloured Print by Shōkei." But it was A. D. Ficke who rekindled her interest in Japan about 1915. In her letter to Ficke, an ukiyoe collector and poet in Chicago, she wrote:

> Once more let me thank you for your "Chats on Japanese Prints." I have read it again since I came home from Chicago, and always with renewed pleasure. It has even inspired me to write a number of little 'Hokku' poems—for no reason whatever except that you put me so in the mood.[21]

In 1919 she wrote to Richard Aldington that she had been writing the short lyrics, which were to be collected in her *Pictures of the Floating World*, "at odd moments for the last four years."[22] It can be assumed that most of those short lyrics were written after her acquaintance with Ficke's *Chats on Japanese Prints* (1915).

Ficke's book is a brief history of ukiyoe with illustrations and comments, and with a number of poems on paintings and prints. Of a portrait of a woman by Utamaro, Ficke writes:

> In robes like clouds of sunset rolled
> About the dying sun,
> In splendid vestures of purple and gold
> That a thousand toiling days have spun
> For thee, O imperial one!

It is a verbal description of, and free fantasies about, the prints in verse form. It is this sort of poetry that stimulated Amy Lowell most. But to write a poem to a painting, or to draw a painting to a poem, was a common practice in Japan, especially among ukiyoe painters, haiku poets, and Zen priests. It may be that this practice inspired Ficke, who inspired Lowell.

Many of the heavily rhymed poems in Ficke's *Chats on Japanese Prints*, however, are tediously descriptive and frivolously fantastic, as in "The Pupil of Toyokuni."

> I walk the crowded Yedo streets,
> And everywhere one question greets
> My passing, as the strollers say—
> "How goes the Master's work to-day?
> We saw him sketching hard last night
> At Ryogoku. . . ."
> Yes, I am pupil to the great
> How well he bears his famous state![23]

Amy Lowell tried to write her poems about ukiyoe—not for ukiyoe, but independent from it—with more concentration, "brevity and suggestion." She may have achieved it successfully because she had imagist training, which Ficke did not. She eliminated irrelevant descriptions, and by using personae, as she learned from Pound, re-created the emotional equivalents of the pictures in her poems. "One of the 'Hundred Views of Fuji' by Hokusai" has re-created a Japanese sense of humor, as in discovering Mount Fuji in the small cup of sake. A dreary sense of nothingness behind nightingales on plum trees is re-created in her "Desolation." In the poem "A Year Passes," while the reader is shown the images one by one removed farther from him, he realizes that the scene has moved the speaker to the point where he already has felt pain.

> Beyond the porcelain fence of the pleasure garden,
> I hear the frogs in the blue-green rice-fields;
> But the sword-shaped moon
> Has cut my heart in two.

An emotion conjured by the scene is condensed into an intense moment. The idea behind all this is the same as that of ukiyoe painters: the fragility of beauty and life.

The greatest influence, however, on Amy Lowell in her understanding and recreation of ukiyoe probably was Percival Lowell's account of Japanese art in his influential book, *The Soul of the Far East*, with which she had long been familiar.

A Japanese painting is a poem rather than a picture. It portrays an emotion called up by the scene, and not the scene itself in all its elaborated complexity. It undertakes to give only so much of it as is vital to that particular feeling, and intentionally omits all irrelevant details. It is the expression caught from a glimpse of the soul of nature by the soul of man, the mirror of a mood, passing, perhaps, in fact, but perpetuated thus to fancy. Being an emotion, its intensity is directly proportional to the singleness with which it possesses the thoughts.[24]

Amy Lowell's poetry of Japan is an attempt to portray "an emotion called up by" Japanese art. It is the expression "caught from a glimpse of the soul" of Japanese art. And its intensity is "directly proportional to the singleness with which it possesses the thoughts," as in the haiku. The main theme of the book by Percival Lowell is that the chief characteristic of the Japanese people and their art is "impersonality." The emotion in Amy Lowell's poetry is made impersonal by her use of personae. And here she is in the poem but ironically outside it as well.

Toward the end of her life, Amy Lowell wrote more poems on Japanese culture and in Japanese forms, which she continued to love and admire: "Free Fantasia on Japanese Themes," "Twenty-Four Hokku on a Modern Theme," and "Tanka." And certainly her understanding of Japanese culture grew deeper. But through out her life she never immersed herself in Japanese culture to the extent that Fenollosa, Pound, Rexroth, and Gary Snyder did. She did not accept the Japanese way of life but stuck to American values. She wrote in her "Free Fantasia on Japanese Themes,"

> I would experience new emotions—
> Submit to strange enchantments
> Bend to influences,
> Bizarre, exotic,
> Fresh with burgeoning.

She would "submit to strange enchantments" awhile. But as a poet of "the Yankee will"[25] she would never let herself remain enchanted.

In one of her poems of later years collected in *What's O'Clock* (1925), she wrote about lilacs in New England.

> Lilacs
> False blue.
> White,
> Purple,
> Colour of lilac,
> Your great puffs of flowers
> Are everywhere in this my New England.

.   .   .

> Maine knows you,
> Has for years and years;
> New Hampshire knows you,
> And Massachusetts
> And Vermont.
> Cape Cod starts you along the beaches to Rhode Island;
> Connecticut takes you from a river to the sea.

.   .   .

The "great puffs" stretch "from Canada to Narragansett Bay." The assumption is that the beauty of lilacs in America lies not in the blossoms or leaves of a single tree, but in the whole mass of trees in abundance and variety, stretching for hundreds of miles, a vision not easily contained in a short poem. This seems peculiarly an American sensibility. She ends her long poem, in a Whitmanesque way, with her glorification of, and identification with, her country.

> Heart-leaves of lilac all over New England,
> Roots of lilac under all the soil of New England,
> Lilac in me because I am New England,
> Because my roots are in it,
> Because my leaves are of it,
> Because it is my country
> And I speak to it of itself
> And sing of it with my own voice
> Since certainly it is mine.

Amy Lowell remained an American and a New Englander. She kept her American, and more particularly New England, sentiments.

Her poetry was most powerful when she wrote about American subjects, in looser forms, with personal feelings. Her poetry was most delicate and beautiful when she wrote short, imagistic, haikulike poems, often with Japanese subjects. Her poetry was at its best when the two types of poetry were merged and functionally superposed in "polyphonic prose" as in *Guns as Keys: And the Great Gate Swings*, where the narrative of Commodore Perry's voyage was interspersed with the short poems about peaceful Japanese scenes.

The Cinquains of Crapsey

In her earlier years, Adelaide Crapsey (1878–1914) wrote longer poems, such as "Birth-Moment" (1905) about Aphrodite's approach to the shore, and "The Mother Exultant" (1905) about a happy, young farm wife on a Mediterranean vineyard. When Crapsey again visited the Mediterranean, she wrote another long poem, "John Keats" (1909). A former colleague, Esther Lowenthall, recalls that, while teaching poetics as an instructor at Smith College between 1911 and 1913, Crapsey was still "working very hard on the metric, counting all the syllables in *Paradise Lost*, *Samson Agonistes*, the longer poems of Tennyson, Thompson, Swinburne, and nursery rhymes." [26]

But between 1911 and her death, Adelaide Crapsey wrote a number of short poems in her freshly delicate poetical form, which she called cinquain, consisting of five lines, usually of two, four, six, eight, and two syllables.

Shadow

A-sway,
On red rose,
A golden butterfly.
And on my heart a butterfly
Night-wing'd.

Louis Untermeyer called her "an unconscious Imagist." [27] Certainly we find fragile and imagistic beauty and compression, often associated with Japanese art, in such a poem as "The Guarded Wound."

If it
Were lighter touch
Than petal of flower resting
On grass oh still too heavy it were,
Too heavy!

Mary Elizabeth Osborn investigated Crapsey's library and found that she owned a copy of William N. Porter's *Hundred Verses from Old Japan* (1910), a translation of *Hyaku-nin-isshu*,[28] in which each poem was rendered in five lines. Earl Miner observed that "Anguish," one of her cinquains, "echoes" Porter's translation of a tanka by Mibu no Tadamine:

I hate the cold unfriendly moon
That shines at early morn
And nothing seems so sad and gray
When I am left forlorn
At day's returning dawn.[29]

Anguish

Keep thou
Thy tearless watch
All night but when blue-dawn
Breathes on the silver moon, then weep!
Then weep!

According to Hideo Kawanami, three of the autographed copies of the poems in French and England found in Crapsey's notebook proved to be her copies of the poems found in Michel Revon's *Anthologie de la littérature japonaise des origines au XXe siècle* (1910) and Yonejirō Noguchi's *From the Eastern Sea* (1903, 1910). Kawanami guessed that "Revon's influence on Crapsey is greater than Porter's," as seems to be reflected in her naming of the form "cinquain."[30] Susan Sutton Smith, upon closely examining Crapsey's manuscript notes on Revon, suggested that Crapsey's "Anguish" is closer to the French translation of the tanka by Sato Norikiyo [Saigyō Hōshi]:

Tandis que je pense
A des choses tristes, est-ce la lune
Qui m'a dit: "Pleure!"
Sur mon visage inquiet,
Hélas! mes larmes![31]

(Nageku to te
Tsuki ya wa mono o
Omowasuru
Kakochigao naru
Waga namida kana)

Crapsey's version in her cinquain may be an echo of work by Mibu no Tadamine, by Saigyō, or both. It may also be an echo of other tankas in *Hyaku-nin-isshu*, which is replete with such poems as those by Akazome Emon and Shun-e Hōshi, supposedly written on the watches of the night. One might suspect that Crapsey, a devoted daughter of a Christian minister, may have taken those poems as the Oriental versions of such Western songs of lovers' separation at dawn as the Provençal "Alba," who reproachfully cries out at the "tearless" rascals, "then weep! / Then weep!" But the poem is more probably a reflection of her own experience of sleepless nights, restlessly recollecting in bed the pleasant days of her youth. As Crapsey was suffering seriously from tuberculosis toward the end of her life, when these poems were written, we may suspect she endured many such nights.

Examining the cinquains, Susan Sutton Smith notes that "some indeed involve a superposition of ideas or intersection between the eternal and the momentary, the motionless and the moving." "Roma Aeterna," Smith thinks, "contrasts the evanescent perceptions of the moment—the warmth of sunlight and the sound of birdsongs—with the timeless, changeless presence of Rome's site and its mythical founder." Another cinquain, "Blue Hyacinths," she says, "summons up another contrast between the transitory and the permanent."[32] Certainly there also is tension between two different reactions to attitudes toward life in "Anguish," represented by the contrast between pleasure and sorrow, night and dawn. Smith goes on to point out that Crapsey's manner of contrasting the opposites "foreshadows" Ezra Pound's theory of superposition, showing that one of the translations by Revon in Crapsey's notes has superpositry structure. While Pound was inspired by haiku, Smith is suggesting that Crapsey had derived a similar idea of superpositry structure from tanka, not from haiku. Certainly the superpositry method is found both in tanka and haiku; and since Crapsey's use of superposition, or "intersection," is more starkly straightforward, lacking the kind of subtle wit of haiku, she might quite possibly have found tanka more congenial.

There are two additional points concerning the cinquains. The first is that the form of the cinquain is more rigid than the form of the Japanese tanka. As the number of syllables increases in each succeeding line of the cinquain, the emotional voltage tends to mount to the climactic fourth line, where suddenly it fades off into the frail two-syllable last line, producing an astonishing effect not unlike that of anticlimax or even bathos. In other words, the form itself suggests a meaning, and a tragic sense. It suggests laborious effort for attainment, tersely terminated by the wholly unanticipated. "November Night" is, in that sense, a successful cinquain.

> Listen . . .
> With faint dry sound,
> Like steps of passing ghosts,
> The leaves, frost-crisp'd, break from the tree
> And fall.

When a suitable subject is chosen to be contained in this structure, the form is an extremely effective, brief, yet poignant vehicle to convey the sense of tragedy. But when the content is diluted to fit the form, the poem as a whole seems flaccid.

> The sun
> Is warm to-day
> O Romulus, and on
> Thine olden Palatine the birds
> Still sing.

It seems that the sense of "Roma Aeterna," though praised by Smith, could have been expressed more concisely and effectively in haiku form, or even in free verse.

The second point to be made is that in discussing the cinquain we must take into consideration that Crapsey's view of life seems to have undergone a thorough change as she began to exploit the delicate cinquain form. Manager of the basketball team while a student at Vassar, she was active after her graduation in 1901, helping her father with his church and community center in Rochester, N.Y. Between 1902 and 1904, she taught history and literature at Kemper Hall. In 1904, she was in Europe studying archaeology, for some time staying in Rome. Her poems written in her youth reflect her energy and passion. In her "Birth-Moment" (1905), the speaker cries out to Venus coming to the shore, as if she were another young Venus.

> I too am young;
> I too am all of love!

Crapsey learned in 1911 that she "suffered from tuberculin meningitis,"[33] and collapsed in July 1913; recovery seemed virtually impossible. As her health steadily declined, she left a witty but serious epigram before her death in 1914:

> If illness' end be health regained then I
> Will pay you, Asculapeus, when I die.

By that time she seems to have recognized the transiency of life. All of her cinquains are overshadowed by images of death, blight, and fragility.

Triad

These be
Three silent things:
The falling snow . . . the hour
Before the dawn . . . the mouth of one
Just dead.

Moon-shadows

Still as
On windless nights
The moon-cast shadows are,
So still will be my heart when I
Am dead.

She seems to be obsessed by death, understandably by her own death, as she knew it to be so near. The images which represent "the momentary" in contrast to "the eternal"—the falling snowflakes, the hour before the dawn, and the moon-cast shadows—all seem symbols of her own "momentary" existence. Other similar images are those of the falling leaf in "November Night," of the bird singing on the Palatine Hill in "Roma Aeterna," and of the wan and evanescent moon above the crashing water in "Niagara Seen on a Night in November." Apparently what she wanted to say in her last moments was that her life, and that of every human being, was short and fragile but beautiful.

In her elaboration of the cinquain, Crapsey tried to create the form that might best express her sense of life's evanescence, stimulated by the delicate Japanese classical poems; and she succeeded, after arduous "prosody work," in fashioning that form and structure that suited her purposes better than might the original form and structure of Japanese poetry.

In *After Strange Gods*, T. S. Eliot explains why he did not "make Confucius a mainstay," though he had "the highest respect for the Chinese mind."

Just as I do not see how anyone can expect really to understand Kant and Hegel without knowing the German language and without such an understanding of the German mind as can only be acquired in the society of living Germans, so *a fortiori* I do not see how anyone can understand Confucius without some knowledge of Chinese and a long frequentation of the best Chinese society.... I do not believe that I, for one, could ever come to understand it [i.e., Chinese civilization] well enough to make Confucius a mainstay.

As for Eliot's opinion of Sanskrit and Hindu philosophy:

I am led to this conclusion partly by an analogous experience. Two years spent in the study of Sanskrit under Charles Lanman, and a year in the mazes of Patanjali's metaphysics under the guidance of James Woods, left me in a state of enlightened mystification. A good half of the effort of understanding what the Indian philosophers were after—and their subtleties make most of the great European philosophers look like schoolboys—lay in trying to erase from my mind all the categories and kinds of distinction common to European philosophy from the time of the Greeks.... And I came to the conclusion ... that my only hope of really penetrating to the heart of that mystery would lie in forgetting how to think as an American or a European: which, for practical as well as sentimental reasons, I did not wish to do.[34]

To Eliot, European and non-European philosophies seemed incompatible, impossible to amalgamate with his experiences. Probably it is why he called *The Waste Land* a "chaotic poem."[35] His sense of self-identity as "as American or a European" kept him from "penetrating to the heart of that mystery" of the non-Western civilizations.

Both Amy Lowell and Adelaide Crapsey seem to have had "analogous experiences." Crapsey studied Japanese prosody. Lowell had some knowledge of Japanese art. Crapsey adopted a Japanese poetical form. Lowell decorated her poetry with Japanese images, tried some Japanese forms, and used a Japanese subject as one of the themes of a fugal poem. But still, Lowell remained a New Englander and Crapsey an Episcopalian. It is probably because both of them felt, as Eliot did, that they could never "come to understand" the Oriental philosophy "well enough to make it a mainstay." They had little confidence that they could ever "penetrate to the heart of that mystery" of Japanese art. Such poets as Pound and Rexroth, however, seem to have accepted more readily the assumption that they could amalgamate, as Whitman did, the Eastern with Western values.

3
Ezra Pound

Pound's Interest in the Orient

Ezra Pound (1885–1972) was brought up in Philadelphia after his father, moving his family from Hailey, Idaho, in 1889, began to work for the U.S. Mint as an assistant assayer. The Centennial Exhibition had been held in Philadelphia in 1876, and thousands of people had crowed into the Japanese "dwelling," where they were quite amazed at the Japanese *objets d'art*, especially the wooden house itself, "as nicely put together as a piece of cabinet work." The citizens of Philadelphia had welcomed the seventy-seven envoys from Japan in 1860 with a parade and balloons. They were familiar with the Japanese coins with square holes, some "of oblong shapes," which the Japanese embassy had given out to the crowds. Newspapers had informed them of the "intelligence and acuteness," which the Japanese had displayed in "delicate and difficult investigations" while using an ivory "steelyard" to calculate the gold content of coins of both countries, during their visit to the United States Mint.[1]

While Pound spent his boyhood there, occasionally visiting his father's office, it is quite possible he heard something about Japan, and saw Japanese coins, wallpaper, furniture, screens, or fans, some of them brought by the envoys, and others imported about the turn of the century by such companies as Tiffany and Yamanaka Shōkai. In 1897 a Philadelphia lawyer, John Luther Long, published the novel *Madame Butterfly*, which, as mentioned earlier, was made into a successful play in 1900 and an even more successful opera in 1904. It is quite possible that Erza Pound, who, like his mother, was interested in music, saw, read, or at least heard of a version of *Madame Butterfly*.

When Pound began writing poetry seriously during his under-graduate years at the University of Pennsylvania and Hamilton College, he was mainly interested in Browning, the pre-Raphaelites, Provençal poets and the nineties. He was still interested in them while teaching Romance languages as an instructor at Wabash College, Indiana. But soon after he went to England in 1908, Pound realized that he and Whitman had "one sap and one root."[2] In "What I Feel about Walt Whitman" (1909), he wrote:

> From this side of the Atlantic, I am for the first time able to read Whitman, and from the vantage of my education and—if it be permitted a man of scant years—my world citizenship: I see him, American's poet. . . . The vital part of my message, taken from the sap and fibre of America is the same as his. Mentally I am a Walt Whitman. . . .[3]

It is significant to note that Pound's claim of "world citizenship" is linked to a reappraisal and identification with Whitman, whom he had "detested . . . long enough."[4] To be an American was, for Pound, as it had been for Whitman, to be a cosmopolitan. This awareness seems to have led him from dilettantism to "Passage to more than India," sailing consciously in search of knowledge of world civilization, ancient and modern, Western and Eastern.

On March 15, 1909, Pound heard a lecture by his friend Laurence Binyon on "Oriental and European Art," and found it "intensely interesting." In the same year Pound was introduced to the dining and talking club at Café Tour d'Eiffel, where he met T. E. Hulme, F. S. Flint, and their circles, and was informed of their "program for a modernization of poetry" through "the emphasis on free verse, the appeal to the visual," and also of "the Japanese haiku."[5]

It was most probably in the spring of 1911 that Pound wrote a "*hokku*-like poem" himself for the first time.[6] It is a well-known episode in the history of imagism.[7] Ezra Pound got out of a metro train at La Concord in Paris. He suddenly saw bright and beautiful faces of women and children coming out of the dark, one after another, like white petals dancing in the soft wind. He wanted to write a poem on the sensation he experienced, which came like a flash but lingered in his mind. When he returned home to 92 rue Raymouard that evening he "found, suddenly, the expression."

> I do not mean that I found words, but there came an equation
> . . . not in speech, but in little splotches of colour. . . . I realized
> quite vividly that if I were a painter, or if I had, often, *that kind*
> of emotion, or even if I had the energy to get paints and brushes
> and keep at it, I might found a new school of painting, of
> "non-representative" painting, a painting that would speak
> only by arrangements in colour.

Since he was a poet, he tried to put the "equation" of the experience
into words. He wrote "a thirty-line poem," but destroyed it, because
he thought it was a work "of secondary intensity."[8] Six months later
he composed "a poem half that length." But he thought it still lacked
the intensity of the original, "that kind of emotion."

He then was reminded of a story that his French-English friend
Victor Plarr once told him. According to Plarr, he was walking along
the London streets on a snowy day with a young Japanese naval officer,
most probably Hiroharu Kato.[9] They noticed a cat's freshly imprinted
footsteps crossing the path in the snow. "Stop, I am making a poem,"
the officer said. And in a short while he wrote, and showed him, a
haikulike poem:

> The footsteps of the cat upon the snow:
> Plum-blossoms.

No one would say that this witty, or rather playful, occasional haiku is
a good poem. But Pound, on hearing the story and recollecting a few
other haiku he knew,[10] thought seriously that there must be some
"theory" in the haiku. There was an image of the footprints of a cat
on the snow in the first line, and another of plum blossoms in the
second. Though quite different, the two images, when "superposed,"
became metaphors amplifying and clarifying each other, until the two
seemed to dissolve into a one-image poem. Pound thought that the
haikulike, one-image poem was "a form of superposition."

> I found it useful in getting out of the impasse in which I had
> been left by my metro emotion.[11]

And he composed a two-line poem, in which the "equation" of the
moment of his sensory experience with "splotches of colour" was,
as it were, frozen into a picture with a rhythm.

> The apparition of these faces in the crowd;
> Petals on a wet, black bough.

In September 1912 he met and became interested in Rabindranath Tagore, "the very great Bengali poet."[12] Pound edited, and wrote an introductory essay to, six of Tagore's poems, which appeared in the December 1912 issue of *Poetry*.

> The Bengali brings to us the pledge of a calm which we need overmuch in an age of steel and mechanics. It brings a quiet proclamation of the fellowship between man and the gods; between man and nature.... There is a deeper calm and a deeper conviction in this eastern expression than we have yet attained. It is by the arts alone that one people learns to meet another far distant people in friendship and respect.
>
> I speak with all gravity when I say that world-fellowship is nearer for the visit of Rabindranath Tagore in London.[13]

This passage, which Whitman could have written if he had known Tagore, reveals Pound's conviction that "a deeper calm" of mind and "the fellowship between man and gods" are "overmuch" needed in our age and that there is much to learn from Oriental arts and religions. Just as in Whitman's idea of cosmopolitan brotherhood, which was closely related to his idea of fraternity in "religious democracy," we find religious overtones in Pound's need for "injection" from heterogeneous cultures to create "a renaissance in America."[14]

Pound then tried to translate the fifteenth-century Hindi poet, Kabir, with the assistance of Tagore's pupil, Kali Mohan Ghose.[15] In 1913 when Tagore became the first Asian poet to receive the Nobel Prize in literature, Pound, while busy launching imagism, met Mary Fenollosa at the London house of Sarojini Naidu, an Indian poet and a friend of Tagore's.

Mary Fenollosa was the widow of Ernest Fenollosa, who, while teaching at universities in Tokyo, had taken private lessons in Japanese painting from Kano school masters, learned about Chinese poetry from Kainan Mori, and studied Nō plays with Minoru Umewaka. At his death Fenollosa had left "a quantity of manuscripts including a great number of rough translations (literally exact) from the Chinese,"[16] based on the interpretation of the great sinologist in Japan at that time.

After such poems by Pound as "Tenzone," "Condolence," "The Garret," "Salutation," "Dance Figure," and "In a Station of the Metro," were published in the April 1913 issue of *Poetry* (subsequently collected in *Lustra*), "Mrs. Fenollosa recognized that in Pound the Chinese manuscripts would find the interpreter whom her husband would have wished."[17] The meeting between Pound and Mary Fenollosa proved mutually stimulating. According to Mary Fenollosa, "Pound questioned her at length about her husband's work and their life in Japan and was so enthusiastic about Fenollosa's literary researches that Mrs. Fenollosa promised, on her return to America, to send him whatever translations and notes she had."[18] According to Pound:

> Well, she said that Fenollosa had been in opposition to all the profs and academes, and ... said I was the only person who could finish up these notes as Ernest would have wanted them done. Fenollosa saw what needed to be done but he didn't have time to finish it.[19]

When Pound received the manuscript notebooks, he was delighted. He showed them to his wife and to the poet and playwright William Butler Yeats, and from Stone Cottage he wrote to his close friend, William Carlos Williams, on December 19, 1913.

> I am very placid and happy and busy. Dorothy is learning Chinese. I've all old Fenollosa's treasures in mss.

Pound worked first on a Nō play Nishikigi, which he found "too beautiful to be encumbered with notes and long explanation."[20] It was published in Poetry in May 1914.

Those poems by Pound with Chinese subjects such as "After Ch'u Yuan," "Fan-Piece for Her Imperial Lord," and "Liu Ch'e," which had appeared in the February 1914 issue of Glebe, were not worked from Fenollosa's notes but from H. A. Giles's English translations of Chinese poems in his History of Chinese Literature (1901), as was pointed out by K. K. Ruthven and as evidenced by the transliteration of the proper names.[21] Pound probably worked on them as a kind of exercise or étude while awaiting the arrival of the notebooks of Ernest Fenollosa from Mary Fenollosa, who had described to him how they looked.

Pound then worked on some Chinese poetry contained in Fenollosa's notes, publishing fourteen of them in Cathay in 1915.

Pound and Fenollosa: Cathay

Ever since its publication in 1915, Cathay has won favorable criticism. T. S. Eliot remarked that, with this book of translations from Chinese classics, Pound "enriched modern English poetry as Fitzgerald enriched it." F. R. Leavis acknowledged it as "authoritative." Yvor Winters, though not always sympathetic with Pound, praised the work.[22] Certainly *Cathay* is a charming collection of poems, some of which have been anthologized often; and it is not hard to imagine the impact the freshness, simplicity, and beauty of these poems had on the audience at the book's first apearance in London.

"Song of the Bowmen of Shu" is a poem spoken by a soldier of the Chinese army sent to the northern border about three thousand years ago to defend the country against the "barbarians." While picking young ferns in the early spring, the speaker deplores the "sorrowful" condition of the troops far from their homes.

> Here we are, picking the first fern-shoots
> And saying: when shall we get back to our country?
> Here we are because we have the Ken-nin for our foemen,
> We have no comfort because of these Mongols.
> We grub the soft fern-shoots,
> When anyone says 'Return,' the others are full of sorrow.
> Sorrowful minds, sorrow is strong, we are hungry and
> 　　　thirsty.　　　　　　　　　　　　　　　(lines 1–7)

As the seasons pass, their anxiety deepens. Their defense "is not yet made sure." Their horses are "tired," though they were once strong and "well trained." They "have no comfort," though their generals' arrows and quivers are beautifully ornamented. All the soldiers are depressed and frustrated, for "the enemy is swift" and they must fight "three battles a month." The poem ends on a note of resignation: "who will know of our grief?" With the repetition of the word "sorrow," the despair seems overwhelming, contrasting with the ferns that grow hardier with the passage of the seasons.

Strangely enough, however, the original Chinese poem, "Ts'ai wei" ("Saibi" in Japanese) is not a discouraging poem. Though it may have been written by several hands over a period of time, "Ts'ai wei" as a whole is an "inspiring" poem. It was written, "reputedly by Bunno [Wên wang]," to encourage rather than discourage his soldiers. The speaker, a soldier, is more fully aware of the meaning of the war. Though he begins with a depressing tone, in the middle of the poem, observing the stately general on horseback and the splendid war equip- ment of the royal power, he suddenly realizes the significant role he is playing in defending his country; he therefore refreshes himself and prepares himself for the coming battles.

> The horses are already hitched to the chariot;
> The four horses are vigorous.
> How dare we repose?
> We must conquer the enemy three times a month.
>
> (lines 15–16)

The speaker, imagining a miserable retreat in the snow, asks a rhetorical question, "Who will know of our grief?" The answer assumed is that, though nobody would know of their grief, yet he will persevere and fight. Though there are other interpretations of the poem, the author still being unidentified, yet at least Fenollosa's notebook, from which Pound translated the poem, gives an authentic interpretation.

Fenollosa's notebooks, unavailable to scholars until recently, and erroneously thought to have been full of errors, proved to contain almost exact, literal renderings of the original Chinese poems, although the English is quite awkward. The introductory notes to the poem in Fenollosa's notebook, which Pound must have read, state that the poem was composed "by Bunno," "the commander-in-chief of the Western princes, . . . as if he was one of the soldiers to show his sweet sympathy to them and to soften their grief and pain." [23] The speaker is aware of the significance of the war. "We must be prudent for our affair (which is the order of the emperor): we have no leisure to sit down comfortably," the speaker says. "We must conquer the enemy even three times in a month." Fenollosa's version of the whole poem runs as follows:

						so	
采	薇	采	薇。	薇	亦	作	止。*
sai,	bi,	sai,	bi,	bi,	eki,	saku,	shi,
pick off,	a kind of edible fern,				also to grow		

We pick off the "Warabi" which first grow from the earth.

*The letter 止 is [*sic*] no meaning, no use, but each phrase being composed of 4 letters, this is put at the last of the phrase.

				日	莫	暮	
				sun	bo not		
日	歸	日	歸。	歲	亦	莫	止。
etsu,	ki,	etsu,	ki,	sai,	eki,	baku,	shi,
to say,	to return,			year, also,	come to last.		

We say to each other "when will we return to our country?"—
It will be the last of the year.

The rhime [*sic*] is 作 saku and 莫 baku.

靡	室	靡	家。	玁	狁	之	故
bi	shitsu	bi	ka	ken	in.	shi	ko
without room		house				of	because

Here we are far from our home because we have the "ken-in" as our
enemy.

室, 家 have figurative sense. I.e. 室 means *wife* for the part of husband,
家 means *husband* for the part of wife. "Ken-in" was a Turkish tribe
who lived in the Mongolian desert. "Ken-iku," "Ken-in," "Kyō-
do" are the same tribes, many European scholars approved that
"Kyōto" is quite same to "Hun"; but it is very difficult question,
some professors are quite opposite.

不	遑	啓	居。	玁	狁	之	故
fu,	ko,	kei,	kyo,	ken	in	shi	ko

not to have, leisure, to sit down, to stay.

We have no leisure to sit down comfortably, (as we did at home)
because we have ken-in as our enemy.

N.B.—The gardians [*sic*] go to the boundary of the empire in the
last of spring when the "Warabi" grow from the earth. They
return to the country in the winter of the *next* year. It is very
disagreeable to be so far from their home during almost two years,
but they shall not be angry against the emperor, because the army
of "ken-in" is very formidable and to protect the country against
the enemy is their duty.

采	薇	采	薇。	薇	亦	柔	止。
sai	bi	sai	bi	bi	eki	jū	shi
						soft	

We pick off the "Warabi" which are soft.

日	歸	日	歸。	心	亦	憂	止。
etsu	ki	etsu	ki	shin	eki	yu	shi

When we say the *returning* our mind is full of sorrow.

憂	心	烈	烈。	載	飢	載	渴
yu,	shin,	retsu,	retsu,	sai	ki	sai	katsu
Sorrowful,	mind,	strong,		then to be hungry			thirsty

We are very sorrowful, we are hungry and thirsty.

我	戍	未	定。	靡	使	歸	聘
ga	ju	mi	tei	bi	shi	ki	hei
our,	defense,	not yet,	finish,	not,	let,	return,	to ask

But our defence is not yet settled, so we cannot let our friends return to our country and ask how our family lives.

采	薇	采	薇。	薇	亦	剛	止。
sai,	bi,	sai,	bi,	bi,	eki,	gō,	shi
						rough	

We pick off the Warabi which have become already rough.

日	歸	日	歸。	歲	亦	陽*	止
etsu	ki	etsu	ki	sai	eki	yo	shi
						October	

We say to each other "when will we return to our Country?"—It will be October.

*In "Eki" the Symbol of October is ䷁ i.e. all lines are "In."

There is not "yo" at all, but "yo" comes under the earth, therefore October is called contrarily "the month of Yo."

王	事	靡	盬。	不	遑	啟	處。
wo	ji	bi	ko	fu	ko	kei	sho
royal,	affair,	not,	easy,	not,	to have leisure,	sit down,	stay

We must be prudent for our affair (which is the order of our emperor); we have no leisure to sit down comfortably.

憂	心	孔	疚。	我	行	不	來
							liu
yū	shin	ko	kiu	ga	ko	fu	lai
sorrowful,	mind,	very,	sick,	we,	go,	not,	return

The rhime of this piece is 疚 and 來. The scholars who prefer the new commentary by Shushi (朱子) read 疚 —*kyoku* and 來 —*lyoku* to accord rhime; but I think it forced the sound of words. In my own view, it is much better to read 疚 —ki and 來 —li; because *lai* contract [*sic*] to li, and kiu contract to ki; but I don't know what is the opinion of Prof. Mori.

Our sorrow is very bitter, but we would not return to the country.

彼　爾　維*　何。　維　　常　　　之　　華。
hi　dei　wi　ka　wi　　jo　　　shi　ka
that, blooming, what this, a kind of cherry, of, flower
What is that blooming flower?—That is "Niwazakura."
*維 is used for emphasizing the meaning of phrase.

彼　路　斯　何。　君—子　之　　車。
hi　lo　shi　ka　kun-shi　shi　sha
that, chariot, is, what, prince, of, carriage
Whose is that chariot?—That is our generals.

　　　　　　　　　　　　　　horse　stout
戎—車　既　　　駕。　四　牡　業—々
ju sha　ki　　　ga　　shi　bo　gyō　gyo
chariot, already, to tie the horse, four
The horses are tied already to the chariot. They seem to be vigorous.

豈　敢　定—居。　一　月　三　捷
gai kan　tei kyo　ichi getsu san　shō
how dare　repose　one month　three　victory
Why shall we repose? We must conquer the enemy even three times
in a month.

　　駕　彼　四　牡。　四　牡　騤—々
　　ga　hi　shi　bo　shi　bo　ki—ki
to tie horse, that, four, horse, four, horse, strong
That [*sic*] four horses are tied; they are very strong.

君—子　所　依。　小—人　所　腓。
kun shi　sho　i　sho-nin　sho　hi
prince, that which, ride, subject,　depend.
The *generals* are on their back, and the soldiers are by their side.

　　　　　　　　　　　　　　quiver
四　牡　翼—々。　象　弭　　魚　服。
shi　bo　yoku-yoku,　sho　ji　　gyo　fuku
four　horse　skillful　ivory, edge of arrow,　fish
The four horses are well educated; the generals have the ivory arrows
and the quivers that are ornamented with the skin of fish.

豈　不　日　戒。　玁狁　　孔　棘
ga　fu　jitsu　kai　ken-in　　kō　kyoku
how, not, daily, make attention, very quick
We must be careful every day, because the enemy is very quick.

昔　我　往　矣*。　楊柳　　依々。
Seki　ga　wo　i　yo—liu　i—i
other time, went　　willow　drooping
Other time [sic] when we started the willows are [sic] drooping by spring wind.
*矣 is no meaning, occupy the place only.

今　我　來　思*。　雨—雪　霏　々。
kon　ga　lai　shi　wu-setsu　hi　hi
now, we, come,—　it snows, much,
But now we come back when it snows.

行　道　遲々。　載　　渴　　載　飢
kō　dō　chi—chi　sai　katsu　sai　ki
go road　slowly　then to be thirsty　hungry
We go very slowly and we are thirsty and hungry.

我　心　傷—悲。　莫　知　我　哀*
ga　shin　shō—hi　baku　chi　ga　ai
our, mind, to be sorrowful, not, know, our, grief
Our mind is full of sorrow, who will know our grief?
*哀 contract to single "*i*"

Note how Pound changed and dropped some words in line 15. "The horses are tied already to the chariot. They seem to be vigorous"— Fenollosa's line—is changed to: "Horses, his horses even, are tired. They were strong." The tone of the whole line becomes exactly the opposite. In Fenollosa's version, the horses are ready to go out to the battlefield any moment, but in Pound's they are not. Compare the next lines in the two versions:

> how dare repose one month three victory
> Why shall we repose? We must conquer the enemy even
> three times in a month. (Fenollosa)

> We have no rest, three battles a month. (Pound)

Though the two seem similar on the surface, the speaker in the Fenollosa version is expressing his strong determination to engage in three battles. But in Pound, the speaker seems to be complaining about fighting too many battles.

Fenollosa's next line is: "That [*sic*] four horses are tied; They are very strong." But it is changed to "By heaven, his horses are tired," by Pound, the latter half of the line, "They are very strong," being cut out. And again "tied" is changed to "tired." By emphasizing the sorrow, uncertainty, and anxiety of the soldiers throughout the poem, Pound is building an antiwar poem from the Chinese war poem. Pound earlier had romanticized the war, as in his "Sestina: Altaforte." But 1913 was "a watershed," and, as Peter Makin rightly says, with the outbreak of World War I, and with the news he got from the front, Pound "began to change his ideas on the nature of war, and to look for the rot in the commonweal that could have produced such a monster." [24] Since the poem was published during World War I, and since Pound was against "any war" as reflected in "Mauberley" and his broadcasts, it can be said that Pound boldly "translated" the poem as a persona of his, giving voice to his own feeling about the misery and grief of war.

But examination of Fenollosa's notebooks in relation to Pound's "translations" reveals that the Chinese poems Pound selected for *Cathay* mostly were the ones that present sorrowful or lonely figures who speak out as if to overcome their sorrow or loneliness—"Exile's Letter," "Lament of the Frontier Guard," "The River-Merchant's Wife: A Letter," "Four Poems of Departure," and "To-Em-Mei's 'The Unmoving Cloud'." These poems reflect a state of mind similar to that in his book *Lustra.* That is, "Tenzone," "Ité," "The Rest," "Further Instructions," and three "Salutations" are all confessions by spiritual exiles of their sufferings and crucial emotional experiences. And that this choice may reflect Pound's own state of mind at the time seems apparent in his scribbled note on the last page of *Cathay*:

> If I give them [i.e., more poems], with the necessary breaks for explanation, and a tedium of notes, it is quite certain that the personal hatred in which I am held by many, and the *invidia* which is directed against me because I have dared openly to declare my belief in certain young artists, will be brought to bear first on the flaws of such translation, and will then be merged into depreciation of the whole book of translations. [25]

Pound was fully aware that he was beginning to be known as a center of the new poetical movement and that he would have to suffer the slings and arrows of his fortune. His fear that he might be more isolated from both American and English societies seems reflected in his selection of the poems in *Cathay*.

"The City of Choan," included in *Cathay* as one of the "Four Poems of Departure," also is a poem in which the speaker is a lonely exile. The original Chinese poem is Li Po's "Climbing the Phoenix Terrace in Chin-ling." At the southwest corner of the old city of Chin-ling (Kinryo in Japanese), now called Nankin, was the monument of the Phoenix Terrace, built in the period of Sung 宋(六朝), according to the legend, in celebration of the happy visit of the paradisiac birds on the terrace. Li Po (Rihaku), who became a government official at Chang-an (Chōan) when he was 42, only to be dismissed when he was 44, is supposed to have composed the poem when he visited the Phoenix Terrace after he left the capital. Although Achilles Fang maintains that "the title 'The City of Choan' is erroneously derived from the last line ... of the poem,"[26] Pound's change of its title to "The City of Choan" seems to be the key to the additional meaning that he tried to attach to his translation.

On the surface, "The City of Choan" is a nostalgic poem. It begins with a fantastic image of the phoenix "at play" on the terrace. It then describes the barren terrace, and the river still flowing around it, as if connecting the past and the present.

> The phoenix are at play on their terrace.
> The phoenix are gone, the river flows on alone.
>
> (lines 1–2)

The speaker imagines the old courtly life in Wu (Go) and Chin (Shin), though these places now are covered with clay.

> Flowers and grass
> Cover over the dark path
>   Where lay the dynastic house of Go.
> The bright cloths and caps of Shin
> Are now the base of old hills.
>
> (lines 3–7)

Pound is carefully avoiding the past tense, in order not to overemphasize the past and be too sentimental. The speaker is then reminded of the present capital, Chang-an, and ends his monologue with his nostalgic reaction to being denied a view of the beloved city.

> Now the high clouds cover the sun
> And I cannot see Choan afar
> And I am sad.
>
> (lines 11–13)

Since nobody can see Chang-an from Nankin anyway, whether cloudy or not, it is obvious that the poem has another level of meaning that the speaker is suggesting in his last lines. As the sun is traditionally the symbol of the Chinese emperor—and Chang-an being the capital—the speaker is trying to suggest that the cloud, which obscures the sunlight, is something around the emperor that is distressingly darkening the world. Thus, "The City of Choan" is not only nostalgic but also a lament.

The original Chinese poem also suggests the two levels of meaning.

> 鳳凰台上鳳凰遊
>
> 鳳去台空江自流
>
> 吳宮花草埋幽徑
>
> 晉代衣冠成古邱
>
> 三山半落青天外
>
> 二水中分白鷺洲
>
> 総爲浮雲能蔽日
>
> 長安不見使人愁

Even the images of the mountains and the river are charged with symbolic meaning here. In lines 5 and 6 the speaker is describing the scenes from the terrace: the three distant mountains, their feet hidden by mist, seem out of balance and ready to fall down to the bottom of the space at any moment. The speaker then gives another unstable image of the scene: the "two waters" of the river flowing around the island of White Heron. The island might be washed away anytime into the river. These images convey to the reader a sense of tension and uneasiness.

Pound's emphasis in his translation of these lines is more on the sense of rapid and sharp motion.

> The Three Mountains fall through the far heaven,
> The isle of White Heron
> > splits the two streams apart.

> > > > (lines 8–10)

But the two lines of the original Chinese poem suggest that some disastrous upheavals might happen at any moment. Describing dark "clouds" as before a storm, they suggest that something drastic might happen in Chang-an also.

Fenollosa dictated in his notebook the interpretation of the poem by his teacher, Kainan Mori.

> This seems like best poem so far in the quality of being charged with double meaning. . . . Mr. Mori thinks that there are 3 different aspects in last two lines—
> 1st   it is a cloudy day—looking west, Choan, invisible.
> 2d   because Genso, altho wise in himself, was weak enough to listen to false accusations. So Rihaku himself was banished from Choan.
> 3d   because such men as Anrokusan ban all in power, the Capital Choan is the town as if it did not exist at all.

The clouds, in other words, have three different levels of meaning: actual clouds, Emperor Hsüan-tsung's (Genso's) weak points, and "such men as Anrokusan (An Lu-shan)." Mori also suggested, "Because of clouds Choan is not visible, but this can be compared to fact that evil men obscure the power of Genso."[27] To Mori, then, the "evil men" are "such men as Anrokusan."

But it would narrow the poem to confine the meaning of the sun to Emperor Hsüan-tsung and the clouds to An Lu-shan. It would give a more universal meaning to the poem to interpret the clouds as any form of political injustice or evil, such as a politician's loss of historical insight caused by his ambition for power, or something which is a block between the governing and the governed. It would be more natural to assume that Li Po saw the germs of corruption and decay in the seemingly maturing civilization of the T'ang dynasty.

It is probable that Pound chose this poem from the Fenollosa notebook because he thought he was in a situation similar to that in which Li Po had found himself. Again, the speaker may be Pound's persona. As he read Mori's footnote to the poem, "This history recalls to Rihaku the present Choan," [28] and understood that the motive for his writing the poem was his lament for the dark clouds in Chang-an, Pound, too, might have felt some nostalgia for his home in America.

Pound had been familiar with the life of Li Po through his readings in H. A. Giles and Fenollosa's notebooks. He had composed an epitaph for Li Po, who was said to have drowned while trying "to embrace the moon" in the water.[29] As exile and poet, Pound must have felt sympathy for Li Po, who also was proud and depressed, wandering and homesick, sorrowfully taking leave of friends.

When Pound found in Fenollosa's notebook that Li Po was comparing the "clouds" to the "evil men in the capital," Pound might well have thought of the "evil men" in his own country—the university "profs," the politicians and "the appalling fungus of our 'better magazines'," causing "the diseases of American letters," all of which long had felt his critical lash.[30] Civilization under the "flowers and grass" might well have reminded him of the European heritage, from which Pound had "dug up" Bertran de Born, Arnaut Daniel, Dante, and Simon Zelotes. Underlying his translation may be Pound's secret wish that America, which he loved, would not follow the destiny of the city of Chang-an. And this seems to be one of the main reasons Pound chose his title, "The City of Choan," rather than the original title, "Climbing the Phoenix Terrace in Chin-ling."

The source of the poem in Fenollosa's notebook is as follows:

golden tomb

To	*kin*	*rio*	*ho*	*o*	*tai*
Climb up	Nan	Kin	phoenix		terrace

Ho	*o*	*tai*	*jo*	*ho*	*o*	*yu*
phenix		terrace	above	phenix		play

Above the ho terrace the hos used to play

Ho	*kio*	*dai*	*ku*	*ko*	*ji*	*riu*
phenix	away	terrace	vacant	river	of itself	flow

The hos have fled, the terrace bare, the river flows away by itself alone (seen from above)

Go	kiu	kwa	so	mai	yu	kei
dynastic	palace	flower	grass	bury	sombre	path

go

Where the go palace stood flowers of grass bury up the sombre path

Shin	dai	i	kwan	sei	ko	kiu
dynastic	dynasty	garment	caps	become	old	hill

Shin   [here buried]

Where the Shin dynasty [courtiers] have lived (clothes & caps) the foundations of those houses have become old hills.

San	zan	han	raku	sei	ten	gai
3	mts	half	fall	blue	heaven	outside

name

The triangle mt is half disappearing beyond the blue sky

Ni	sui	chu	bun	haku	ro	shu
2	water	middle	divide	white	heron	island

name

And the white heron island divides the waters into two

So	i	fu	wun	no	hei	jitsu
all together	because	floating	clouds	well	cover	sun

everywhere of

Because everywhere the floating clouds can cover up the sun

Cho	an	fu	ken	shi	jin	shu
City	Capital	not	see	let	man	sorry

So Choan is invisible and makes men sad.[31]

"The River-Merchant's Wife: A Letter," perhaps one of the "most anthologized" examples of Pound's translations, is, as Sister Bernetta Quinn remarks, "a charming interior monologue by a teen age 'war bride' who is longingly expecting her husband, 'My Lord You'."[32] It is a poem again spoken by a lonely and "sorrowful" figure. But the poem is celebrated also because the speaker, a sixteen-year-old wife, is so infinitely naive, tender and "charming." A. R. Orage thought the poem to be "simple and straight-forward."[33] Ford Madox Ford admired it as "delicate" and "beautiful." He wrote:

The poetry of great quality is that without comment as without effort it presents you with images that stir your emotions; so you are made a better man; you are softened, rendered more supple of mind, more open to the vicissitudes and necessities of your fellow men. When you have read "The River-Merchant's Wife" you are added to. You are a better man or woman than you were before.[34]

Pound himself, apparently satisfied with the work, wrote in the April 1918 issue of *Today*:

I can add nothing, and it could be an impertinence for me to thrust in remarks about the gracious simplicity and completeness of the poem.[35]

This remark by Pound will be given consideration later.

The poem opens with a recollection of the young wife's childhood.

> While my hair was still cut straight across my forehead
> Played I about the front gate, pulling flowers.

While she is playing with the flowers, the boy, who is later to become her husband, comes to her on his bamboo stilts and walks around her. They go on living in the village of Choan "without dislike or suspicion" until

> At fourteen I married my Lord you.
> I never laughed, being bashful.
> Lowering my head, I looked at the wall.

At fifteen she stops "scowling," and wishes her dust "to be mingled with yours / Forever and forever and forever." At sixteen, however, her husband departs up the river on a boat. She feels that "the leaves fall early this autumn," for he has been gone for five months. She sees a pair of butterflies flying in the garden, and laments, "They hurt me. I grow older." The line is highly praised by Donald Davie for its brevity, rhythm and "poignancy."[36] The poem ends as if ensuring hope in a simple and tender tone of voice. "If you are coming down through the narrows of the river Kiang, / Please let me know beforehand. / And I will meet you / As far as Cho-fu-sa."

But "Chang-kan Hang" ("Chokanko" in Japanese) the original

Chinese poem by Li Po, gives us a more frigid impression. It is written in the rigid form of *wu-yen chüeh-chü* (*gogon zekku*), with eight lines and with five characters in each line, a strict structural and rhyming pattern. Among many other characters, *ch'ieh* (*shō*) is chosen for the speaker to denote the first person singular pronoun *I*. For the second person singular, *lang* (*rō*) is used. In the T'ang period, *lang* meant a high official of the government, and it was used by Li Po to denote the husband with a tone of reverence. *Ch'ieh* was used to show the wife's humility toward her husband. By carefully selecting these characters, Li Po made the speaker appear to be a prudent woman who knows how to use the proper language and has common sense. Pound in contrast created the image of a young wife, full of love but naive and simple, who does not know much about social custom.

In Li Po, moreover, the speaker is presented as an educated woman who is well versed in classical Chinese literature. She says:

> At fifteen I began to stretch eyebrows
> And wished to live with you together like dust and ash.
> I always had faith like a man who died holding the pillar.
> I never thought of climbing up the husband-look-out-terrace.

Here she is alluding to an episode in *Shih Chi* (*Shiki*) about a man called Wei-sheng (Bisei), who promised to meet a girl at a pillar under a bridge. The river was at flood stage and the girl did not appear. But he stayed there clinging to the pillar and died. The speaker also alludes to a "husband-look-out-terrace," said to be common all over China, one of which is supposed to be fifty or sixty miles south of Chung-chou (Chushu). According to one legend, a woman watching from the terrace for her husband's return for many years finally became petrified.[37]

Pound translated the passage as if there were no allusions in it at all, by omitting the whole line about the man holding the pillar, and by changing some expressions in the passage.

> At fifteen I stopped scowling.
> I desired my dust to be mingled with yours
> Forever and forever and forever.
> Why should I climb the look out?

By ingeniously substituting the omitted line with the repetitions of "forever," Pound creates the image of an extremely tenderhearted woman, instead of re-creating the image of an educated woman.[38]

A look at the passage in the Fenollosa notebook will make it clear that the change is deliberate.

ju	*go*	*shi*	*tem*	*bi*
15	first time	open	eyebrows	

At fifteen I first opened my brows
I first knew what married life meant—now she opens her eyebrows. i.e. smoothes out the wrinkles between her brows. She now began to understand love, and to be happy.

gan	*do*	*jin*	*yo*	*bai*
desire	same	dust	together with and	ashes

And so I desired to live and die with you even after death, I wish to be with you even as dust, and even as ashes—partially together

Jo	*son*	*ho*	*chu*	*shin*
eternally	preserve	embrace	pillar	faith

I always had in me the faith of holding to pillars.

ki	*jo*	*bo*	*fu*	*dai*
why should	climb	lookout	husband	terrace

And why should I think of climbing the husband looking out terrace.

On the other side of the page are notes to the passage:

> referring to story of a yangster [*sic*] called Bisei who once promised his love to be waiting for her below a bridge—she was late in coming, and the water gradually rose in tide, yet faithful to promise he clang onto the pillar and was drowned.

> Referrence to story where a wife, looking out for her husband, who was late in returning, she died in that position and was petrified. The rock still pointed out and was called Bofutai.

Though pencil written, the notes are clear, and Pound could not have failed to read them while translating the passage. Pound rejected these allusions and sliced off the "educated" side of the speaker's character.

There is another passage in Li Po's original poem where the speaker is displaying her knowledge. Fenollosa's notebook gives its literal rendering into English:

Ju   roku   kun   en   ko
 16   you   far   go
At 16, however, you had to go far away

fearful   riverside   both yen & yo are adj; expressing
                                  form of water passing over
                                  hidden rocks

ku   to   yen   yo   tai
  name   yenyo-rock
of locality   eddy?
(towards Shoku passing through the difficult place of Yenyotai at Kuto.)

Go   getsu   fu   ka   shoku
 5   month   not   must   touch
In May not to be touched.
The ship must be careful of them in May.

En   sei   ten   jo   ai
monkeys   voices   heaven   above   sorrowful
Monkeys cry sorrowful above heaven.

Kutō [Chü-t'ang] is said to be the entrance to the three narrows in the upper Yangtze, through which one must pass to go to Shu. Enyotai [Yen-yü tui] is the name of the huge rock in the river at Kutō, soaring high above the water during winter, and hidden below the surface during the flood season in May. The speaker strangely has full knowledge about Kuto and Enyotai. She knows that the monkeys make sorrowful cries on the cliffs over the rapids, though she would not have heard them herself. Moreover, she warns in her letter that one must not touch the rock in May. Pound radically changes the passage; he does not allow his speaker to say much about the narrows.

> At sixteen you departed,
> You went into far Ku-to-yen, by the river of swirling
>   eddies,
> And you have been gone five months.
> The monkeys make sorrowful noise overhead.

The young wife in Pound's version says the monkeys cry over her head, not his. She does not give directions to her husband, or warn him not to touch the rock "in the fifth month." But instead she laments that he has been gone "for five months." She naively and erroneously coins Enyotai Kuto into Ku-to-yen. Pound is carefully molding her character as an innocent, modest, helpless, and lonely woman.

"I can add nothing," Pound wrote. "And it would be an impertinence for me to thrust remarks about the gracious simplicity and completeness of the poem." It is apparent that by "completeness" he did not mean that his translation was completely exact and flawless. It is complete because he could achieve "the gracious simplicity" in his translation that he desired; he cannot delete or add anything. He is implicitly suggesting that he thinks he has succeeded in presenting his own image of an Oriental woman in his translation, different from the image of the prudent and wise woman in the original and in Fenollosa's versions.

It seems that Pound has shaped his image of the innocent, tender, and lovely Oriental woman from some models he knew. One of them might have been Umeko, the heroine of the novel *The Dragon Painter* (1906) by Mary Fenollosa. It is possible that Pound read it about the time he met the author in London. The novel is about a Tokyo painter named Kano, who chooses a young painter Tatsu as his successor and as the husband of his beautiful only daughter, Umeko. After marriage, Tatsu begins to neglect his studies and quarrels with his father-in-law. Umeko, who loves both Tatsu and her father, disappears, and her wooden clogs are found by the Sumida River. Tatsu jumps into the river, but is saved from drowning by his father-in-law. After recovery, Tatsu resumes taking lessons from Kano in the house but is lonely with Umeko gone. One evening when the two visit the grave of Kano's decreased wife at a nunnery, they hear a woman sobbing nearby in the dark. They discover it is Umeko; the three then take up a new life together.

In the novel Umeko is described as a modest, beautiful, obedient, innocent, and tenderhearted woman. Although she is a talented painter, she modestly refrains from displaying her ability. She patiently waits at the nunnery until her rebellious husband mends his ways. The river-merchant's wife in Pound's version is, like Umeko, young, married, tenderhearted, and patiently awaiting her husband's return.

Another model by which Pound may have shaped his image of an Oriental woman is the heroine of *Madame Butterfly*, with which he most probably was familiar. Pinkerton sails away and Butterfly waits for his return, gazing down at the harbor from her house on the hill, which is like a "lookout." She, too, is pretty, young, innocent, and tenderhearted. She speaks in broken English, "I'm marry to Lef-ten-ant B. F. Pik-ker-ton," which resembles the expression, "Ku-to-yen." Mention of "the yellow butterflies" in Fenollosa's notebook might have reminded Pound of *Madame Butterfly* while he was translating.[39]

Even if Pound had not read or seen *The Dragon Painter* or *Madame Butterfly*, he must have been exposed to quite a few other, similar stories, for a number of works of Japonisme, containing beautiful descriptions of stereotypical Japanese women, were written in the early twentieth century in America.

Following Provençal models, Pound had been interested in portraying various types of women in his poetry. "Na Audiart," "Erat Hora," "The House of Splendour," and "Portrait d'une Femme" are examples of such works. Translations such as "The Beautiful Toilet" and "A Ballad of the Mulberry Road," included in *Cathay*, also offer portraits of women. It was Pound's "fundamental passion," as his persona reveals in a passage in "Hugh Selwyn Mauberley,"

> to convey the relation
> Of eye-lid and cheek-bone
> By verbal manifestations;
> To present the series
> Of curious head in medallion—[40]

It can be said that Pound is presenting another portrait in "The River-Merchant's Wife: A Letter"—an amalgam of Li Po's image of a T'ang period Chinese woman and the image of the idealized Japanese woman in America during the period of Japonisme. Though a hybrid, the portrait of the river-merchant's wife is curiously charming, infinitely tender, beautiful, and "complete," as Pound imagined—to which he could "add nothing."

The whole poem in Fenollosa's notebook is as follows:

Chokanko

regular 5

Chokan = $\dfrac{\text{name of town}}{\text{place}}$ ko = uta = narrative song

long-Mt. side

Sho	*hatsu*	*sho*	*fuku*	*gaku*
mistress	hair	first	cover	brow

Chinese lady's I or my beginning
My hair was at first covering my brows.
     (Chinese method of wearing hair)

Setsu	*kwa*	*mon*	*zen*	*geki*
break	flowers	gate	front	play

Breaking flower branches I was frolicking in front of our gate.

rō	*ki*	*chiku*	*ba*	*rai*
Second person	ride on	bamboo	horse	come
masculine				
you, young man				
lit. young man				

When you came riding on bamboo stilts

Gio	*sho*	*ro*	*sei*	*bai*
going round	seat	play with	blue	plums (fruit)

And going about my seat, you played with the blue plums.

Do	*kio*	*cho*	*kan*	*ri*
Same	dwell	cho	kan	village

Together we dwelt in the same Chokan village.

rio	*sho*	*mu*	*ken*	*sai*
double	small	not	dislike	suspicion
"the two"				

And we two little ones had neither mutual dislike or suspicion.
     (no evil thots or bashfulness)

ju	*shi*	*i*	*kun*	*fu*
Fourteen		became	lord's	wife
			your	

At fourteen I became your wife—

shu	*gan*	*mi*	*jo*	*kai*
bashful	face	not yet	ever	open

Bashful I never opened my face (I never laughed)

Tei	*to*	*ko*	*am*	*peki*
lowering	head	face	black	wall

but lowering my head I always faced toward a dark wall ashamed to
    see anybody—she sat in dark corners

Sen   kan   fu   itsu   kai
thousand   call   not   once   look back
And though a thousand times called, not once did I look around......

ju   go   shi   tem   bi
    15   first time   open   eyebrows
At fifteen I first opened my brows
        i.e.
I first knew what married life meant now she opens her eyebrows.
i.e. smoothes out the wrinkles between her brows. She now began
to understand love, and to be happy.

Gan   do   jin   yo   bai
desire   same   dust   together with   ashes
                                      and
And so I desired to live and die with you even after death, I wish to
be with you even as dust, and even as ashes—partially together.

Jo   son   ho   chu   shin
eternally   preserve   embrace   pillar   faith
I always had in me the faith of holding to pillars.

Ki   jo   bo   fu   dai
why should   climb   look out   husband   terrace
And why should I think of climbing the husband looking out terrace.

ju   roku   kun   en   ko
    16   you   far   go.
At 16, however, you had to go far away.

fearful   riverside   both yen & yo are adj. expressing form of
                                      water passing over hidden rocks

Ku____to   yen   yo   tai
    name   yenyo-rock
of locality   eddy?
(towards Shoku passing through the difficult place of Yenyotai at
Kuto.)

Go   getsu   i   ka   shoku
    5   month   not   must   touch
In May not to be touched.
The ship must be careful of them in May.

En	*sei*	*ten*	*jo*	*ai*
monkeys	voices	heaven	above	sorrowful

Monkeys cry sorrowful above heaven.

Mon	*zen*	*chi*	*ko*	*seki*
gate	front	late	go	footstep
		reluctant		

Your footsteps, made by your reluctant departure, in front of our gate.

itsu	*itsu*	*sei*	*rioku*	*tai*
one	one	grow	green	mosses

one by one have been grown up into green moss.

Tai	*shin*	*fu*	*no*	*so*
mosses	deep	not	can	wipe away

These mosses have grown so deep that it is difficult to wipe them away.

Raku	*yo*	*shu*	*fu*	*so*
Fallen	leaves	autumn	wind	early

And the fallen leaves indicate autumn wind which (to my thought only) appears to come earlier than usual.

		male	female	
Hachi	*gatsu*	*ko*	*cho*	*ko*
8th	month		butterflies	yellow

It being already August, the butterflies are yellow.

So	*hi*	*sei*	*yen*	*so*
pairs	fly	western	garden	grass

And yellow as they are, they fly in pairs on the western garden grass.

Kan	*shi*	*sho*	*sho*	*shin*
affected (by) this		hurt	(female)	mind
		normal	my	
		pained		

Affected at this, (absence) my heart pains.

Za	*shu*	*ko*	*gan*	*ro*
gradually	lament	crimson	face	decay—older
				become old.

The longer the absence lasts, the deeper I mourn, my early fine pink face, will pass to oldness, to my great regret.

So	*ban*	*ka*	*sam*	*pa*
sooner (or) later		descend	three	whirls

                                          name of spot on Yangtse Kiang,
                                          where waters whirl

If you be coming down as far as the Three Narrrows sooner or later.

Yo	*sho*	*shō*	*ho*	*ka*
beforehand with		letter	report	family-home

Please let me know by writing

Sho	*gei*	*fu*	*do*	*yen*
mutually	meeting	not	say	far
	coming to meet			

For I will go out to meet, not saying that the way be far.

                                  carring

Choka	*chi*	*cho*	*fu*	*sa*
directly	arrive	long	wind	sand

                          a port on the Yangtse

And will directly come to Chofusha.

    (the port just this side of Sampa)[41]

The English translation by Pound of "The River Song" is a strange blend of two Chinese poems. The first part is the translation of Li Po's "Chiang-Shang Yin" ("Kōjōgin")—"Song on the River"—and between the first and the second halves there is the following passage:

> And I have moped in the Emperor's garden,
>   awaiting an order-to-write!
> I looked at the dragon-pond, with its willow-coloured water
> Just reflecting the sky's tinge,
> And heard the five-score nightingales aimlessly singing.

>   (lines 19–22)

But this passage is actually a rendering in verse of the long title of the second poem by Li Po: "Shih-ts'ung Ichün-yüan . . . " ("Jijū Gishun-yen . . .")—"Poem Composed at I-chün Garden. . . ." Indeed one may wonder if it was one of Pound's "howlers" as some sinologists and critics have speculated.[42] In Fenollosa's notebook, from which Pound made his translation, the two poems are successively rendered into awkwardly literal English and almost look like one long poem. Pound penciled in "#129" to "Kōjōgin," the first poem, but he did not assign any number to the second, "Jijū Gishunyen...."[43]

However, there is some evidence that Pound knew the two were independent poems. At the end of the first poem, Fenollosa comments, "having come to conclusion," suggesting that it is the end of the poem. The title of the second poem on the next page in Fenollosa's notebook is merely a word-for-word translation, without rough sentence-to-sentence translation, and, moreover, the first letter of each line is not capitalized there. At the end of the title, Fenollosa jots in a comment, "All this is name, or rather description of circumstances of production, instead of name." Though one might attribute the confusion of "title" and "name" to Nagao Ariga's awkward English, it is hard to believe that anyone could make the mistake of taking the second poem as the continuation of the first poem, since the distinction surely would be apparent to even a casual reader of the notebook.

It seems more likely that Pound, at his first hasty reading, while numbering the poems in the notebooks, confused the two poems. By the time he got to serious work on them, he surely was aware of their differences in form, tone, and meaning, and was trying deliberately to make one poem out of two in the form of superposition.[44]

"Kōjōgin" is said to have been composed when Li Po was enjoying a day on a boat in a large river, most probably the Han (Kanko). In the first stanza of the original poem, the speaker richly describes the surroundings of his boat drifting on the river. The boat itself is built with fragrant magnolia and rare *shato* wood. (According to one of the commentaries, a boat built of *shato* does not sink, and if one eats the red fruit of the tree, one can never drown.[45]) On the boat are plenty of good wine and women, while the musicians are said to have jeweled flutes and gold pipes.

The speaker then, in successive couplets in the second stanza, indirectly expresses his feeling by comparing himself to a legendary *hsien-jên* (*sennin*) who waited for the yellow stork to come down from the cloud and flew away on it, and also to a boy who innocently played with the sea gulls at the shore. Suddenly the speaker directs our attention to the great poetry of Chien Yüan (Kutsugen), bright and eternal as "the sun and the moon," in contrast to "the mountains and hills," which were once gorgeous palaces and gardens of the king of Ch'u (So), whom Chieh Yüan had served but who had expelled him from court.

The last stanza is a more direct utterance of the speaker. He exclaims that, if he should drop his pen on paper at the height of his pleasure, China's five mighty mountains would tremble. He declares that he will recite the poem when completed and his joy and pride will surpass anything in the paradisiac island in the eastern sea. The speaker concludes: It is as unlikely that fame and wealth could last forever as it would be for the River Han to flow backward to the northwest.

Following is Fenollosa's version of the poem.

kiang

Ko   jo   gin   (1) (one number)

[one word illegible] river   above   sing   (gin = song without music)

by

"Song at the River"

generic

sand dry Kaido = do = tree like Kaido

Moku   ran   shi   yei   sha   to   shu

magnolia   no   side of   name of a tree   boat

boat   possibly like Keyaki

A (fine) boat of shato wood, with sides of *mokuren*

Gioku   sho   kin   kan   za   rio   to

jewel   flute   gold   pipe   sit   both   heads

instrument of   both sides

wood

Jeweled flute, and gold pipe, and (musicians) sitting in row on both sides.

Bi   shu   son   chu   chi   sen   goku

Fine   wine   wine tub   in   put   1000   a

measure

= 100 *sho*

(and) with fine wine put in casks to amount of 100 *sho*

Sai   gi   zui   ha   nin   kio   riu

carry   courtesan   follow   waves   confide oneself   go away   stop

singer   to

passive let

things go

laisser fair [*sic*]

Carrying also *singing girls*, and following passing course of

With   those that sit   waves, going or stopping as
          on both sides   the boat will.

Sen   *nin*   *yu*   *tai*   *jo*   *ko*   *kaku*
  Sennin   is   wait   ride   yellow   stork
Sennin is in need of a yellow stork to ride on

Kai   *kaku*   *mu*   *shin*   *zui*   *haku*   *o*
sea   guest   not   mind   follow   white   gull
                no
(Whereas) a sea man, without intention, follows the white gulls
                              (whether they go or come)

Kutsu   *pei*   *shi*   *fu*   *ken*   *jitsu*   *getsu*
  Kutsugen   prose   song   hang on   sun   moon
  Kuppei   lit. words measured
                rhymed prose
Kutsugen's prose and poems hang together with sun & moon i.e. (are
handed down to posterity never changing in brightness, fame, like sun &
moon)

So   *o*   *dai*   *sha*   *ku*   *san*   *kiu*
So province   King   terrace   palace   vacantly   mountain   hill
(whereas) the terraces of palaces of the King of So have left nothing behind
but mountains & hills.

Kio   *kwan*   *raku*   *hitsu*   *yo*   *go*   *gaku*
pleasure   at its height   let fall   pen   make   five   peaks
merriment   brandished   move
                            rapidly
At the height of the merriment, I sweep my pen, and write poems in such
powerful strokes as to cause the 5 peaks to tremble.

Shi   *sei*   *sho*   *go*   *rio*   *so*   *shu*
poem is made   laugh   pride   compete   blue a group of islands
                assume proud   with   archipelago
                countenance   prevail
                (a verb)
The poem now being made, I laugh with all pride in my heart, pride which
spreads over (as wide as) the blue islands beyond.

Ko   *mei*   *fu*   *ki*   *jaku*   *cho*   *zai*
merit   fame   wealth   nobility   if   long   exist

If merit, fame, wealth and nobility were to last forever

Kan	*sui*	*yeki*	*o*		*sei*	*hoku*	*riu*
Kan	water	also	will		west	north	flow
name of the			ought to				
Kan ko							
Han river							

The water of this Han River ought to flow North West (instead of S. E. as now.)[46]

The speaker's belief in the eternal values of poetry, his pride in his own talent, and his delight in his unfettered imaginative power may be reflections of Li Po's own confidence as a poet. It seems natural that Pound observed in this Chinese poem something that resembles romantic poetry in Western literary history.

On the other hand, the second poem, "Jijū Gishunyen, ... " ("Poem Composed at I-chün Garden ... ") is an occasional poem composed while Li Po was a court poet in Chang-an. As its long title suggests, the emperor ordered him to write a poem on the occasion of his visit to the detached palace in early spring.

The poem begins with an exquisite description of the idyllic scenes at the palace. The willows are half green, and their pendant branches are softly rubbing against the "carved railings of the balconies" of the colorfully painted palace, while the birds are singing to one another. The emperor leaves the palace accompanied by a retinue of his guards in glittering armor. He then enters the detached palace, and takes a turn around the garden. He gazes at the dancing storks at Horai [Penglai], a legendary island in the eastern seas on which *hsien-jêns* are supposed to be living, but here meaning the island in the pond of the garden. (Penglai may mean one of the buildings so named in the detached palace, as some commentaries suggest.[47]) The emperor then observes the nightingales flying over the garden, and listens to their song. They sing as if they might blend their melodies with the music of the court musicians.

Here is the Fenollosa version of the poem:

appropriate spring				
Ji	*ju*	*gi*	*shun*	*yen*,
waiting upon	at gi	shun	garden	
(Emperor)				

ho	sho	bu,
following	decree	compose (poem)
	order	

	riu	chi	riu	shoku	sho	sei
(on the	dragon	pond	willow	color	(for first time)	blue
subject of)						

cho	shin	o	hiaku	ten	ka
hear	new	nightingale	100	warble, the song about
		uguisu		
		(lark?)		

All this is name, or rather description of circumstances of production, instead of a name. (With Genso.)

name, Supposed
Sennin abode

To	fu	ki	rioku	yei	shu	so
Eastern	wind	already	green	yei	island	grass

The eastern wind has already made green the grass of yeishu Island

Shi	den	ko	ro	kaku	shun	ko
purple	hall	crimson	storied	feel	spring	balminess
	palace		house	(recon conscious)		

On purple hall, and crimson story we can feel the spring balminess
(of aspect)

Chi	nan	riu	shoku	han	sei	sei
pond	south	willow	color	half	blue	blue

South of the pond (sunny) the willows are already half blue.

Kei	yen	cho		na	futsu	ki	jo
twining	smoke	tender men		tenderness of	sweep	varied	fortress
about	mist	(of female drapery)		female body		colored	in
				grace		cloth	imperial
				[personal]		(beautiful)	abode

Their tender threads entwine about the mist or brush against the brocade-like palace (on the roof)

Sui	shi	hiaku	shaku	kei	cho	yei
hang down	threads	100	feet	hang on	carved	balcony
						rail

hanging in threads of 100 feet (long) they hang on the carved railings of
the balconies   cling

Jo   yu   ko   cho   sho   wa   mei
above   there are   lovely   birds   mutually   harmonizing   sing
Above (these willows) are seen lovely birds singing in mutual harmony

"kwan   kwan"   so   toku   shun   pu   jo
⎛onomatopoeia for⎞   early   acquired   spring   wind   emotion
⎝singing of birds ⎠
Then "kan kan" already resounds the emotion of the spring winds.—
(foretell-) (spring not yet come)
(They get the feeling from the wind)

Shun   pu   ken   niu   heki   wun   kio
spring   wind   roll   go in   blue   cloud   pass away
As the spring wind (carrying in itself these harmonious sounds) blow up
into the sky, and pass away—

Sem   mon   ban   ko   kai   shun   sei
1000   gates   10000   doors   all   spring   voice
(So these sounds are heard) at every one of the gates and doors (of the
palaces) filling them with spring tone

Shi   ji   kun   wo   zai   ko   kei
This   time   master   king   is   old name   capital
                                stops   for Choan
                                lives
This time the Emperor is in the K. Capital

Go   wun   sui   ki   yo   shi   sei
five   cloud   hang   brightness   shine   purple   clean
                    down   against
And the five clouds (sign of peace) hang above and shine against the
purple sky.

Jo   shutsu   kin   kiu   zui   jitsu   ten
imperial   going out of   gold   palace   following   sun   turn
guards
troop
The guards first appear coming out of the golden palace, and then
        armor's glitter against the sun (so following)
                motion

Ten	kwai	gioku	ren	gio	ka	ko
heaven	turn	jewel	sedar [*sic*]	going	flower	proceed
			chair	round		
			or			
			hand chariot of			
			Emperor			

Heaven (Emperor) courses his jewel (hand drawn) chariot to make de-tour
—going [turning] about where flowers are

Shi	ko	ho	rai	kan	bu	kaku
at first	going		Horai	sees	dancing	stork
	towards		name given to			
			part of garden			

First it (the chariot) proceeds toward Horai, and (the Emperor) sees the
dancing stork (flapping wings)

			orchid			
Kwan	kwa	sai	seki	tei	shin	wo
going back	pass by	name of a rock		hear	new	nightingale
		in garden				uguisu

Returning he passes by the Sai rock where he for the first time catches the
noise of the new nighting[a]le.

				high forest		
Shin	wo	hi	gio	jo	rin	yen
new	nightingale	fly	going round			garden
				name of whole	garden	

This (fresh new spring) nightingales, seeing the Emperor coming, fly about
the whole garden (not stay on willows)

Gwan	niu	sho	sho	zatsu	ho	sho
wishing to	enter	flute	tune	mixed	phenix	flute
			melody	with	bird	

As if they wished that their melody might enter into (harmonize with)
the flutes tune, and mixed with the mouth organ (12 pipes, form shape of
Ho's tail) (The two Shos are played together)

Why? because not only is instrument an imperial instrument but the bird
is the King of birds.[48]

"Hori" in some versions of Pound's translation should be "Horai";
"Kwan, Kuan" might better be rendered as "kwan kwan" or "Kan
kwan"; and "Jo-run" should be "Jo-rin" [shang-lin], (though the dot

for the i in "jo rin" is almost undiscernible in Fenollosa's manuscript.)

The second poem as a whole is less personal than "Kōjōgin." The statement is more indirect, with several metonymic expressions. (Shang-lin was the name of the imperial garden in the Han dynasty, but here it denotes the detached palace, Ch'ü-chiang (Kyokko), where the emperor is visiting. "Gishunyen" in the title was the name of the imperial garden at the time of Ch'in, which here also denotes Ch'ü-chiang. Kokei [Hao-ching] was the name of the capital in the Chou (Shu) period, but here it is used to denote Chang-an, the present capital, as Fenollosa's manuscript suggests.) The elegance of effect gained by the use of metonymy is augmented by the elegant description of nature, the fine weather, the softly blowing breeze; we even find the wild birds behaving gently and "properly" as if domesticated. It may be natural that Pound noticed some elements pertaining to English neo-classical literature in this courtly poem by Li Po.

When Pound deliberately superposed the two poems, he stressed the romantic aspects in the first poem; for the second, he stressed the neoclassical elements. Pound translated the first with a number of run-on lines, but the second without any.

> Yet Sennin needs
> A yellow stork for a charger, and all our seamen
> Would follow the white gulls. . . .

> And the Emperor is at Ko.
> Five clouds hang aloft, bright on the purple sky,
> The imperial guards come forth from the golden house
>   with their armour a-gleaming.

In both of the originals, and in Fenollosa's rough English translations of them, each line is a sentence. Pound is coloring the first poem by using this style often adopted by romantic poets. The "blue" in Pound's version,

> And I have joy in these words
>   like the joy of blue islands,

seems to suggest the remoteness and happiness of the "blue bird" of Maeterlinck. The luxurious boat of fragrant "magnolia" (line 1), with "rich" wine (4), "singing girls" (5), and musicians with "jewelled" and "gold" instruments (2), which "drift with drifting water" (5), all seem to suggest the sensuousness, hedonism, and loss of direction of the late romantic period. And Pound writes as if there were more musicians on the boat than there seem to be in Fenollosa's version.

> Jeweled flute, and gold pipe, and (musicians) sitting
> in row on both sides.

> (Fenollosa, line 3)

> Musicians with jeweled flutes and with pipes of gold
> Fill full the sides in row.

> (Pound, lines 2–3)

On the other hand, the second part of "The River Song," in which everything is in subtle harmony and order in the original, is rendered by Pound with neoclassical coloring. Furthermore, Pound uses the "end-stopped lines" and makes a rococo-style variation by changing the "tender threads" of the willows to "vine-strings" (line 27), giving the scene of the court a greater variety of decoration.

> South of the pond the willow-tips are half-blue and bluer
> Their cords tangle in mist, against the brocade-like
> palace.
> Vine-strings a hundred feet long hang down from carved
> railings,
> And high over the willows, . . .

Pound's use of the strong verb "inspect" (line 35) for the emperor's "making de-tour" (Fenollosa's manuscript), and his use of such an expression as "awaiting an order-to-write!" (19), reflect his attempt to imply subtleties of social relationships characterized by belief in the great chain of being.

At the time he was translating the *Cathay* poems, Pound was searching seriously for new poetic forms and devices. He had invented superposition, applying it to his "In a Station of the Metro." He was aware of the limitations of imagism. He wrote "April," published in the November 1913 issue of *Poetry*, in which he superposed a kinetic image in the first four lines on top of a static image in the last line.

> Three spirits came to me
> And drew me apart
> To where the olive boughs
> Lay stripped upon the ground.
> Pale carnage beneath bright mist.

The two images grow more concrete and vivid as they are forced to transform themselves into metaphors for each other. The whole poem is a slightly longer one-image poem. But it is still imagistic. Pound then made a bold attempt in "Liu Ch'e," published in February 1914 in the *Glebe*, in which he picked up the fourth line of the original Chinese poem, rewrote the line, and put it at the end of the poem, in conformity with his notion of superposition. For Pound, literal faithfulness to the original in translation was far less important than experimenting with new poetic contrivances. "The River Song" reflects this attitude.

It should also be remembered that, in the beginning of the twentieth century, there were long and heated discussions in literary circles on romanticism versus classicism. The vehemence of T. E. Hulme's violent philosophical attack on romanticism, echoing in the chapter called "Romanticism and Classicism" in his *Speculations*, probably was appreciated and supported by most of his "dining and talking" group, which met every week at Café Tour d'Eiffel in 1909, a little after Pound's arrival in London.[49] Pound may have listened to Hulme's argument that romanticism was the culmination of humanism, which regarded man as the omnipotent center of the limitless universe, or that romanticism was "an awful disease," while the "classical ideal ... [was] a living thing." As T. S. Eliot later recalled in his "What is a Classic?" the "pair of terms" were "belonging to literary politics, and therefore arousing winds of passion which I ask Aeolus, on this occasion, to contain in the bag."[50]

Though not a stark classicist, Pound belonged to the classicist camp, and attacked the epigones of the romanticists. When Lascelles Abercrombie, a Georgian poet and critic, wrote "an article advising young poets to ... study Wordsworth," Pound sent him a note: "Stupidity carried beyond a certain point becomes a public menace. I hereby challenge you to a duel, to be fought at the earliest moment that is suited to your convenience." Pound, on the one hand, believed in classical values, "dry and hard" images, "perfect control," impersonality, and "objectivity."[51]

On the other hand, Pound was "possibly" a romanticist at heart, as he has confided.[52] He began his literary career in the wake of D. G. Rossetti, the Provençal troubadours, and Robert Browning. His aspiration for beauty, his interest in "sudden revelation," "brevity," "Risorgimento," and the personal feelings in the "moment of song" hidden behind his personae show that he shared some sentiments with the romantics.[53] Pound, in other words, was pragmatic in believing in some values of both classicism and romanticism, and used them as tools for composition.

In "The River Song," Pound "superposed" the two streams of thought. "The River Song" is thus like the river on which were reflected two sets of images, ideas, styles, and values.

But the experiment, was only partly successful. It succeeded in that Pound could suggest that there were ways of dealing with the problem of romanticism *versus* classicism other than by fighting "political" battles over them. Also, Pound seems to have become confident of his ability to deal satisfactorily with the complexly contrasting elements in a much longer poem, a still larger framework: the *Cantos*.

The experiment was unsuccessful, on the other hand, in that Pound only superposed the two streams in the poem, left them reflecting each other. He apparently was unable to synthesize and sublimate them into a really new, inclusive, but idiosyncratic stream. It was unsuccessful also because, ironically, it gave the wrong impression that he was quite incompetent in Chinese. For some years, therefore, he seems to have been reluctant to attempt further translations from the Chinese until he thought he had studied it well enough.

However unsuccessful, "The River Song" is an important milestone in Pound's formation of ideas that ultimately would shape the structure of the *Cantos*. It is also an important work because it forced reflection as to whether romanticism and classicism are mere tags for certain periods in literary history, or represent sets of inherited values still relevant for us.

The poems included in *Cathay* are, as T. S. Eliot once remarked, the "personae" of Erza Pound.[54] Through these translations Pound tried to speak with various experiments in form and other devices.

"The Chinese Written Character as a Medium for Poetry," edited and prefaced by Pound in 1918, was one of the essays included in Fenollosa's manuscript notebooks. Pound had read the essays sometime before June 1916, for he wrote at that time to Iris Barry suggesting which parts of the essay might be most valuable to her as well as to him.

> You should have a chance to see Fenollosa's big essay on verbs,
> mostly on verbs. . . . He inveighs against "is," wants transitive
> verbs. "Become" is as weak as "is." . . . I think the theory is a
> very good one for poets to go by.[55]

According to Fenollosa, "a large number of primitive Chinese characters . . . are shorthand pictures of actions or processes," and those characters present vivid images at the same time they denote associated
ideas. The process from the image to the idea, "from the seen to the
unseen," Fenollosa speculates, is the same as the process of the metaphor,
in which "the known interprets the obscure. . . . The chief work of
literary men in dealing with language, and of poets especially, lies in
feeling back along the ancient lines of advance."[56]

In the argument, Fenollosa points out that many of "the Chinese
words are alive and plastic because *thing* and *action* are not formally
separated"; and "the eye sees noun and verb as one: thing in motion,
motion in thing." And then a passing remark is made on translating
Chinese literature.

> In translating Chinese, verse especially, we must hold as closely
> as possible to the concrete force of the original, eschewing
> adjectives, nouns and intransitive forms wherever we can, and
> seeking instead strong and individual verbs.[57]

But the passage written in Fenollosa's idiosyncratic scrawl can be
found in his notebook:

> Especially in translating Chinese verse we must hold as closely
> as may be to the concrete force of the original, in eschewing
> adjectives, nouns and intransitive forms, wherever it is possible
> to substitute in English a strong, individual verb.[58]

This original text of Fenollosa is slightly different from the published
version. One may safely assume that Pound changed the passage when
he edited and sent his copy of the text to the publisher. But one may as
readily speculate that Pound had already read the essay while he was
working on the *Cathay* poems, and consequently was inspired by
Fenollosa's ideas in translating the Chinese poems. Pound replaced
some verbs in Fenollosa's rough English translation with still "stronger"
ones. To give a few examples:

Ko	*kwan*	*gio*	*fu*	*sha*
north	gate	much	wild	sand

"Regions around Fort gate against barbarios [*sic*]
    abound in wind and snow."
                    (Fenollosa, "14th Kofu")

By the North Gate, the wind blows full of sand.
        (Pound, "Lament of the Frontier Guard")

"Abound" is changed to "blow" with the change of the sentence structure. ("Snow" is correctly dropped out.)

      Blue cow, white horse, seven, fragrant, carriage
                          woods   (wheeled)
                          incense
cows and horses are drawing these chariots made of
fragrant wood.
blue cow is for carriage white horse for rides.

                .   .   .

      (horse eating
      bag)
Dragon swallow precious canopy receive morning sun
Dragon munching costly (sun shade)
    means the dragon on tip of the handle
    The precious canopy with the dragon swallow[59]
              (Fenollosa, "Old Idea of Choan")

Dark oxen, white horses,
    drag on the seven coaches with outriders.

                .   .   .

The canopy embroidered with dragon
    drinks in and casts back the sun.
    (Pound, "Old Idea of Choan by Rosorin")

"Draw" is changed into "drag" in the first line, and "receive" into "cast back" in the second, though both "receive" and "cast back" seem to lack adequate strength. Pound probably thought that to strengthen the verbs was what Mary Fenollosa wished him to do: to "finish up these notes as Ernest would have wanted them done." But Pound himself must have welcomed Fenollosa's ideas, for Pound at that time was searching for a way to give poetry strength and motion, like a vortex.

During his London years (1908–20), Pound literarily gew up, as it were, by sloughing off some parts of what he had absorbed. Under Hulme's influence he dropped off much of the genteel style—"thous" and "thees," refrains, and complex sentences—which he had picked up from the pre-Raphaelites, the Victorians, and the troubadours. He even managed to escape from Browning's "mesmerism," though it took him some years.[60] Between 1912 and 1914 Pound was able to write a number of "dry and hard," "granite"-like imagistic poems with utmost brevity and precision.[61] But in 1913, while he was still editing *Des Imagistes*, he began writing "more intense," "naked," "whirling," and "energetic" vorticist poetry.[62] Pound stopped writing short, classical, haikulike, imagist poems, especially after he had quarrels with Amy Lowell and launched vorticism with Wyndham Lewis and Henri Gaudier-Brzeska, by publishing the *Blast*, no. 1, in June 1914.[63] Pound was "very placid and happy" upon receiving Fenollosa's manuscript as a "windfall"[64] at the crucial time he was moving from imagism to vorticism.

While working on the translation of the Chinese poems in 1914, Pound often adopted the imagist technique,[65] but he as often experimented more boldly with the new, vorticist ideas inspired by Fenollosa. He used the "strong verbs." With a hint from Fenollosa's essay on Chinese characters, he invented the "spotlight method," presenting blocks of images with "cinematic effect,"[66] sometimes without grammatical links, to resemble a flow of Chinese ideograms:

> Desolate castle, the sky, the wide desert.
> ("Lament of the Frontier Guard")

> Surprised. Desert turmoil. Sea Sun.
> ("South Folk in Cold Country")

> The red and green kingfishers
> flash between orchids and clover.
> ("Sennin Poem by Kakuhaku")[67]

Behind the quick motion from one "intense" image to another in these lines seems to be hidden the action of dynamic forces whirling like a vortex. Pound amalgamated the ideas of vorticism with Fenollosa's ideas about the Chinese written character and experimented with this in his translation of the *Cathay* poems. His work in turn enriched the vorticist poetry.[68]

Furthermore, Pound added to his gallery of portraits, the exotic, Oriental "curious heads" in *Cathay*. He experimented with his superpository theory in a larger framework. But the most important thing Pound got from Fenollosa's notebooks was the discovery that there were rich sources of inspiration in the Oriental culture, which convinced him of the significant role it would play in the stormy *risorgimento* of the twentieth century, which he had dreamed would come. He wrote in 1915, "The first step of a renaissance, or awakening, is the importation of models for painting, sculpture or writing. . . . It is possible that this century may find a new Greece in China." Pointing to "the great Roman vortex," he suggested that "any city which cares for its future can perfectly well start its vortex."[69] For Pound, the new vortex of awakening in our age was, and should be, started by the "injection" from the East.[70] A prophetic advocate, Pound himself went on to further study of Oriental civilization—Nō plays, Confucianism and other classical literature.

Nō Plays and The Cantos

In Fenollosa's notebooks, Pound also found the rough English translation of several Nō plays. He read them, and edited some of them and Fenollosa's comments on them, between 1914 and 1917. Pound published *Nishikigi* in *Poetry* in May 1914; *Atsumori, Kinuta,* and *Hagoromo* in *Quarterly Review* in October 1914; *Sotoba Komachi, Kayoi Komachi, Suma Genji, Kumasaka, Shojo, Tamura,* and *Tsunemasa* in *Drama* in May 1915; and *Awoi no Uye* in *Quarterly Notebook* in June 1916. Four of the Nō plays were collected and published by the Cuala Press as *Certain Noble Plays of Japan* in September 1916, with an introduction by W. B. Yeats. Fourteen of them were collected under the title of *'Noh' or Accomplishment* and published with Pound's introduction by Macmillan in England and Alfred Knopf in America in 1917.

On reading some of "these beautiful plays," Yeats was inspired to write a play, *At the Hawk's Well,* as he confessed in his introduction to *Certain Noble Plays of Japan*:

In fact with the help of these plays "translated by Ernest Fenollosa and finished by Ezra Pound" I have invented a form of drama, distinguished, indirect and symbolic, and having no need of mob or press to pay its way—an aristocratic form. When this play and its performance run as smoothly as my skill can make them, I shall hope to write another of the same sort and so complete a dramatic celebration of the life of Cuchulain planned long ago.[71]

With the help of Michio Ito, a Japanese dancer, Edmund Dulac, costume and mask designer, Lady Cunard, and Ezra Pound, the performance of *At the Hawk's Well* in London in April 1916 turned out to be "smooth" and successful.[72] Pound, too, became so enthusiastic about Nō plays as to write in 1916 that "the Noh is unquestionably one of the great arts of the world, and it is quite possibly one of the most recondite."[73] But Pound was not interested in writing plays under the influence of the Nō as Yeats was. Apparently under the influence of the Nō, especially by what is called *Fukushiki Mugen nō*, or "double structural visionary Nō," Pound was inspired to write a new type of poetry.

The "double structural visionary Nō" is the two-scene play in which most of the best works of Nō are written, such as *Suma Genji*, *Kakitsubata*, *Aoi no Ue*, and *Nishikigi*, all of which Pound has translated. In *Suma Genji*, a traveling priest from the southern province of Japan meets a humble, old woodcutter by the Suma seashore (now a part of Kobe city), where, as the priest is reminded, the hero of the well-known classical Japanese novel *The Tale of Genji* once had lived and had a love affair. The priest persistently asks the woodcutter, "But tell me exactly where he lived. Tell me all that you know about him." The woodcutter replies ambiguously, "If you will wait for the moonlight, you might see it all in a mist," and disappears. By the hints from the chorus, the priest realizes that the woodcutter "was Genji himself," and he listens to "the waves filled with music" till night comes. In the second half of the play, "a bright apparition of Genji in supernatural form" (dressed like the protagonist of the original story) appears, dances to the waves of Suma, and tells his story.

This kind of Nō play is composed of two definite parts. (1) *Waki*, in this case a wandering priest, comes to a historic site, often a deserted place. He meets *Shite*, or the hero, usually in a humble attire of the locality, who tells him a popular legend about the place. Then Shite turns out to be the spirit of the hero of the legend. (2) Shite reappears as the ghost of the legend's protagonist. Waki dreams, or sees in a vision, the ghost dancing and passionately recounting his own version of the story. At the end, which is sometimes omitted, Waki wakes up, prays for the ease of his soul, and the ghost departs for the other world. Throughout the play the time shifts back and forth between the past and present.

Shite may be a warrior, a poet, a courtier, or a god, male or female, Japanese or foreign, real or fictitious, but often he is a figure from the classic Japanese literature. This type of Nō play is called "double structural" because in the first half of the play, Shite appears as a kind, rustic, and well-informed inhabitant of the historic site, but in the latter half he reappears radically changed into a transcendental but passionate ghost, relying on his personal memory.

Although Pound may not have known the term, some of his poems and his *Cantos* resemble the Nō play written in this form.[74] In Canto 4, for instance, with fragments of stories from Greek mythology, Ovid's *Metamorphosis*, Provençal tales, Chinese poetry, and the Nō play, Pound seems to be calling back the ghosts of the past to the present.

One of the most ghastly stories in this canto is that of Itys, young son of Tereus and Procne. Tereus seduces his wife's sister, Philomela, and cuts out her tongue. Enraged and determined to get revenge, Procne kills Itys and serves his flesh as food to her husband. Procne then tries to kill herself but is changed into a swallow. Pound is concerned only with the last moments of the story in the canto:

> Et ter flebiliter, Itys, Ityn!
> And she went toward the window and cast her down,
>   'All the while, the while, swallows crying:
> Ityn!

Following this passage is the fragment of another grim story of illicit love and of cannibalism. Guillem de Cabestanh, a twelfth-century troubadour, was not unjustly suspected of unseemly dalliance with the Lady Seremonda, wife of Raymond of Chateau Roussillon. "According to Chabaneau, Pound's source, Raymond killed Cabestanh and served his cooked heart to Seremonda."[75] Again Pound gives only the last moments of the story:

> And she went toward the window,
>
> . . .
>
> Swung for a moment,
>   and the wind out of Rhodez
> Caught in the full of her sleeve.

Pound is concerned not with "the prose part," but with the "momen of song,"[76] the beautiful fluttering fall, and sudden metamorphosis at the critical moments for a new start of life. But, when superposed, the fragmentary moments of beauty in the "archetypal human situations" point up a moral issue: the "futility" of any kind of "violence in love," and the misery caused by disorder.[77]

The passage on Cabestanh is followed by another on Actaeon, who, for having observed Diana bathing in the pool in the wood, is changed to a stag, chased by his own hounds, and killed. Then there are allusions to the pines in the Nō play "Takasago,"[78] to a Chinese poem, "Ode on Wind" by Sō-Gyoku [Sung Yü],[79] and, in the last part of the canto, to the "Ideal City" of Ecbatan, with terraces in seven different colors of stars, suggesting perfect order and harmony. Walter Baumann interprets the canto as "the march of civilization from the passion which destroys men and cities to affection which is in harmony with great mysteries of this world."

> After many glimpses at human cruelty under the influence of passion, after several highlights of human divine love, having gone through the whole of the light-process, and carrying with us the vision of the Ideal City, we reach the sphere of the contemplation of spiritual beauty. The progression of values has attained that serene height which allows men to view the great harmony of this world.[80]

The canto certainly reflects Pound's idea of the structural outline of the whole *Cantos*, which may reflect his own view of the world: man "descends into Hades" for spiritual rebirth, undergoes a series of transformation through purgatorial experiences in the "events" of the time, and attains "the Triumph of Love," order, and beauty.[81] But the canto seems also to reflect Pound's fascination with the Nō play.

Published separately in the fall of 1919, soon after Pound's return with his wife from their trip to southern France,[82] Canto 4 is interspersed with passages from his travel accounts. But these accounts actually are pilgrimages to the past. The speaker, wandering like Waki, visits the historic sites where the ancient troubadours used to live and love, and the woods and lakes where the legends about nymphs and gods might have originated. And then he expects the apparition of the legendary protagonists to appear before his eyes. He imagines he hears the songs of the nymphs and the footsteps of satyrs.

> The silver mirrors catch the bright stones and flare,
> Dawn, to our waking, drifts in the green cool light;
> Dew-haze blurs, in the grass, pale ankles moving.
> Beat, beat, whirr, thud, in the soft turf
> > under the apple trees,
> Choros nympharum, goat-foot, with the pale foot alternate.

The speaker meets the ghosts in imagination. He does not converse with them. But as on the Nō stage, one by one the dead from the past return to the present—Tereus, Procne, Raymond, Marguerite, Diana, Actaeon, Piere Vidal, Persephone, Salmacis, Hermaphroditus, the old couple in Takasago, Sennin, Polhonac, Danaë, and Cavalcanti. Pound inserts his travel accounts, and time flies back and forth between the past and the present. Finally the ghosts, like Shite, disappear as "we sit here . . . / there in the arena." Prose and poetry are interwoven, and the protagonists are capable of attaining beauty and meaning through struggles and sacrifice. The canto is in that sense a multiple structural visionary Nō play.

However, it should be noted that the "double structural visionary Nō" is not the only source of inspiration for the structure of Canto 4. "Have I dug him up again?" we find Pound asking in the epigram to his "Sestina: Altaforte." In his earlier short poems, he had "dug up" Bertran de Born ("Sestina: Altaforte"), Baucis and Philemon ("The Tree"), Psyche ("Speech for Psyche in the Golden Book of Apuleius"), Nikoptis ("The Tomb at Akr Çaar"), and a number of other historical and fictitious figures from the tumuli of the past. By having them speak in modern English in his poems, Pound has brought them to the present. Pound was interested in the visionary re-creation of the dead, as Browning was in his dramatic monologues. And this idea of "digging up" the figures in the past is certainly the basic idea of Canto 4. But Pound had been using these figures as his personae in the earlier poems. As he confided to William Carlos Williams, "I paint my man as I conceive him. Et voilà tout!"[83] In Canto 4, however, the ghosts are not his personae. That is, Pound does not speak through their masks, but rather watches them speak, as does the wandering priest in the Nō play. Pound is dramatizing those values of the past that he has been concerned with by using the Nō form.

In Canto 4 Pound also adopts the effect of the Nō chorus. "All the while," he writes, the swallows are crying like a chorus, "Ityn, ... Itys, Itin!" Such half-sympathetic but timeless voices as "Hither, hither, Actaeon," and "Pergusa ... pool ... Gargaphia, / Pool ... pool of Salmacis" seem meant to be spoken, not by the protagonists or by the narrator, but by the chorus.

Pound even imitates the rhythm of the Nō play. We find echoing beginning the lines of the canto:

> Gold, gold, a sheaf of hair,
> Thick like a wheat swath,
> Blaze, blaze in the sun,
> The dogs leap on Actaeon.
> Stumbling, stumbling along in the wood,
> Muttering, muttering Ovid. . . .

These repetitions seem to reflect an attempt to recapture the effect of the Nō's rhythm:

> Blue-grey is the garb they wear here,
> Blue-grey he fluttered in Suma.
>   ("Suma Genji")
>
> Is it illusion, illusion?
>
>   .   .   .
>
> Cruel, ah cruel!
>   ("Nishikigi")
>
> Sorrow!
> Sorrow is in the twigs of the duck's nest
>
>   .   .   .
>
> Sorrow between mandarin ducks.
>   ("Kinuta")

Influences of the Nō play can also be found in other cantos. In Canto 3, the narrator "sits" like Waki on the Dogona's steps in Venice, watching "the Buccentoro," in which the legendary wedding of the Adriatic to Venice is acted out symbolically. He also watches the gallant

Myo Cid galloping back from the past, beating "the studded gate between two towers" with his "lance butt," as in the dance of Shite in the Nō. In Canto 5, the narrator, again like Waki, sees "again the vision." In Cantos 74, 77, and 79, *Hagoromo*, *Awoi no Uye*, and *Kumasaka* are alluded to, as was *Takasago* in Canto 4. In the "Pisan Cantos," Pound appears, not as Waki anymore, but as Shite, like a passionate ghost with his own memories of the humbling and yet delightful past. All these cantos, however, lack the essential *yūgen* of the Nō play, but Canto 49 successfully recaptures yūgen, the uniquely Japanese, "most recondite," emotional atmosphere.

The Seven Lakes Canto

"The interesting portion" of one of Ezra Pound's letters to his father, quoted by Hugh Kenner in his "More on the Seven Lakes Canto," *Paideuma*, vol. 2, no. 1, reveals some aspects of the creative process of Canto 49. The rough English translation of the eight Chinese poems in the letter certainly contains many of the images of the first part of the canto. It is natural that Kenner should comment that "these paraphrases, not the Chinese, would appear to be what Canto 49 was made from."[84]

Before discussing the matter, however, I would like to start by filling in some gaps between the facts. The facts are basically as follows: Ezra Pound's parents owned an old Japanese manuscript book of Chinese and Japanese poems illustrated with paintings on eight famous scenes of Hsiao-Hsiang all written and drawn by the Japanese. The eight Chinese poems in it were paraphrased into English and were either sent, or meant to be sent, to his father Homer Pound by Ezra on July 30 (year unspecified). "Mary de Rachewiltz thinks it was 1929," Kenner notes. Pound's Canto 49, written some time later, was published in 1937.

First I agree with Kenner's guess that it was "a visitor" who paraphrased them. Most probably he was Chinese, not a Westerner, and not Pound himself. The manuscript poems are written in various styles of penmanship. With some exceptions, it is extremely difficult to decipher them without some historical knowledge of Japanese penmanship. Pound would have been able to identify several individual ideograms, but would not have been able to read a line himself. A Western sinologist of that period would never have been satisfied with paraphrases so full of errors. The translator was most probably not

Japanese either, for he did not try any Japanese poems in the manuscript. Moreover, he transcribed the name of the famous lake in China in Chinese pronunciation, "Tong Ting." If the paraphrases had been done by a Japanese, it seems likely that he would have attempted a translation of at least some Japanese poems, which he would have found easier to read, and undoubtedly rather than "Tong Ting," the lake would have been written "Do-tei" in the Japanese fashion, or possibly "Tung-ting." The translator was most probably a Chinese with some knowledge of Japanese penmanship.

Second, I would imagine "the interesting portion" of the Pound letter most probably was the note of the translator, or the note that Pound took as dictated without examining the original Chinese. The crossed-out lines are there, and some obvious errors remain uncorrected. For instance, "empty rain" should be "empty river." "Sai Yin" should be "San Yin." These errors could have been avoided by Pound if he had only checked the original. The ideograms for "river" and "mountain" must have been easily recognizable by Pound at that time.

Third, however, I would imagine that Pound reexamined the Chinese and Japanese texts in the manuscript book before he actually composed Canto 49. Many errors in the paraphrases are corrected in the canto. For instance, "rooks" and "shrimps," which appear in the original Chinese poems but not in the paraphrases, are in the canto. There are some images in the canto that reflect some parts of the Japanese poems. Pound might have had someone reexamine the manuscripts. Noel Stock gives an account, told by Dorothy Pound, of a Miss Tseng's visit to Rapallo sometime about 1934–35. Miss Tseng was a school teacher in central China, and was staying with a friend of Dorothy Pound's.

> One afternoon when the two women came to tea Pound sat on his rooftop terrace with Miss Tseng and asked her to translate from a small "book" of Chinese poems which belonged to his parents; it was made of silk and each poem was accompanied by a painted scene. Miss Tseng obliged and Pound took notes. From the notes he later wrote Canto 49 which has a resonance such as is not to be found in any other of the cantos.[85]

If Dorothy Pound's memory about the date is accurate, and Mary de Rachewiltz's correct, Tseng would be the person whom Pound asked to reexamine the manuscripts. However, it is also probable that Tseng's version of the translation might have been the paraphrases that Pound inserted in his letter to Homer, and which Kenner quoted. Dorothy Pound describes the manuscript book as "made of silk." But it is actually made of silk and rice paper. Although there still is the problem of the dates, considering the similarity of Miss Tseng to the translator we assume responsible for the paraphrases, I would guess that Miss Tseng was more probably the author of the paraphrases.

Whomever it may have been who provided Pound with translations, the fact remains that the first part of Canto 49 (lines 1–32) is closer to the original Chinese poems than to the paraphrases. Obviously Pound went over the originals himself, or had someone reexamine them, sometime after he acquired the paraphrases and before he amalgamated his experience to compose the canto. This indicates that the original manuscripts need as close attention as the paraphrases.[86]

The eight famous scenes of Hsiao and Hsiang are along the Hsiao, the upper part, and the Hsiang, the lower part, of the river that pours into Lake Tung-ting in central China. This scenic area has inspired a number of poems and paintings both in China and Japan. Especially between the late Muromachi and Edo periods in Japan, many Zen priests, courtiers, and some common people tried their versions of stylized poems in Japanese and Chinese on the eight famous scenes, or "Shō-shō Hakkei" as known in Japan. The scenes are as follows:

1. Wild Geese Plummeting to the Flat Sands
2. Sailboats Returning to Far-off Shores
3. Mist over a Mountain Town
4. Snowfall over the River
5. Autumn Moon on Lake Tung-ting
6. Night Rain in Hsiao-Hsiang
7. Evening Bell of a Misty Temple
8. Sunset Glow over a Fishing Village

The set of manuscripts in Pound's parents' possession, which looks like a book and folds like a screen, contains a version of poems in Chinese and Japanese, and paintings in black ink, each corresponding to one of the eight scenes, all composed and drawn by the Japanese in Japan.[87]

To the three poems in Japanese corresponding to scenes 2, 6 and 7 are attached slips of paper written by a connoisseur. The poems are attributed to three courtiers: Asukai Masatoyo (1664–1712), Sono Motokatsu (1663–1713?) and Takakura Eifuku (1657–1725). The judgment by a connoisseur is not always correct. But if we trust him, the manuscripts date back to the late seventeenth or early eighteenth century. Another key to the dating is in the Chinese poem on the last scene. The autograph signature in it is that of Genryū, the name under which a book of wood-block prints was published in 1683. Its title is *Poems in Chinese and Japanese on the Eight Famous Scenes by Genryū.* And it contains exactly the same version of the Chinese and Japanese poems on "Shō-shō Hakkei" that Pound's manuscript book contains.[88] The paintings are entirely different. The styles of penmanship are different. But the poems are exactly the same. It even includes those lacking in Pound's set of photographs, and, in addition, some commentaries on all the poems. One may assume that the manuscript of the eight Chinese poems in Pound's possession signed by Genryū was written about 1683 and that the whole set of manuscripts was edited also about that time.

The poems Pound saw, a part of which he undoubtedly read himself, are as follows. (Translations are mine.)

1.　　　　平沙落雁

古字書空淡墨横

幾行秋雁下寒汀

蘆花錯作衡陽雪

誤向斜陽刷凍翎

Wild Geese Plummeting to the Flat Sands
They dot the sky with old ideograms in thin black ink.
The autumn geese in lines fly down to the cold beach.
Reed blossoms in Koyo look much like snow.
Deceived they shake their frozen feathers in the
　　　setting sun.

まづあさる蘆べのともにさそはれて

空行くかりもまたくだる也

Attracted by their friends
Feeding first on the reedy shore,
The wild geese in the sky
Are also coming down.

2.　　　遠浦帰帆

　　　鷺界青山一抹秋

　　　潮平銀浪接天流

　　　帰檣漸入蘆花去

　　　家在夕陽江上頭

　　Sailboat Returning to Distant Shore
The white herons tinge the blue mountains with
　　autumn.
The water is flat but the silver waves flow along
　　the sky.
A returning mast comes slowly into reed blossoms
　　and off.
His home is above the river toward the setting sun.

　　風むかふ雲のうきなみ立つと見て

　　　つりせぬうちに帰る舟人

　　　　　（飛鳥井殿雅豊卿）

Noting the floating waves of clouds
Portending winds and high waves,
The boatman makes for home
Fishing abandoned.
　　(Attributed to Asukai Masatoyo)

3.　　　山市晴嵐

　　　一竿酒斾斜陽裏

　　　　数簇人家煙嶂中

　　　山路酔瞑帰去晩

　　　　太平无日不春風

　　Mist Over a Mountain Town
A wine flag on the pole is in the slanting sun.
Some houses are in the mist.
Intoxicated on the mountain road,　　I come home late.
Not a day is without peace and spring wind.

　　松たかき里よりうへの峰晴て

　　　あらしにしづむ山もとの雲

The mountain peaks are clear
Above the village with a tall pine tree.
Below at the foot are the clouds
Sunk in the storm.

4.　　　江天暮雪

雲淡天低槮玉塵

扁舟一葉寄吟身

前湾咿軋数声櫓

疑是山陰乗興人

Evening Snowfall Over the River
From the colorless clouds in the low sky, the jewel
　　dust is flying.
I crouch in a small leaflike boat in a poetic mood.
From an inlet above, the squeaking of an oar.
I imagine another man in rapture there behind
　　the mountain.[89]

あしの葉にかかれる雪もふかき江の

みぎはの色は夕ともなし

With the deep snow on reed leaves
The water of a deep inlet near the shore
Shows the color
That is not quite the color
Of the twilight.

5.　　　洞庭秋月

西風剪出暮天霞

万頃煙波浴桂花

漁篷不知羈客恨

直吹寒影過蘆山

Autumn Moon on Lake Tung-ting
The west wind drives the mist against the evening sky,
The hazy waves on the vast water are bathed in the
　　fragrant olive blossoms.[90]
The whistling from the fishing boat has none of
　　the traveler's gloom.

A breeze just wafts the cold silhouette and
    ignores the reed blossoms.

秋にすむ水冷じくさよふけて

月をひたせる沖つ白波

The water is clear in autumn
And cold at night.
The moon is soaked
In the white waves in the open sea.

6.   瀟湘夜雨

先自空江易断魂

凍雲黏雨濕黃昏

孤灯篷裏聴簫瑟

祇向竹枝添涙痕

Night Rain in Hsiao-Hsiang
The empty river first of all grieves my soul so
    easily.
Frozen cloud is sticking to rain dampening the
    twilight.
Under the lonely lamp beneath the thatch I hear
    pipes and strings.
I only turn to a bamboo branch and add my teardrops.[91]

ふねよする波に声なき夜の雨を

苫よりくぐる雫にぞしる

（園殿基勝卿）

Only the drops of water
Leaking through the thatched roof
Tell me of the night rain
Voiceless to the waves against the boat.
    (Attributed to Sono Motokatsu)

7.   煙寺晩鐘

雲遮不見梵王宮

殷殷鐘声訴晩風

此去上方猶遠近

為言只在此山中

Evening Bell of a Misty Temple
Hidden in the cloud,   the temple invisible
Sends the boom of its bell to tell the evening wind
That it is not near nor far above,
That it is deep in the mountain.[92]

暮かかる霧よりつたふかねのおとに

遠かた人も道いそぐなり

（高倉殿永福卿）

At the resounding evening bell
Down from the mountain,
A traveler
Hurries his way.
(Attributed to Takakura Eifuku)

8.   漁邨夕陽

薄暮沙汀惑乱鴉

江南江北鬧魚蝦

呼童買酒大家酔

臥看西風咢荻花

（玄竜）

Sunset Glow Over a Fishing Village
Twilight bewilders the crows that swarm on the
    sandy beach.
North and south of the river clamor of fish and
    shrimps.[93]
Calling a boy to buy wine, we all get drunk.
Sprawling I see the west wind set the reed blossoms
    dancing.

波の色は入日の跡に猶みえて   (Genryū)

磯ぎはくらき木がくれの宿

The waves are colored
By the wake of the setting sun.
And the cottage by the shore
Is dark under the tree.

The fact that only one of these poems is signed, and not easily
identifiable with the author, is reflected in the first line of Canto 49,

"by no man these verses." Certainly "no man" alludes to Odysseus on the island of the cyclopes, as Pearlman has pointed out.[94] The voyaging protagonist "of no fortune, and with a name to come" now wanders through the Oriental Lake District. It may also allude to the traditional "Nobody" such as Jorg Schan's Niemand, who says, "Nobody is my name; what everybody does, for that I am blamed."[95] The speaker in Canto 49 would be ready to accept any criticisms on the iniquities of others, including the mistranslations of the paraphrases. But considering the fact that two old Chinese poems, transliterated and translated in the second half of Canto 49, also are anonymous and impersonal, the phrase in line 1 seems to suggest that the whole canto is intended to be as impersonal, and as whimsical on the surface, as an anonymous poem.

Lines 2–6 of Canto 49 are suggested by the "Night Rain in Hsiao-Hsiang." The unusual combination of images, "rain," "empty river," "frozen cloud," "twilight," "under the cabin roof," "one lantern," "bamboo," and "weeping" are all literal translations of the main ideograms used in the Chinese poem. Most of them are literally the same as those in the paraphrases. But the "empty river" is "empty rain" in the paraphrases, as already mentioned. The image of the "voyage" may have come from "travel" in the paraphrase, which is an erroneous reading of "easily." But it also may have come from the picture of a boat on the water in the ink painting. "Under the cabin roof" may have come from "inside boat cover" (i.e., a sort of shelter, not an awning on a small boat) in the paraphrase. But it might have come from the "thatched roof" in the Japanese poem corresponding to the scene. "Fire" in the "fire from frozen cloud" is not in the original. It is obviously from the paraphrase. It is hard to guess why "fire" has been inserted into the paraphrase. But if we assume that Pound took notes while the Chinese visitor translated, she might have said "adhere" for the ideogram meaning "stick," which Pound might have heard as "fire." "The reeds are heavy; bent" does not appear in the "Night Rain in Hsiao-Hsiang," either. But it may have been suggested by the image of the reeds bent by the wind or snow in such lines as "With the deep snow on reed leaves" in the Japanese poem about the fourth scene.

Lines 7–12 are suggested by "Autumn Moon on Lake Tung-ting." "Autumn moon" obviously is taken from the title. "Hills rise about lakes against sunset" is the image of the painting. "Evening is like a curtain of cloud" comes from "the mist in the evening sky," but the conventional image is changed by Pound into a fresher metaphor, "like a curtain of cloud." It might be that the inaccurate translation in the paraphrases, "screen off evening cloud," was a happy suggestion. But the curtain suggests a theatrical end of the day. "Though it sharp long spikes of the cinnamon" is a strange image. The cinnamon has no spikes, and it has nothing to do with the context in the original Chinese poem. But obviously it comes from "yü kuei-hua." For kuei (kei) is occasionally referred to as cinnamon. However, it here means the Japanese Judas tree, supposed to grow on the moon, and kuei-hua (keika) denotes the blossoms of the fragrant olive, connoting the moonlight. Yü kuei-hua here means, therefore, "bathed in the moonlight." The error originates from the paraphrase, "ten thousand ripples send mist over cinnamon flowers." The painting, however, to "Autumn Moon over Lake Tung-ting" depicts a sharp, tall pine tree through haze. It may be that Pound intentionally created a witty and strange image out of the paraphrase from the Chinese poem and a part of the painting. It may be that the "sharp long spike of the cinnamon" refers to color, perhaps of hills or mountains poking through the mist of a painting. Or perhaps the cinnamon spikes here are a reference to the spicy pungence, the sharp odor of cinnamon; or perhaps the tones of the flute, sharp and piercing as cinnamon. "A cold tune amid reeds" (line 12) is a distillation of the last two lines of the paraphrase, "Fisherman's flute disregards nostalgia / Blows cold music over cottony bullrush"; and the Chinese poem, "The whistling from the fishing boat does not know the traveler's gloom. / A breeze just wafts the cold silhouette and passes the reed blossoms by."

Lines 13 and 14 are suggested by "Evening Bell of a Misty Temple." And thus lines 16 and 17 are suggested by "Sailboat Returning to Distant Shore"; and lines 18 and 19 by "Mist over a Mountain Town." Lines 20–24 are suggested by "Evening Snowfall Over the River"; lines 25–27 by "Wild Geese Plummeting to the Flat Sands"; and lines 28–32 by "Sunset Glow over a Fishing Village."

As the passage goes on, however, Pound's adaptation sticks less strictly to the original. There can be found no corresponding phrase in the original or in the paraphrase to the line, "Sail passed here in April; may return in October" (line 15). It may be that the line alludes to the boat in "The River Merchant's Wife: A Letter," which the young, tender wife is waiting for. Neither is there the source in Hsiao-Hsiang poems for line 31: "In seventeen hundred came Tsing to these hill lakes." By "Tsing" Pound probably means the second emperor, K'ang-Hsi (Kōkitei), of Ch'in. Pound's spelling shows that he already has been familiar with de Mailla's *Histoire générale de la Chine*. But he seems to have acquired the knowledge of the emperor's visit there from some other source. The emperor energetically traveled around his country during his reign (1661–1722). He made six trips to the southern part of China, mainly to oversee the embankment works, and, according to Bouvet, to meet his people. He seems to have visited the Seven Lakes area on his trip of 1699–1700 with the empress.[96] The line, however, significantly links the first part of the canto to the second.

As a whole, the first part of Canto 49 is a succession of translations of fragments of the Chinese and Japanese manuscript poems, sometimes literal and sometimes very loose, occasionally with free associations. Although it may seem a fragmentary and incomplete pastiche on the surface, it significantly pins down the essential quality of the original manuscript poems and paintings.

In the originals we find expressed what is called *yūgen* in Japanese art history. It is a concept of aesthetics discussed since the late Heian period, and has been one of the most difficult terms to define. It is the abyssal and mysterious kind of beauty, most found in the poems and Nō plays of the Muromachi period. Yūgen in art is the abstruse beauty in calmness of a work that is dark but elegant, mysterious but suggestive. "Night Rain in Hsiao-Hsiang," for instance, describes a lonely traveler who feels moved by the peculiar concatenation of the empty river, the frozen cloud, the rain, and the bamboo at night. He believes he hears, beyond his cabin roof, something resembling the pipes and strings telling of the sorrowful fate of the ancient princesses, whose shrine he is visiting. The poem suggests that there is something invisible but working on us beyond our world. In "Evening Snowfalls over the River" the lonely speaker in the boat thinks someone else is up the river behind the mountain on a dark snowy evening. In both the Japanese and Chinese versions of "Evening Bell of a Misty Temple," the sound of the bell is heard from somewhere in the evening mist. By presenting something visible or sensible in an uncanny atmosphere, all the poems of "Shō-Shō Hakkei" suggest that there is something invisible and mysterious lying behind the scene. The settings are either in the evening or at night, either in the autumn or winter. The reader is expected, as in Nō plays, to feel that, in the profound and abstruse atmosphere, nature surrounding him must be wider, deeper and richer than he sees it.

Curiously, Pound manages to recreate yūgen in his Canto 49. He presents a series of unusual combinations of images, such as "rain" and "empty river," "fire" and "frozen cloud," "wine flag" and "sunset," "cloud" and "the hole of the window." In contrast to the previous cantos telling of usury, disorder and ugliness, the world of the Seven Lakes is certainly one of calmness and beauty. But this world also seems charged with an abstruse atmosphere. Pound then suggests there is another world beyond this visible one. "Boat fades in silver" into somewhere far off. "The monk's bell" is "borne on the wind" from somewhere "behind hill." "Wild geese swoop to the sand-bar" from, and "line out with autumn" into, somewhere far away. "A light" that moves on the north and south "sky lines" appears from somewhere behind the horizon. There is no evidence that Pound was familiar with the term yūgen. Yet what it signifies is there in the first half of the canto. Pound seems to be particularly interested in suggesting that there is something mysterious behind the seeming calm of nature.

Pound begins the second half of the canto with a warning that a state will be driven to disaster if it increases its debts as it accumulates its riches. Reference is then made to Yang-ti (Yō-dai) (605–18) of Sui (Zui), who built canals for his pleasure. For Pound, in an ideal society what a king does for his pleasure is good for the people. Pound seems to adumbrate that some power working behind economic and social life plays an important role in the history of a nation. The idea becomes clearer with the introduction of two Chinese poems.

The first, beginning with "KEI MEN RAN KEI," (lines 37–40) is a transliteration of the Japanese *on* pronunciation of a classical Chinese poem. The source has been pointed out by American graduate students since 1954.[97]

卿雲歌

卿雲爛兮	The auspicious clouds bright and colorful
糺縵縵兮	Twist and spread.
日月光華	The sun and the moon shed their rays
旦復旦兮	Morning after morning.

But the version of the poem Pound read is titled, "Kei Wun Ka," with comments, transliteration, and translation in one of Fenollosa's notebooks. Fenollosa had for some time taken lessons in Chinese poetry from Kainan Mori in Tokyo. In his note for June 4, 1901, he writes:

> Last time spoke of Shun at his 9 provinces. Shun finally decided to hand the power to Wu just as he had received it from Gio. Wu is descendent of Kotei.
>
> Wu gave for the first time to the 9 provinces as a whole a single name, and called it Ka—"summer," meaning in this case "wide-broad." To that date belong that poem here given. Said to be composed by Shun himself at time of transmission. (Many things in this book which are not in She King found in Shosho Daiden.)[98]

Fenollosa seems to have tried to pencil every word quickly in his notebooks as his interpreter put the master's lectures into English. Consequently the notes are sometimes extremely cryptic. No wonder that Pound made the error of reading "Wun" for "MEN."[99] As indicated in Fenollosa's note, the poem is attributed to the legendary Emperor Shun at his retirement. He has chosen his successor with the consent of his ministers. He is said to have recited the poem, and listened to them recite it. Hence the poem has been considered a hymn to the ideal polity under an ideal king.

The next passage of five lines beginning with "Sun up; work" is a translation of another Chinese poem. The source has also been identified by the graduate students working under the direction of Norman H. Pearson at Yale.

擊壤歌

日出而作

日入而息

鑿井而飲

耕田而食

帝力于我何有哉

An English translation of the poem is in H. A. Giles's *History of Chinese Literature*, which Pound was familiar with.

> Work, work; from the rising sun
> Till sunset comes and the day is done

> I plough the sod,
> And harrow the clod,
> And meat and drink both come to me,
> So what care I for the powers that be?[100]

The Cambridge professor of Chinese literature translates the poem with a Victorian moral: work hard and "meat and drink both come." But there is no word for "meat" in the original. Pound could not have been satisfied with this diluted, heavily rhymed rendering. He might again have consulted the Fenollosa notebook for the direct source to the canto.

Geki beating	*jo* soil	*ka* song	no special meaning but to comment "and [one word illegible]" (denotes a succession either in time or in thought)
nichi sun	*shutsu* go out	*ji* and	*saku* work
nichi sun	*niu* enter	*ji* and	*soku* rest
saku dig	*sei* well	*ji* and	*in* drink
ko till	*den* field	*ji* and	*shoku* eat

Tei Emperor's	*rioku* might power	*u* for	*ga* we	*ka* what	*yu* is	*sai* ?

> This is called an earth beating song, because old folks beat the ground (for music) in singing this song.[101]

The simplicity of a folk poem in Pound's translation is achieved through his reliance on the Fenollosa notebook. The original Chinese poem has long been interpreted in Japan as expressing an ideal state of society where the people are content with their life and feel no coercion from the emperor or even an awareness of any government presence at all. The poem has been considered a eulogy of an ideal government by the emperor. Pound's interpretation of the poem is the same. He writes his own comment on the poem in the last page of the Fenollosa notebook: "dig and eat / evidently / salutations to the emperor / & folk refrains." One can associate it with Pound's frequent quotation in his essays of a Jeffersonian dictum, "the best govenment is that which governs the least."

The two ancient Chinese poems transliterated and translated in Canto 49 both describe ideal societies and suggest the workings of the emperor behind the scenes. The first poem describes an orderly scene wherein the ministers are working in beautiful harmony with one another like the bright and colorful clouds twisting and spreading in the sky. The second describes the serene life of a farmer peacefully living on his farm. But both suggest that there is an imperial power lurking behind the visible world and supporting its orderly and peaceful condition.

One is reminded of the idea in the first half of Canto 49 that there is something beyond the natural world that gives a mysterious calmness and profundity to the scenes in nature. In the second half, there is the idea that there is an imperial power working behind the scenes of social life, invisible, omnipresent, and influencing daily life. In both, Pound is suggesting that some pivotal power in the nonphysical world keeps our world in harmony and order.

The meaning of the last two enigmatic lines of the canto now is clearer. "The fourth; the dimension of stillness" is the pivotal center in the world beyond this world, from where a power for order and love comes, without which the three-dimensional world is in chaos, like that of the "wild beasts." Canto 49 is not a mere nature poem. It is not only a social and political poem, but it is in a sense a religious poem, for it points to a vision of paradise as well as of hell. And that is the theme Pound developed in his later cantos.

Pound like a magician has exposed the theory of superposition latent in Japanese haiku. Like a wizard he has been "bent resolutely on wringing lilies" out of the Chinese classical poems and the Japanese Nō plays in Ernest Fenollosa's notebooks. Though disappointed at what "the age demanded" ("Better mendacities / Than the classics in paraphrase"), he has tried further translations from Chinese classics.[102] He has written some poems under the influence of Nō plays. He has re-created the kind of world charged with a yūgenlike abstruse atmosphere.

But, compared with that of Kenneth Rexroth, Pound's understanding of Oriental culture is limited. Certainly Pound's appreciation of Far Eastern cultures is admirably multifaceted and his achievement and influence should never be minimized. Yet, cosmopolitan Odysseus that he was, Pound nevertheless did not penetrate very far into the Japanese cultural hinterland.

4

Kenneth Rexroth

In his essay, "The Influence of Classical Japanese Poetry on Modern American Poetry" (1973), Kenneth Rexroth (1905–82) compares the difference between the prewar and postwar attitudes of the American poets toward Japan.

> In the last twenty-five years the influence of Japanese poetry has become far more pervasive than it has been. The postwar development has been quite different, a difference of distance. Japan was once for the West a far away world of lotus dreams, a paradise of decadent sensualists. Whatever it is now, it is certainly that no longer.

He then traces the influence of Japanese tanka, haiku, Nō plays, and Zen on the American poets and translators mainly after World War II, such as Louis Zukofski, Robert Creeley, Gary Snyder, Philip Whalen, Cid Corman, and Francis Densmore. Rexroth's assumption is that it was in part in search of the new values and a solution for the problems modern Western civilization had brought into American society, that so many American poets were attracted by the classic Oriental literature. In conclusion, he writes:

> It can be safely said that classical Japanese and Chinese poetry are today as influential on American poetry as English or French of any period, and close to determinative for those born since 1940. I have tried to explain why this is so. Classic Far Eastern poetry speaks for all those elements of a complete culture, or factors of the human mind, of man at his most fulfilled, which are suppressed or distorted by Western civilization.[1]

Rexroth does not mention his own poems in the essay. But, by "explaining" the Japanese influence on contemporary American poets, he seems to be suggesting that he, too, was one of them, though his role was somewhat different from most of them.

He was the bridge between the prewar generation dreaming of the "far away world of lotus" and the postwar generation seriously studying Zen Buddhism, Shinto religion, or Japanese and Chinese classics. He has kept his concern with Japanese classics during the critical period between the Japanese invasion of Manchuria and World War II, when enthusiasm for Japonisme rapidly cooled off, and he passed the baton to the next generation by reinterpreting the Japanese values as new sources of poetic inspiration. He kept up his studies in Japanese poetry and Shingon Buddhism, visiting Japan several times after World War II, and translating more than two hundred Japanese poems, both classic and modern. He thus has been a bridge between the classical Japanese poetry and his contemporary American readers. Naturally his original poems, many of which show outstanding artistic mastery, reflect his familiarity with Japanese classics. He was also a synthesizer of the cultures.

But Rexroth was not influenced only by the Far Eastern classics. He read very widely and lived through some extraordinary personal experiences. He was interested in French poetry, especially in Pierre Reverdy, whose poems he translated and later published in *Pierre Reverdy: Selected Poems* (1955). He wrote essays on Homer, Sophocles, Thucydides, Plato, Petronius, the Mahabharata, Tu Fu, Chaucer, Rabelais, Machiavelli, Cervantes, Shakespeare, Stendhal, Marx, Dostoevski, Chekhov, and many others, some of which are collected in his *Classics Revisited* (1965). Having lost his mother when he was ten, his father dying two years later, and having known the sorrow of a young wife's death, he was possessed by the idea of death and the meaning of life, and was desperately in search of love. On the other hand, he also was concerned with social justice and was for some time actively interested in the labor movement. All these experiences, echoing in his various short poems, are blended into such longer poems as *The Phoenix and the Tortoise*.

The Phoenix and the Tortoise

Just as Pound's *Cantos* do, Rexroth's *The Phoenix and the Tortoise* (1944) begins with a description of the sea.

> Webs of misery spread in the brain,
> In the dry spring in the soft heat.
> Dirty cotton balls of cloud hang
> At the sky's edge; vague yellow stratus
> Glimmer behind them. It is storming
> Somewhere far out in the ocean.
> All night vast rollers exploded
> Offshore; now the sea has subsided
> To a massive, uneasy torpor.
> Fragments of its inexhaustible
> Life litter the shingle, sea hares,
> Broken starfish, a dead octopus,
> And everywhere, swarming like ants,
> Innumerable hermit crabs,
> Hungry and efficient as maggots.

The protagonist of *The Phoenix and the Tortoise*, however, does not "set keel to breakers, forth on the godly sea," but walks along the California seashore, trying to put in order the problems clinging to his brain numbed by the "webs of misery."

> Of what survives and what perishes,
> And how, of the fall of history
> And waste of fact—[2]

The solemn announcement of the poem's theme, reminding us of that of Milton's *Paradise Lost*, "Of man's first disobedience," is followed by the presentation of various aspects of man's life and death. The first figure the reader encounters is the dead body of a Japanese sailor.

> A group of terrified children
> Has just discovered the body
> Of a Japanese sailor bumping
> In a snarl of kelp in a tidepool.[3]

The drowned sailor drifting in the ocean is not the symbol of regeneration here, as in T. S. Eliot's *The Waste Land*. He is eventually to become one of the "fragments of its inexhaustible life," like the "broken starfish" or "a dead octopus." In contrast, however, the protagonist, watching the deaths, is the real living existence "seeking the continuity ... of history," and searching for the "lyric" as evidence of life among the epical series of events.

> Me—who stand here on the edge of death,
> Seeking the continuity,
> The germ plasm, of history,
> The epic's lyric absolute.

The protagonist's contemplation upon the lyric in the epic, the personal voice in history, and the life among the deaths is developed into a drama of love in the desert.[4]

The speaker kisses his wife by the campfire, goes to bed, and meditates on "Yin and Yang," "danger and desire," and "fact and value." Before falling asleep, he sees beautiful visions in fragmentary images and thoughts. When he wakes up next morning, he finds his wife, who has gone swimming before sunrise, coming toward him naked, and the morning sun shines upon them. One of the conclusions that the protagonist reaches is, as Morgan Gibson points out, that "only through loss is transcendence possible; only through destruction is creation possible."[5]

In the long, meditative passage in which the protagonist contemplates various subjects in the canvas under the stars, some Japanese images intermittently appear.

> It is past midnight and the faint,
> Myriad crying of the seabirds
> Enters my sleep ... Amida,
> Kwannon, turn from peace. As moonlight
> Flows on the tides, innumerable
> Dark worlds flow into splendor.
> How many nights have we awakened—
> The killdeer crying in the seawind.[6]

"Amida" and "Kwannon" will be discussed later. Rexroth published *One Hundred Poems from the Japanese*, in which we find his translation of a Japanese tanka by Minamoto no Kanemasa.

> Guardian of the gate
> Of Suma, how many nights
> Have you awakened
> At the crying of the shore birds
> Of the Isle of Awaji?[7]

The translation closely resembles the last two lines quoted earlier. The tanka is inlaid, as it were, into the context of the poem as if it were a concealed picture puzzle. The method is similar to that of Eliot and Pound. Just as Eliot quotes a passage from Dante in *The Waste Land* and expands his world by double-exposing the world of the *Divine Comedy*, Rexroth juxtaposes the world of the California beach at night with that of the Suma beach at night during the Heian period in Japan. In Eliot, the wasteland of modern society is compared to, and explained in terms of, the world of the Inferno, where "Death had undone so many." In Rexroth, the experience on the California beach is associated with the world of the tanka on Awaji Island so far away that they seem to be reflecting each other rather than interpreting each other. Rexroth, in that sense, is closer to Pound than to Eliot. In the *Cantos* the images are often superposed and contrasted as in *The Phoenix and the Tortoise*.

Part 3 begins with the scene where the protagonist hears an owl before dawn lying beside his "wife's canvas chrysalis."

> Softly and singly an owl
> Cries in my sleep. I wake and turn
> My head, but there is only the moon
> Sinking in the early dawn.[8]

If one replaces "owl" with *hototogisu*, or cuckoo, this passage very closely resembles the well-known tanka by Gotoku Daiji. And this tanka, too, is translated by Rexroth.

> A Cuckoo calls,
> When I look there is only
> The waning moon
> In the early dawn.[9]

Both of the tankas that Rexroth uses in his poem are included in the *Ogura Hyakunin Isshu*, a popular anthology of tankas edited by Fujiwara no Teika. It can be guessed that Rexroth was familiar with the anthology by the time of his composition of *The Phoenix and the Tortoise*. Indeed, the tankas included in the anthology appear one after another toward the end of Part 3, translated and transformed in various ways:

> Would it have been better to have slept
> And dreamed, than to have watched night
> Pass and this slow moon sink? My wife sleeps
> And her dreams measure the hours

As accurately as my
Meditations in cold solitude.
I have lain awake while the moon crossed,
Dragging at the tangled ways
Of the sea and the tangled, blood filled
Veins of sleepers. I am not alone,
Caught in the turning of the seasons.
As the long beams of the setting moon
Move against the breaking day,
The suspended light pulsates
Like floating snow. Involuntary,
I may live on, sustained in the web
Of accident, never forgetting
This midnight moon that already blurs
In memory.
            As certain
As color passes from the petal,
Irrevocable as flesh,
The gazing eye falls through the world.
As the light breaks over the water
One by one, pedetemtim,
The stakes of the nets appear
Stretching far out into the shallows,
And beyond them the dark animal
Shadow of a camouflaged cruiser.[10]

At least four tankas from *Hyakunin Isshu* are half-concealed here. The first three lines are based on the poem by Lady Akazome Emon, and the second half of the passage is composed of the poems by the Emperor Sanjo, the poetess Ono no Komachi, and Fujiwara no Sadayori. All of these are also translated into English by Rexroth and included in his *One Hundred Poems from the Japanese*.

I should not have waited.
It would have been better
To have slept and dreamed,
Than to have watched night pass,
And this slow moon sink.
            (Lady Akazome Emon)

Involuntary,
I may live on
In the passing world,
Never forgetting
This midnight moon.
　　(Emperor Sanjo)

As certain as color
Passes from the petal,
Irrevocable as flesh
The gazing eye falls through the world.
　　(Ono no Komachi)

As the mists rise in the dawn
From Uji River, one by one,
The stakes of the nets appear,
Stretching far into the shallows."
　　(Fujiwara no Sadayori)

The sources of the Japanese poems in Rexroth's *Phoenix and the Tortoise* are, thus, evidently the tanka included in *Hyakunin Isshu*, translated by Rexroth himself.

Rexroth had been interested in Japanese poetry since his adolescence. In the preface to *One Hundred Poems from the Japanese*, he wrote:

A few of these translations date back many years, one to my adolescence (it happens to be perfectly literal) so there is a certain amount of inconsistency in the degree of literalness.[12]

He recalls that he owned a pack of cards of *Hyakunin Isshu* in San Francisco, where he helped edit a newspaper for Japanese immigrants, and that after they were sent to the concentration camps he worked on them by himself with the dictionaries and such books as listed in the bibliography of *One Hundred Poems*.[13] By the time he wrote *The Phoenix and the Tortoise*, he had translated a certain number of the Japanese poems and was so charmed by some of them that he quoted and alluded to them in his own poem. He then probably reworked the translations he had done and added still more translations before selecting and publishing them in book form in 1955. The title *One Hundred Poems from the Japanese* seems to echo the *Hyakunin Isshu*, which literally means one poem each by a hundred poets, which may also reflect his deep indebtedness.

Rexroth's understanding of Japanese poetry is surprising. It is much deeper and sharper than some poets, such as Amy Lowell and Ezra Pound, who had been interested in it before and during World War II. And he re-creates its beauty in compressed and explosive English, by using the imagist method he had learned from them. The tanka is alive in his language. As he confesses, he translated them "in conversation with the poet behind each poem." [14]

But more suprising is his effective use of Japanese poetry in *The Phoenix and the Tortoise*. He uses it as a kind of yeast to swell and enrich the meaning of his poem with wit, fantasy, and suggestiveness. And it seems that this richness is a reflection of the complexity, synthesis and discordant harmony of the international and multicultural society of a modern city like San Francisco.

Beyond the Mountains

After *The Phoenix and the Tortoise*, Rexroth published *The Art of Worldly Wisdom*, a collection of early short poems, in 1949, and *Beyond the Mountains* in 1951, a collection of four plays in which some influence from Japanese Nō plays can be traced.

Of the four plays, centered on such classical figures as Phaedra, Iphigenia, Hermaios, and Berenike, the second play, *Iphigenia at Aulis*, seems the purest and the best. The story is based on Greek mythology.

When Agamemnon comes with his fleet to Aulis, the seaport in Boeotia, central Greece, on his way to Troy, he finds he is unable to move his ships any farther because of the calm. The prophet tells him that calm is caused by the anger of Artemis, and that in order to soothe her, he needs the blood of a virgin. Agamemnon sends for his daughter, Iphigenia, on the pretext that she is to be married to Achilles. When Iphigenia arrives at the seaport with her mother, Clytemnestra, Achilles tries to save her life. Iphigenia, too, entreats her father to change his mind. But finally she decides to sacrifice herself.

In Ovid's *Metamorphosis*, Artemis pities Iphigenia, sends down a cloud upon the altar, and changes her into a deer. In Euripides's *Iphigenia in Tauris*, Iphigenia, carried off on the cloud, is made Artemis's priestess in Crimea. The plot in Euripides's *Iphigenia at Aulis* is more complexly interwoven with the story of Menelaus, whose wife, Helen, has been carried off to Troy by Paris.

But Rexroth's version is much simpler in plot, with only three characters and two choruses on the stage. Iphigenia, Achilles and Agamemnon, however, are presented as characters with modern sensibility. Agamemnon loves his daughter so much that he remains indecisive for three months, while she and Achilles enjoy romancing on the beach.

> How she loves to swim.
> She'd spend all her time swimming and hunting
> If she could.We used to swim together
> When she was little, just a few years ago.
> Now she has a lover to swim with her.
> A girl turns to a woman overnight.
> When she was born he was a puppy. . . .

While Agamemnon is still wondering whether his army could "march overland, conquering the country as we go," and could "make it an empire," Achilles praises Iphigenia in sensual terms.

> Do I love your body's beauty . . . ?
> Do I love the different perfumes
> Of your breasts and armpits and thighs,
> And the honey of your mouth and sex,
> And your limbs that clasp me about?

But Iphigenia, who "can command the wind," having "the power of Artemis," decides to sacrifice herself "When the Moon's disc slides into full."[15] And the father consents, without a word, to the dance with her, symbolizing the tacit understanding between the two. The following dance of Iphigenia and Achilles, with "terrific violence under tremendous restraint," reaches "climax after climax." Finally Iphigenia orders in tears to prepare her "for pure act." Surrounded by fire, she cries out, "I conquer Troy," and the knife shines "black with her blood."

Iphigenia's love for her father and her nation culminates in her death, and it is suggested that her love for Achilles is consummated in heaven after his death for the country: the perfection of love is the voluntary self-sacrifice. Morgan Gibson rightly summarizes the characteristic of the play common also to the four plays in *Beyond the Mountains*:

> Iphigenia, Hyppolytus, Phaedra, and others achieve transcen-
> dence through the mysteries of erotic union and sacrificial

death. In no work does Rexroth communicate more profoundly the meaning of love as universal responsibility and the integral person as the source of community.[16]

As has been mentioned earlier, traces of the Nō play can be seen in the play. Rexroth had been interested in the Nō since he produced Yeats's *At the Hawk's Well* soon after it was published, and acted the part of Cuchullain in Chicago.[17] Later when he visited Japan and saw some Nō plays, he praised *Kakitsubata* and *Nishikigi*, translated by Pound, as "far better than any other scholastic translations." His essay in the *New York Times* in 1971 shows his continuous interest in and deep insight into the Nō play.

> There was nothing like Japanese Nō drama in the West until Thomas Sturge Moore and William Butler Yeats imitated the first Pound-Fenollosa translations. *Iphigenia at Aulis* and *Salome* bear a faint resemblance to Nō, but there is a fundamental difference. They are plays of action and of the developing interaction of persons, and they culminate in dramatic climax. The typical Nō play contains no action at all but rather the recollection of action, and although it commonly culminates in a dance, the dance is not a climax but the manifestation of the crystallization of the realization that has grown and pervaded the play.[18]

He explains further in the essay that, as the "revenants" are released from "the endless re-enactment of dead fate and consequence," by the prayers of the pilgrim priest, the audience realizes the meaning of Karma and "a crystal called release."

Rexroth does not mention his own plays in his essay on the Nō play. In *Iphigenia*, however, can be traced what he has seen as the characteristics of the Nō play. The dance of Iphigenia and Achilles toward the end is not the dramatic climax in the traditional sense. But it is the "crystallization" of the emotional struggle restrained and sublimated.

Yet Rexroth writes practically the same thing in the preface to his *Beyond the Mountains*.

> The first two plays [*Phaedra* and *Iphigenia*] do not culminate in dramatic resolution or climax; rather an atmosphere is created, a general situation developed, and dramatic realization occurs

as a sort of precipitated crystal from the saturated solution of dramatic tensions—not a kind of happening, but a state of being. Iphigenia marches straight to transcendence.[19]

What are regarded as the characteristics of the Nō play in one essay are regarded as the characteristics of his own plays in another place. Obviously Rexroth was conscious of the Nō play when he wrote his plays.

If one looks into his plays more closely, one can find more of their resemblances to the Nō: simple stage setting, a limited number of characters, subtle dramatic responses between the chorus and the characters, concern with the past, and allusions to classical literature. He was not particularly interested in the double scene structure and visionary aspects of the Nō play as Pound was. He was not interested in what the legendary protagonists really wanted to say after their deaths. But he was interested in creating "an atmosphere" in the process toward consent and crystallization of emotion by transcendence. In later years, Rexroth became interested in the esoteric Buddhism of the Shingon sect, and wrote *The Heart's Garden / The Garden's Heart*, (1967) in which the narrator seeks love and religious truth. He also wrote "On Flower Wreath Hill" (1976), in which a mysterious atmosphere is created quite close to yūgen. Behind these works, which will be discussed later, can also be found the echo of the Nō play.

San Francisco Renaissance

In 1952, Rexroth published, *The Dragon and the Unicorn*. It is a long poem in which, as the protagonist wanders from San Francisco through New York, Liverpool, and the historic sites and bombed cities in England, he speculates on love, community, and history, just as in *The Phoenix and the Tortoise*. He attempts to systematize his theory especially of the community bound by love.

The political stance of the poems never changes—the only absolute is the Community of Love with which Time ends. Time is the nisus toward the Community of Love.[20]

His idea of "the Community of Love" led him to help organize the poets and artists in the San Francisco Bay area into a community. Rexroth is not solely responsible, but from that community in 1955 came the cultural movement known as "beat."

Rexroth established a poetry center, began poetry readings and welcomed poets arriving in San Francisco: Lawrence Ferlinghetti, Lew Welch, Michael McClure, David Meltzer, Lenore Kandel, Allen Ginsberg, Gregory Corso, Jack Kerouac, and others. However, the crystallizing historical event was the big poetry reading in 1955 at the Six Gallery in the Marina, where Ginsberg read his *Howl*. Kenneth Rexroth, who was the moderator, praised it as great prophetic literature in the biblical tradition. Other participants in the reading were McClure, Philip Lamantier, Ferlinghetti, Gary Snyder and Philip Whalen. Ferlinghetti and Peters recollected:

> Certainly the most international literary soirée in San Francisco in the 1950's and early 1960's was that held almost weekly at Kenneth Rexroth's large second-floor flat at 250 Scott Street above Jack's Record Cellar on the edge of the mostly black Fillmore district. The halls of the flat were lined to the ceiling with apple boxes containing one of the finest collections of literature (Western and oriental, classical and modern, in several languages), much of it review copies in many fields (poetry, geology, astronomy, art, sociology, philosophy, political history, and radical thought in general).... Writers from many countries plus migrant East Coast and Northwest poets found their way to Rexroth's where they encountered many of the resident San Francisco radical community, the heart of which was made up of World War II conscientious objectors and poets active in the Berkeley Renaissance of the late 1940's and published there, especially in *Circle* magazine.[21]

Rexroth publicized the movement and helped give it its historical focus: rejection of the "established" and "academic" culture on the East Coast, revolt against the ethos of "Back to Normalcy" during the 1950s, and creation of a new mode of poetry with a more personal voice opposing mechanized society, freer choice of subject matter, and a higher voltage of emotional power rather than use of technical devices and objectivity. His essay, "Disengagement: The Art of the Beat Generation" (1957), reveals Rexroth's energy and expectation for the new movement.

> The youngest generation is in a state of revolt so absolute that its elders cannot even recognize it. The disaffiliation, alienation, and rejection of the young has, as far as their elders are concerned, moved out of the visible spectrum altogether.[22]

It also reveals the role he played in the San Francisco renaissance. He not only attracted and oriented the revolting poets into a community, but, like a "librarian,"[23] also gave them international perspectives with his wide range of knowledge in world literatures and religions and history of ideas. He published *One Hundred Poems from the Japanese* (1955), *One Hundred Poems from the Chinese* (1956), and *Thirty Spanish Poems of Love and Exile* (1956). It is significant to note that, just when the local movement was growing into, and was converged with, a worldwide phenomenon of "counter-culture," Rexroth injected into it Buddhism and Japanese classical poetry.

The Heart's Garden / The Garden's Heart

In 1967, after traveling through Europe and the Middle East, Rexroth visited Japan for the first time, and stayed in Kyoto, which he had heard about through Gary Snyder, Cid Corman, and Philip Whalen. He went up to Kurama, climbed Mount Hiei, and visited Sanjusangendo, Rokuharamitsuji, and Daitokuji, looking at Buddhist sculptures and gardens. All these experiences are woven into *The Heart's Garden / The Garden's Heart*.

The poem, composed of 12 sections, seems at first glance a series of travel accounts, but it is in effect a restrained love poem, and also a serious religious poem in search of the Buddhist truth. In sections 1 to 4, the scenes of Kurama in late spring are described, in which the protagonist, picking ferns and bamboo shoots, falls into meditation, listening "Deep in his mind to music / Lost far off in space and time." The lost music he recovers first is Oriental.

> The valley's soul is deathless.
> It is called the dark woman.
> The dark woman is the gate
> To the root of heaven and earth.[24]

This passage is a paraphrase from Lao-tzu:

谷神不死。是謂玄牝。玄牝門，是謂天地根。綿綿若存，用之不勤。

> The valley's god does not die. It is called dark
> woman. The gate of the dark woman is the root of
> heaven and earth. It seems to have been there
> continuously. Though it is used, it does not wear
> out.[25]

It seems to suggest that one of the themes of the poem is the mysterious energy of woman. Following the passage, another theme of the poem is introduced.

> Pausing in my sixth decade
> At the end of a journey
> Around the earth—where am I!
> I am sitting on a rock
> Close beside a waterfall
> Above Kurama Hot Springs
> In the hills above Kyoto.[26]

The quest for his identity ("where am I?") on the geographical level is linked to the quest for his spiritual identity. Looking at the rainbow over the waterfall, the speaker discovers within his heart "a pearl" glowing with rainbows around it.

> Millions of pearls in the mist
> Of the waterfall added
> Together make a rainbow.
> Deep in the heart one pearl glows
> With ten million rainbows.

But the meaning of the pearl, and the light that shines upon it in his heart, is left unexplained. It is only vaguely suggested metaphorically:

> Deep in the mountain wilderness
> Where nobody ever comes,
> Only once in a while something
> Like the sound of a far off voice,
> The low rays of the sun slip
> Through the dark forest and gleam
> In pools on the shadowy moss.[27]

Rexroth suggests that another theme of the poem is the quest for the pearl in his heart—his identity.

In sections 5 to 7, fragments of scenes in Kyoto are humorously described as a kind of interlude. Close by the silent dry garden of a temple the protagonist hears the noisy looms and pinball machines. "Should Buddhist monks / Have telephones?" he asks mischievously.[28] The tone of the sections is that of a scherzo, with incongruous juxtapositions. But soon he casts aside the tourist attitude and stops poking fun.

Symbols gain more concrete meaning in sections 8 to 10, where the scenes of Kyoto under the full moon are depicted. Vega and Altair are bright in the clear sky on either side of the Milky Way.

> The air is sweet
> With the scents of a May night,
> And the faint smell of incense
> At each temple gate.

Just as the speaker in "Ode to a Nightingale" smells the sweet flowers in the woods in the "tender" night of May, Rexroth wanders around the temple and feels the air filled with "the scents of a May night." The speaker in Keats wishes to "fade away," "unseen," with the requiem of the nightingale, but Rexroth's speaker, on hearing the temple bells and the chanting of the sutra, suddenly feels as if he is led toward a new life.

> A bell.
> And then gongs sound from every
> Compound, and temple by temple,
> The chanting of monks.

As if invited, he approaches Buddhism. The full moon shines as if promising the attainment of nirvana. Altair and Vega are on the apex and "the Eagle plays the Lyre with his rays."

> The weaving girl dances for
> Her cowboy far across the
> Cloudy River.[29]

As the images of the two stars are repeated and grow pregnant with symbolic meaning, we may imagine that Altair in the eagle, now in Japan, is playing the lyre of Vega in America with his "rays" across the Pacific. Sure enough, toward the end of section 10, the expectation of the rendezvous of the two stars is described in terms of a vision mixed with myth and reality. According to the Japanese myth of Tanabata, the "cowboy" (Altair) and the "weaving girl" (Vega), the two lovers, are allowed to meet once a year on July 7, if the sky is clear.

> Her bracelets tinkle, her anklets
> Clink. She sways at her clattering
> Loom. She hurries to have a new

> Obi ready when he comes—
> On the seventh day of the seventh
> Month. . . .
>   He returns to
> Penelope, the wanderer
> Of many devices, to
> The final woman who weaves,
> And unweaves, and weaves again.[30]

As the weaver is portrayed as waiting at home wearing bracelets and anklets, and as the two stars are compared to Odysseus and Penelope, we cannot but read these lines as the lyrical expression of the particular man in love with a particular woman.

Section 11 depicts a home in California with a waterfall, a garden, song, and love, and section 12 suggests the fire of love burning in the heart of a man who has been wandering over the ocean.

> Love turns the heart to an unknown
> Substance, fire of its fire.
> Not by flesh, but by love, man
> Comes into the world, lost in
> The illimitable ocean
> Of which there is no shore.[31]

The poem as a whole presents the story of courtship and love's fulfillment.

But the poem is not a mere love poem. It is also a poem in search of religious truth. The very passage quoted above also has a religious overtone: only by love, which transforms the human heart into "an unknown/substance," is man capable of self-realization and self-fulfillment. The two themes of seeking love and seeking religious truth are brought together in the last section.

Rexroth has been carefully building the images suggesting his serious interest in Shingon Buddhism. In section 8 he writes:

> The full moon appears on the
> Horizon above the temple
> Of Dainichi as an
> Immense, incomprehensible
> Silence overwhelming the world,
> The orb of wonder, not moving,
> But growing like an obsession.[32]

The full moon is the traditional symbol of spiritual awakening in Buddhism. Dainichi Nyorai (Mahavirocana Tathāgata) is regarded as the incarnation of the supreme wisdom and the fundamental principle of the universe in Shingon Buddhism. Since the moon was semicircular in the previous section, the full moon over the temple of Dainichi may well suggest the promise of fulfillment of his search for the truth and enlightenment.

But Rexroth, though aware of the possibility of faith, chooses to remain uncommitted—and like the protagonist of *The Waste Land* waiting for the final "rain," waits for the last call from Buddha.

> The promise of the vow of
> The Bodhisattva is so
> Powerful the stormy ocean of
> Karma turns to an unruffled mirror.
>
> .   .   .
>
> Where is the three legged crow?
> He is flying across the
> Solar system to the moon—
> The mascot of Dainichi.
> My heart is not a mirror.
> I cannot see myself in it.

His heart is not as transparent yet as "an unruffled mirror," and he does not find his own figure in it. Morgan Gibson rightly comments, "In the heart's garden lies the garden's heart." But Rexroth does not find "the garden's heart" yet in his heart's garden.[33]

> At Daisenji the abbot's
> Garden consists of two cones
> Of gravel heaped to the angle
> Of repose, surrounded by
> A herring bone sea of raked
> Gravel. Between the cones
> Devadatta has thrown an empty
> Film box, red and yellow,
> The colors of fire.

Rexroth seems extremely amused to find an empty film box thrown out onto the famous garden of white gravel in Daisen-in in Daitokuji, symbolizing the ocean of limitlessness. He visits the same garden again the next day. He finds the film box gone, but he witnesses a curious thing happen.

> A baby
> Breaks away from its mother,
> The lady who sells tickets,
> And runs across the limitless sea
> Of raked gravel, just where
> The film box was yesterday.[34]

In describing the central image of the garden in this poem, Rexroth is greatly concerned with the disorder in the supposedly perfect symbol of limitlessness. Most probably Rexroth is trying to show that his heart's garden is as much in disorder and as imperfect as the disturbed garden of limitlessness in Daisen-in, that his heart is not yet as clear as the "unruffled mirror," and that he has not reached the enlightened state of mind yet. According to Shingon Buddhism, every man is inherently capable of attaining suchness (the absolute truth of the universe) and of being identified with, and becoming himself, Nyorai (Tathāgata); but is interrupted and harassed by uneasiness caused by earthly desires. Rexroth's uneasiness seems to be closely related to his inability to identify the true substance of the pearl "deep in his mind" glowing "with ten million rainbows." The key to the meaning is the figure of Marishiten, who appears in the latter half of the poem.

Marishiten usually is represented in Japan by the statue of a young woman sitting on a pedestal that is a figure of a boar, or a few boars. She is worshipped as the protector from calamities, especially by the warrior class since the Muromachi period. There still remain a number of statues of her in various temples in Japan; but "the temple near Rokuharamitsuji with one of those statues," which Rexroth says he has visited, is described in the poem as follows:

> At the end of an avenue
> Of boars, like a line of sphinxes,
> Is the temple of Marichi,
> Patroness of geisha and whores,
> And the goddess of the dawn. The girl
> Beside me tells me she was
> A great Indian prostitute
> Who was really an incarnate
> Bodhisattva. The girl herself
> Turned out to be a Communist.

Rexroth makes a comment on Marishiten in his preface.

> Marichi, an avator of the Shakti of Shiva, has three
> heads: a sow, a woman in orgasm and the dawn. "Goddess
> of the Dawn," as Westerners call her, her chariot.
> drawn by swine, she haunts "The Homestead called
> Damascus" and comes back as a beautiful Communist
> girl in "The Heart's Garden" as does Vega, the jewel
> in the Lyre, the weaving girl who weaves and ravels
> and weaves again.[35]

Just as Pound thought Helen, Aphrodite, and the heavenly maid of
Hagoromo to be the symbols of perpetual female beauty, so Rexroth
presents Marishiten, the communist girl, Vega, and the weaving girl as
symbols of his ideal figure of a lover.

As mentioned earlier, Rexroth has been seriously interested in
esoteric Buddhism of the Shingon sect. One of its branches, the Tachikawa Shingon sect, keeps as its secret Buddha the statue of Marishiten
in her ecstasy on the laps of Dainichi Nyorai. According to its doctrine,
one may awaken and attain nirvana by chanting esoteric incantations
and through sexual intercourse.

In the Kamakura period this sect branched off from the Shingon
sect, which had been established by Kūkai in the Heian period. Kūkai
had been in China, where he learned the esoteric Buddhism of India
from Priest Hui-kuo, a disciple of Ta-k'ung, an Indian Buddhist. In
Chang-an, he found another school of esoteric Buddhism indirectly
brought from India through Tibet. Kūkai synthesized the two schools
of thought into one doctrine and systematized his own Buddhist theology based on his belief in Ryōbu Fuji, literally "twin worlds not two,"
meaning "two worlds without contradiction," the two being Kongō
Kai and Taizō Kai.[36]

This theology included some ideas of Tantrism from Tibet. The
Tachikawa Shingon abstracts and emphasizes this Tantric part of the
Shingon system of thought. Though Rexroth was not a Tantrist, he
seemed particularly concerned with this part of Shingon esotericism.

For Rexroth, the seeker of truth and love, one is able to attain nirvana
by becoming unified with the mysteries of the world and by being
spiritually and physically united with the other sex in "the sea of love."
Even though the full moon shines over the temple of Dainichi Nyorai,
and the bells and chanting are heard from the temple, Rexroth is unable
to attain nirvana insofar as he is unable to see the pearl-like figure of

woman glowing in his heart. When he returns to Mount Calvary in California, however, he sees the figure clearly in his heart's garden, for he sees the woman waiting for him like a Penelope. There, he writes, "the sparrow has found her a home, / the swallow a nest for herself," and "the weaving girl is pregnant / With another year," suggesting the unity and fulfillment with the "garden's heart" in his "heart's garden."

> The sea of circumstance where
> The heart drowns is the sea of love.
> The heart drinks it and it drinks
> The heart—transubstantiation
> In which the One drinks the Other
> And the Other drinks the One.
> The sea of the fire that lights all being
> Becomes the human heart.[37]

The last and the most significant message of Rexroth seems to be that mystic "transubstantiation" of the spirit and body is brought about only by love. This is achieved by enveloping each other, as if "drinking" the heart of each other, when the eternal light of truth flows into the "human heart" like "the sea of the fire." Love and religious faith are thus linked in his climactic assertion.

All the main images in the poem are interlocked like a chain: "the dark woman of the valley," "the limitless sea" of the garden in Daito-kuji, Marishiten, and the "weaving girl" are the symbols of the mystic power and inclusiveness of woman, containing the possibility of the "Holy Wedding"[38] with the principle of the universe through unity in love. Finally, it should be noted that the religious love poem, *The Heart's Garden / The Garden's Heart*, is the product of Rexroth's stay in Kyoto, and might not have been written without his contacts with Japanese culture, especially the gardens, temples, and images of Buddha.

Another trace of Japanese culture's influence on the poem also should be pointed out: the ingenious use of the tanka. Just as in *The Phoenix and the Tortoise*, the English translations of tankas are inlaid like a damascene work, so in *The Heart's Garden / The Garden's Heart*, a number of tankas have been ingeniously incised. In section 6, where the sunset viewed from Mount Hiei is described, Rexroth writes,

> The lower leaves of the trees
> Tangle the sunset in the dusk.
> Awe perfumes the warm twilight.[39]

Anyone who has seen the picturesque sunset from Mount Hiei or from anyplace in the eastern hills of Kyoto would agree that, as the vast basin of Kyoto underneath grows darker, something awesome spreads with the twilight. But the atmosphere created by the passage is quite close to that in the tanka by Sone no Yoshitada, a Heian poet.

> Hi korureba
> Shita wa koguraki
> Ko no moto no
> Mono osoroshiki
> Natsu no yugure.

> After sunset
> Under the trees
> Drifts the darkness,
> The awful uncanniness
> Of the summer evening.

Since Sone no Yoshitada was a conceited poet and courtier, and was coldly treated in the court, one may sense in the poem some weird presentiment of his fearful destiny. But Rexroth translated the same poem into English with the effect of a beautiful painting.

> The lower leaves of the trees
> Tangle the sunset in the dusk.
> Awe spreads with
> The summer twilight.[40]

This translation, however, closely resembles the passage quoted from his poem. Or it may be that he was reminded of his experience on Mount Hiei while translating the tanka and injected the experience into his translation. Whichever the case may be, it is certain that Rexroth skillfully wove the tanka of Sone no Yoshitada into his own poem, suggesting that "awe" may spread in his heart's garden.

In section 4, where the protagonist meditates on Mount Kurama, another tanka is inserted, after the passage about the rainbow over the million pearls of spray in the waterfall.

> Weary of the twin seas of
> Being and not-being, I
> Long for the mountain of bliss
> Untouched by the changing tides.[41]

This passage, with its heavily Buddhist connotations, is the English translation of an anonymous tanka in the Manyōshū. The translation by Rexroth is also included in his *One Hundred More Poems from the Japanese*, as in the case of Sone no Yoshitada's poem.

> Shoji no
> Futatsu no umi o
> Itowashimi
> Shiohi mo yama o
> Shinobitsuru kana.

> I loathe the twin seas
> Of being and not being
> And long for the mountain
> Of bliss untouched by
> The changing tides.[42]

Abruptly and obtrusively inlaid in the context as in a collage, the passage seems to warn the reader that the theme of the meditation is to be developed as in Buddhism.

There are more translations of tankas scattered in *The Heart's Garden / The Garden's Heart*. In section 10, where Vega begins to assume the more concrete image of a particular woman, Rexroth writes:

> I
> Remember a grass hut on
> A rainy night, dreaming of
> The past, and my tears starting
> At the cry of a mountain cuckoo.
> Her bracelets tinkle, her anklets
> Clink. She sways at her clattering
> Loom. She hurries to have a new
> Obi ready when he comes—[43]

The passage is composed of two different tankas: one by Fujiwara no Shunzei and the other by an anonymous Manyō poet. Both of them are translated into English by Rexroth.

Mukashi omou
Kusa no iori no
Yoru no ame ni
Namida na soeso
Yamahototogisu.

Ashidama mo
Tedama mo yurani
Oru hata o
Kimi ga mikeshi ni
Nuiaemu kamo.

I remember a grass hut
On a rainy night,
Dreaming of the past,
My tears starting at the cry
Of a mountain cuckoo.

Her bracelets tinkle
Her anklets clink
She sways at her clattering loom
She hurries to have a new
Obi ready when he comes.[44]

In using the tanka by Fujiwara no Shunzei, Rexroth describes the "hut"
of his weaving girl in America, and, by quoting the anonymous poem
in the *Manyōshū* on *tanabata*, he suggests that the weaving girl is waiting
and longing for him.

Section 10 ends also with a tanka in translation. The passage suggests his departure from the curiously fantastic world of the old capital
of Japan in late spring.

In the moon drenched night the floating
Bridge of dreams breaks off. The clouds
Banked against the mountain peak
Dissipate in the clear sky.[45]

This is a paraphrase of a poem by Fujiwara no Teika.

Haru no yo no
Yume no ukihashi
Todae shite

> Mine ni wakaruru
> Yokogumo no sora.

> The Spring night's
> Floating bridge of dreams
> Breaks off. The clouds banked
> Against the mountain peak
> Dissipate in the clear sky.[46]

The translation is excellently done, as if the translator was in communion with the original poet, and a slightly modified version is found in Rexroth's own poetry, as if to assure that he can, indeed, understand the feeling of Fujiwara no Teika. *The Heart's Garden / The Garden's Heart* is a poem in which Rexroth "drinks" from the sea of the Japanese classical poetry he loved, in which he is "drowned," and in which he clarifies his position as a seeker of love and truth in Buddhism.

Later Poems

It was 1967 when Rexroth visited Japan for the first time and wrote *The Heart's Garden / The Garden's Heart*. His second visit was in 1972 when he was invited by the Japan PEN Club to attend the International Japanologists' Conference. Two years later, he was granted a Fulbright Fellowship and made his third visit to Japan this time for a year. He arrived in Kyoto in September 1974, stayed in that city most of the time, and left Kobe by boat on September 7, 1975.[47] His fourth visit was from April 8 to July 15, 1978, and although he went on a tour to Southeast Asia, he spent the rest of the time in Toyonaka and Kyoto.[48] His fifth visit was for a month from November to December 1980, mainly to give one talk at the International Poets' Conference in Tokyo, and another at the poetry reading by candidates for the Kenneth Rexroth Poetry Award in Kyoto on December 6.[49]

During these years, Rexroth grew closer to Japan, while vigorously writing a number of poems published in *New Poems* (1974), *The Silver Swan* (1976), *On Flower Wreath Hill* (1976), and *The Love Poems of Marichiko* (1978), the last three later collected in one volume, *The Morning Star* (1979). During these years he also translated Japanese and Chinese poetry such as *One Hundred More Poems from the Japanese* (1976), *The Burning Heart: Women Poets of Japan* (with Ikuko Atsumi, 1977), *Seasons of Sacred Lust: Selected Poems of Kazuko Shiraishi* (with Carol

Tinker, Ikuko Atsumi, John Solt, and Yasuyo Morita, 1978), and *Li Ch'ing-Chao: Complete Poems* (with Ling Chung, 1979).

Many of these poems and translations were done in Japan, and most of them reflect aspects of Japanese aesthetics by the maturing poet.

New Poems marked Rexroth's steps toward Buddhism. "Star and Crescent," written in Esfahan, describes the tranquil atmosphere surrounding the speaker, who is engaged in religious meditation. In contrast, "Void Only" focuses on the inner experience of the meditating speaker.

> Time like glass
> Space like glass
> I sit quiet
> Anywhere Anything
> Happens
> Quiet loud still turbulent
> The serpent coils
> On itself
> All things are translucent
> Then transparent
> Then gone
> Only emptiness
> No limits
> Only the infinitely faint
> Song
> Of the coiling mind
> Only.[50]

Visualized here is the state of mind of one in the depth of religious experience, in which one sees no color, no form, no content in all the phenomena of the universe—"void only." As Morgan Gibson suggests, the paradox of the "Prajnaparamite truth that form is void and void is form" is given poetical expression. Gibson goes on to point out its theological background:

> In "Void Only," all things dissolve in the emptiness of the "Song / Of the coiling mind / Only" (p. 22)—a terse union of the two major schools of Mahayana philosophy, the Madhyamika Nagarjuna, in which All is Void (*Shunyata*), and

the Yogachara school of Asanga and Vasubandu, in which All is Mind.[51]

The image of the snake, used to express metaphorically the spiral process of sublimation toward transparency, Rexroth has said, was suggested by Arthur Avalon's *The Serpent Power*. According to Avalon's explanation of *Sat-cakra-nirūpana*, there are six "astral" centers in the human body, each with a specific function.[52] And at the base of the spine is the "Serpent Fire." When "vivified" by the "Fire," these centers "become gates of connection" between the physical and the astral bodies. For instance, at the center between the eyes, "the voice of the 'Master' (which in this case means the higher Self in its various stages) is heard." The center at "the top of the head" enables one "to leave the body in full consciousness."[53]

It may be that the serpent's coil in the poem by Rexroth is the symbol of the mystic, fundamental power that "vivifies" the physical body and enables one to attain nirvana.

In *New Poems*, there are pieces inspired by Japanese art. Rexroth held that "the form of superposition," which Ezra Pound had found in haiku, could also be found in tankas. Such an idea was quite sound.

> Kare yanagi
> Semi shigure shite
> Nishizora wa
> Akaboshi hitotsu
> Hikari sometaru.

The first two lines of this anonymous poem give an image of a dead willow tree with cicadas making a showering sound. The last three lines present another image with Akaboshi beginning to twinkle in the western sky silently in the summer evening. Akaboshi usually refers to the morning star, especially to Venus, but, since it is "beginning to twinkle," it could be Mars, Antares, or any red star in the evening. The poem as a whole suggests the subtle shift of attention from life toward eternal peace and silence. However, one image is superimposed on another, as in Pound's "In a Station of the Metro." Rexroth translated it into a four-line poem:

> The cicada sings
> In the rotten willow
> Antares, the fire star,
> Rolls in the west.

He translated, or transformed, another tanka into a poem more obviously in the form of superposition.

> In the mountain village
> The wind rustles the leaves.
> Deep in the night, the deer
> Cry out beyond the edge of dreams.

> Yama zato no
> Inaba no kaze ni
> Nezame shite
> Yo fukaku shika no
> Koe wo kiku kana.
>   Minamoto no Morotada

In the original poem, the speaker is roused from sleep at night by the rustling of the rice plants and hears the deer cry. But Rexroth deals with the speaker's two experiences as if they were a set of two images, and compresses them into a more objective and intense poem by way of superposition. For Rexroth it is more important that his translations "stand as poetry in English, and even, in a sense, as poetry by a contemporary American poet."[54]

Rexroth applies his idea of superposition to his own poetry in the section called "Earth Sky Sea Tree Birds House Beasts Flowers" in *New Poems*.

> Slowly the moon rises
> Over the quiet sea.
> Slowly the face of my beloved
> Forms in my mind.

The parallelism stresses the form as well as the sense of slowness. Here is another example:

> In the dark forest the whisper
> Of a million leaves.
> On the deep sea the sigh
> Of a million waves.

None of the other poems in the section provide evidence of his use of the superpository form, but they resemble the tanka form in many ways. Rexroth apparently tried to re-create what he found valuable in Japanese poetry. He writes in his introduction to *One*

Hundred Poems from the Japanese that he has "striven for maximum compression," so as "to interfere as little as possible with the simplicity of the Japanese text." Together with "simplicity" and "maximum compression," he re-created the lyricism and a sense of permeating intimacy with nature.

> Moonless night.
> In the black heavens
> The eye goes ten million miles.
> Melancholy fills the heart.

The same can be said of the eleven short poems written in Kyoto, collected in "The City of the Moon—for Kimiko Nakazawa."[55]

The last comment about *New Poems* is on a poem titled "The Flower Sutra." The Flower Sutra, "featuring The Net of Indra," is called Kegonkyo in Japanese. While writing about the curious songs and habits of the wild birds, Rexroth once noted, "The *hototogisu* usually sings in the twilight. Its cry, as well as the *uguisu*'s, is often interpreted by the Japanese as *Hokkekyō*, the name of the Lotus Sutra." "The Flower Sutra" is his parody.

> Deep drowsy shade under the broad leaves,
> The dusty plain far below dim with haze,
> Picking flowers—bush clover, gold banded lily,
> Bell flower, wild pink, while a mountain cuckoo
> Flutters about, watching me and crying,
> "Kegonkyo."[56]

The Silver Swan is a collection of poems and translations "written in Kyoto, 1974–1978" as its subtitle states. One of the best is the four-line poem about a swan on "the lake of the mind." It is simple, presents a beautiful image, and is painfully rich with meaning.

> As the full moon rises
> The swan sings
> In sleep
> On the lake of the mind.[57]

The rising full moon suggests the approaching end, the fulfillment of life, and peace of mind. A single large, white bird on the dark water is a dramatic representation of the loneliness, majesty, and purity of the speaker. According to legend, the swan sings its most beautiful song only once in its life, at its death. And the drama takes place in a "dream" as if in a Nō play, suggesting unworldliness and even uncanniness. The final line, "On the lake of the mind," suggests that his mind is as deep, large, and calm as the lake. The poem as a whole presents a tableau of transcendence, esoteric beauty and religious truth. Morgan Gibson captures the religious overtones of the poem by pointing out that the full moon symbolizes "the realization of Nirvana in Samsara (the world of confusion, desire, and pain), never apart from it." [58]

When asked once what the main characteristic of his poetry was, Rexroth immediately replied, "Personal." Applying that to this poem, it may reflect the religious focus of the poet's mind as he lay weakened with a bad cold and fever in the spring of 1975 in Kyoto—the spontaneous and irrepressible desire to sing out even in "the realization of nirvana in the world of confusion, ... and pain." It is significant that Rexroth expresses the Buddhist sense of transcendence, of the transient, "birth, sickness, old age, and death," and the sense of irrepressibility of the ego's desire by combining, amalgamating, and harmonizing the Oriental symbol of the full moon (nirvana) and the Western symbol of the swan (the poet). [59]

In the same collection of poems is one conveying that delicate mystery of recollection that seems uncannily reminiscent of the opening of a Nō play.

> On the forest path
> The leaves fall. In the withered
> Grass the crickets sing
> Their last songs. Through dew and dusk
> I walk the path you once walked,
> My sleeves wet with memory.

The poem was written in Kyoto in late autumn 1974. Near the 800-year-old Tea House in which he lived was the forest of Senyūji, where he used to walk with his wife, Carol Tinker, along the path leading to Yamashina. As the title of the poem suggests, it is an "adaptation" from an anonymous Manyō tanka, "Asagumori." [60]

> Asagumori
> Hi no irinureba
> Mitatashi no

> Shima ni oriite
> Nagekitsurukamo.

> Cloudy morning
> The sun dim
> I walk in the Palace gardens
> And wept where he had walked.[61]

Rexroth's walk on the forest path may have reminded him of someone in Yamashina, and the Senyūji forest with its imperial tumuli may have reminded him of this Manyō tanka about the palace gardens, which he had translated.

By "adaptation" he might have meant *honkadori*, an old Japanese poetical device of alluding to, or borrowing a passage from, a well-known classical Japanese poem in order to enrich the meaning by association. Rexroth explains it himself in his notes to his more than 200 translations of Japanese poems. In fact, many of the *dodoitsu* he translates are "modeled on," as he points out, classical Japanese tankas. His own poem, quoted above, appears to be Rexroth's English rendition of a *honka*, or the original poem, which is the anonymous Manyō tanka. Thus is Rexroth himself a confessed practitioner of honkadori.

In the longer poem, *On Flower Wreath Hill* (1976), the same theme is expanded and developed in eight parts. And at the same time, surprisingly, a series of honkadori are elaborately interwoven. The poem opens with an allusion to "Asagumori."

> An aged pilgrim on a
> Darkening path walks through the
> Fallen and falling leaves, through
> A forest grown over the
> Hilltop tumulus of a
> Long dead princess. . . .

But it is more like a Nō play than the original "Asagumori," because it presents a "pilgrim" who visits a desolate historic site like a Waki, and also because there are constant allusions to the Nō plays, especially to *Matsukaze*. We find, however, that the poem is filled with more allusions to other tankas.

> Who was this princess under
> This mound overgrown with trees

Now almost bare of leaves?
Only the pine and cypress
Are still green. . . .
        There are more leaves on
The ground than grew on the trees.
I can no longer see
The path; I find my way without
Stumbling; my heavy heart has
Gone this way before. Until
Life goes out memory will
Not vanish, but grow stronger
Night by night.
            Aching nostalgia—
In the darkness every moment
Grows longer and longer, and
I feel as timeless as the
Two thousand year old cypress.[62]

This beautiful passage from part 2 of *On Flower Wreath Hill*, about an
overwhelming nostalgia, is richly tooled and inlaid with echoes of
four classical Japanese tankas.

In the dust the path
You used to come to me
Is overgrown and indistinguishable,
Except for the spider webs
That hang across it
Like threads of sorrow.
            Izumi Shikibu

Evening darkens until
I can no longer see the path.
Still I find my way home.
My horse has gone this way before.
            Anonymous

Until life goes out
Memory will not vanish
But grow stronger
Day by day.
            Anonymous

> Aching nostalgia—
> As evening darkens
> And every moment grows
> Longer and longer, I feel
> Ageless as the thousand year pine.
>
> Anonymous[63]

All these translations have been done by Rexroth and collected in *One Hundred More Poems from the Japanese*. And these tankas are ingeniously inlaid in Rexroth's own poem like a series of honkadori. Rexroth writes in his notes that "the second and third verses of Part II are a conflation of well-known classic Japanese poems, and Part V is entirely so." Indeed, he gives us still other examples of interlocked honkadori in parts 5 and 8.[64]

All through the poem, Rexroth tries to suggest a meaning to life: memories, reverberating in one's mind, like a mountain temple bell, will spread from man to man. So through the poem, various tones of classical Japanese poems reverberate, sometimes like distant echoes and sometimes like peals of thunder.

On Flower Wreath Hill is, in that sense, somewhat different from his earlier works in its use of Japanese poetry. That is, from his early days he has scattered gems of Japanese tankas in his poems. But in *The Phoenix and the Tortoise*, the allusions to Japanese poems are in contrast to the world of California sand dunes at night. The two juxtaposed worlds of old Japan and modern America reflect each other, as it were, from a distance. In *The Heart's Garden / The Garden's Heart* there is a natural reciprocal relationship between the translated passage from the Japanese and the rest of the poem. The East and West are in dialogue, as it were, in this religious love poem. *On Flower Wreath Hill* exhibits a beautiful blend of classical Japanese poetry and Rexroth's world, fused so inseparably by means of the honkadori that the borders of the two worlds blur like overlapping rainbows.

Indeed, he came to be "far more deeply interfused" with Japan. Having in his boyhood sailed out into the "uncharted sea," as he tells us in his *Autobiographical Novel*, Rexroth encountered various values. In his later years, he came to understand Japanese culture more profoundly. One of his messages is clear: if you set sail on a voyage in quest of true values, you will find something precious in the Orient, and especially in Japan.

There is no doubt that, among major American poets, Kenneth Rexroth best understood the Japanese culture. Whitman celebrated the arrival of the first Japanese envoy to the United States in 1860 in "A Broadway Pageant." Longfellow admired the beauty of Imari jars in his "Keramos." But their knowledge of Japanese culture, as we can guess from their writings, was very limited. Whitman seems to have read the New York newspapers, and to have seen the parade of the "two-sworded," "bare-headed, impassive" envoys in Manhattan, and combined the scenes and his panoramic world view. Longfellow received occasional letters from his son Charles wandering through the Far East, and one of the souvenirs seems to have stimulated his imagination.

Amy Lowell loved things Japanese since her childhood. Her brother Percival sent letters and gifts to "dear big Amy" from Japan. The wood-block prints especially inspired her to write a number of short haikulike poems collected in her *Pictures of the Floating World*, the title of which is the direct translation of ukiyoe. Ezra Pound was indebted to haiku in his composition of some imagist poems, such as "In a Station of the Metro" and later "longer one-image poems." Fenollosa's notebooks led Pound to his appreciation of Far Eastern cultures.

But, compared with that of Kenneth Rexroth, their understanding of Japanese culture appears superficial. Lowell remained a New Englander who, quite unaware, held fast to the traditional Yankee values. Odyssean cosmopolitan navigator that he was, Pound nevertheless did not explore far inland from Japanese shores.

Rexroth had a wide range of knowledge of East and West, old and new, but above all he had a surprisingly deep knowledge of various aspects of Japanese life, and, sympathetic with the Japanese mind, Rexroth employed his keen sensibility and mastery of the poet's techniques to re-create in English its intense, fragile, and mystical beauty.

5

Gary Snyder
and
Other Poets

The Postwar United States and Japan

About the time Douglas MacArthur was called back to the United States from the general headquarters in Japan, and the Treaty of Peace and the Security Treaty between the United States and Japan were signed in San Francisco in 1951, a strong interest in Japanese culture was beginning to sweep the postwar United States. The occupation had fostered contacts with Japan, and the Japanese film, *Rashomon*, which won the grand prize at Cannes in 1951, became popular among Americans. That same year, Mark Gayn's *Japan Diary*, widely read in America since its publication in 1948, was on the best-seller list in Japan. In the same year Norman Mailer wrote two stories about the occupation troops in Japan, "The Paper House" and "The Language of Men." *Tea House of the August Moon* by Vern J. Sneider, about the odd relationship between the American Army and the inhabitants of Okinawa, was made into a popular drama. It was chosen one of the best plays produced during the 1953–54 season, and two years later a movie version appeared. Even more successful was James Michener's love story about American soldiers and Japanese women, *Sayonara*, published in 1954.

During these years, Kenneth Rexroth, Allen Ginsberg, Gary Snyder, and other poets later to be labeled the beats were in and out of San Francisco, which suddenly became a lively international city again. The Japanese-Americans had returned from the concentration camps. Both military and commercial ships frequently anchored there from Yokohama, Kobe, Sasebo, and Yokosuka, as well as from other Oriental seaports. Along with Japanese goods, Reginald Blyth's *Haiku* arrived in four volumes, which was to inspire a number of American poets, such as Ginsberg, Richard Wright, and Cor van den Heuvel.

Other books on tea ceremony, flower arrangement, Zen Buddhism, Nō plays, judo, and folklore were to follow. Books by American Japanologists were also beginning to be published: Edwin O. Reischauer's *Japan: Past and Present* (1946), *The United States and Japan* (1950), John Hall's *Japanese History: A Guide to Japanese Reference and Research Materials* (1954), and Donald Keene's *Japanese Literature: An Introduction for Western Readers* (1955). Courses in Japanese civilization were being offered at some universities, and new textbooks for teaching Japanese were being prepared by linguists.

Still, the majority of Americans showed little concern with Japan during this period of *pax americana*. The established newspapers seldom reported on Japan, and people occasionally surprised student visitors from Japan by asking them whether their country had trains.[1]

But the situation in San Francisco was different. Upon graduation from Reed College in 1951, Gary Snyder went to the Graduate School of Indiana University for further study in anthropology, but he left after one semester to return to San Francisco. He was interested in both a primitive way of life and in academia, but he was also anxious to get more stimuli from the Orient than could be expected in the Midwest. He roomed with Philip Whalen, a former classmate at Reed, who was seriously interested in Zen Buddhism and had been writing poetry. Snyder then took courses in Oriental studies at the University of California in Berkeley. In 1955, the two young poets took part in the now historic poetry reading at the Six Gallery in San Francisco's Marina, which was promoted by Rexroth, who had been working on *One Hundred Poems from the Japanese*.

The year 1956 was a turning point, for Japan was admitted to the United Nations. People realized that Japan was now a member of the cultural world, as well as the international political community, no longer a fourth-rate country. Americans and Britons as well as Japanese began to translate Japanese literature into English. Seidensticker's translation of *Snow Country* by Yasunari Kawabata appeared in 1956. Sōseki Natsume's *Kokoro* came out in a new translation in 1957. Takamichi Ninomiya and D. J. Enright's translation, *The Poetry of Living Japan* was also published in 1957.[2] And the two books on haiku most influential on American poets for the next decade were published: Ken Yasuda's, *Japanese Haiku: Its Essential Nature, History, and Possibility in English with Examples* (1957), and Harold G. Henderson's *Introduction to Haiku* (1958). The latter especially was to inspire Richard Wilbur.

Richard Wright and His Haiku

It may seem strange that Richard Wright (1908–60), primarily known as a black novelist, with his *Uncle Tom's Children, Native Son, Black Boy,* and other novels and short stories, should write haiku. But among his unpublished papers were found several thousand short poems in the haiku form written shortly before his death in Paris. Since then, twenty-three of these works have been published. Many of them are excellent pieces of literature. For example:

> Standing in the field
> I hear the whispering of
> Snowflake to snowflake

There is in this poem the delicate, subtle, and sensitive response to nature similar to that in many good Japanese haiku. Wright wrote this kind of short poem on a variety of subjects.

> With a twitching nose
> A dog reads a telegram
> On a wet tree trunk

Here is the kind of humor often found in the early haiku, through personification of a domestic animal. Sometimes the humor is grotesquely reminiscent of Wright's early sympathy with the naturalists.

> The dog's violent sneeze
> Fails to rouse a single fly
> On his mangy back[3]

The poem is closer in its sensibility to *senryu.*

There are some poems with "deeply personal" tones. During the summer of 1959, after visiting Africa, Wright fell ill from amoebic dysentery and stayed in the American Hospital in Neuilly, a western suburb of Paris, where he started writing his haiku.

> An empty sickbed
> An indented white pillow
> In weak winter sun

Hidden under the seemingly indifferent description of the white pillow's cleanliness, in the "weak winter sun," we catch some of the enfeebled, febrile, helpless, and lonesome feeling of the patient.

> I would like a bell
> Tolling in this soft twilight
> Over willow trees[4]

In this beautiful poem, watching the colorful twilight over the willow trees, the speaker wishes he could hear a bell toll. But again the poem seems to reflect something deeper in the poet's mind. Peaceful twilight toward the end of the day suggests calmness and silence. The weeping willow is the symbol of accepting one's fate. It cannot easily be denied that the poem has an overtone of the poet's wish for peace of mind at the time of the bell's knell for him.

Some poems have what may be called reverberations, not only auditory, but olfactory and tactile.

> From across the lake
> Past the black winter trees
> Faint sounds of a flute

> The spring lingers on
> In the scent of a damp log
> Rotten in the sun[5]

> A freezing morning
> I left a bit of my skin
> On the broomstick handle[6]

The sound of the flute, the scent of the damp log, and the coldness of the broomstick handle seem to last for some time in the ear, the nose, and the hand of the reader. This lingering sensory effect may be said to be close to what Basho called *hibiki*, or reverberation.

In all these short poems by Wright, written on a variety of subjects, are some common denominators. Each line in every poem presents an image with a new sense of mild surprise, arousing in the reader's mind a fresh sensation of calmness and beauty. And there is nothing at all of that sense of fear or "the terror of white men" that had dominated his earlier novels and novellas. Nor do we find "the white threat ... hovering near," or "that thirst for violence that was in me, for intrigue, for plotting, for secrecy, for bloody murders," as recollected in his autobiography, *Black Boy*. Each poem is endowed with subtlety, freshness, suggestiveness, delicacy, and a sense of contentment, quite close to Japanese sensibility.

One may wonder why Richard Wright persistently wrote so many of the short poems belonging to a totally different culture from that which he came. He read R. H. Blyth's *Haiku* in 1959, and discovered in it something he had been unconsciously seeking to ease his mind. Just as he "hungered for the sharp, frightening, breath-taking, almost painful excitement" of the novel when he had been told by a schoolteacher[7] a part of the story of *Bluebeard and His Seven Wives*, so he seems to have "hungered" for the world of Oriental poetry when he read the book *Haiku*. The editors of the *Richard Wright Reader* write:

> In 1959, Wright discovered the Japanese haiku. He was entranced by the 17-syllable form and jotted down several thousands of the brief poems, mostly during his treatment at the hospital. "Maybe I'm fooling around with these tiny little poems, but I could not let them go. I was possessed by them," he wrote a friend in May 1960, just six months before his death.

He may have read some haiku in French translation. He may have been familiar with the form through imagism. He may have read Henderson's *Introduction to Haiku* or Yasuda's *Japanese Haiku*. But I would guess that Wright's encounter with R. H. Blyth's *Haiku* was a great event for him. He borrowed the four volumes from a friend, read them, and attempted to write haiku himself.[8]

It is evident that Wright followed very closely what Blyth had written about the haiku.

> This 5, 7, 5 has a wave-like character of flow, suspense and ebb, it is symmetrical, yet in odd numbers. Further, there is a kind of syllogistic nature about the form which gives it the utmost clarity while actually containing no logical elements, often no intellectual connections between the parts.[9]

Wright observes the syllable count of 5, 7, 5 fairly strictly. He sets down the three lines not in logical, syllogistic order, but in what may be called a syllogism of images, by presenting step by step in each line, an independent but related image.

Concerning the *kigo*, or the seasonal reference word, Blyth writes:

There is almost always a season word in haiku. This word may
give the atmospheric background, it may be a kind of seed,
a trigger which releases a whole world of emotion, of sounds
and scents and colours.[10]

There are some liberals in Japan who decline to follow the book of
collected season words, who insist on being freed from their conventional associations. But many haiku poets follow the tradition in
order to render their emotion in the poem still more specifically and
poignantly in terms of the season. Wright probably was unaware of
the existence in Japan of the old, voluminous lists of season words.
But there almost always is a seasonal reference word in each of his
haiku. Most of the time, however, his unorthodox use of the season
words, with Western connotations and associations, accompanies fresh
and unexpected beauty connected with specific seasonal feelings.

Blyth makes a further comment in relation to the classification
by seasons:

Haiku have been for long classified according to the seasons
and the subjects of the verse. There are, as it were, five seasons:
the New Year, Spring, Summer, Autumn and Winter; there
are also a few verses that will not go into any particular season.

Before his death Wright arranged the copies of his typescript haiku,
dividing them into four sections—Spring, Summer, Autumn, and
Winter. In his letter to Margrit de Sablonièr, his Dutch translator,
on March 19, 1960, Wright writes:

During my illness I experimented with the Japanese form of
poetry called haiku; I wrote some 4,000 of them and am now
sifting them out to see if they are any good.[11]

Wright wrote some more haiku in the spring, summer, and fall of 1960,
and before he died in November he "sifted" again, and classified them
into four seasons, in preparation for publication under the title, *This
Other World*. Division by seasons was suggested by Blyth's similar
pattern in his books.

Blyth spends about a hundred pages on the Buddhist influence
on haiku in the section, "Zen, the State of Mind for Haiku," explaining
such terms as "selflessness," "loneliness," "grateful acceptance," "contradiction," "humor," and "simplicity," immanent in the works of
the representative Japanese haiku poets. It is apparent that Wright

read this section very carefully and was greatly influenced by the thought underlying it. "It is a condition of *selflessness*," Blyth writes, "in which things are seen without reference to profit or loss, even of some remote, spiritual kind." He continues:

> This losing of one's life, when attained in the will, is a state of rest and ease. . . . When we are in this condition, we can look at anything and everything and see with its eyes, hear with its ears, fly with its wings.

"Selflessness" and the sense of "rest and ease" prevail in Wright's haiku. His strong and uneasy consciousness in his early years of being a black American is gone. The figure of the poet abstracted from the personae speaking in his haiku is thin in character and almost as transparent as air. To be "selfless" is often compared to being like air. But *selflessness* in Buddhism is *"selffulness,"*[12] and this state of mind is often symbolized by the wind. Though probably unconsciously, Wright often adopts the image of wind in his poems.

> A soft wind at dawn
> Lifts one dry leaf and lays it
> Upon another.

> A leaf chases wind
> Across an autumn river
> And shakes a pine tree.

> Having appointed
> All the stars to their places,
> The summer wind sleeps.

Loneliness is likewise "selffulness." Wright exquisitely expresses the paradox in the image of a soaring, stately mountain peak.

> In the afterglow
> A snow-covered mountain peak
> Sings of loneliness.[13]

It is difficult to calculate how much influence Blyth had on Wright. But the haiku seems to have provided Wright with an important outlet for peace of mind as an enlightened man accepting and transcending his fate, while the novel was the outlet for his violent, black consciousness. The change in his attitude toward life is so remarkable as to seem almost a religious awakening. Indeed, some of his haiku suggest his spiritual rebirth.

> Enough of dawn light
> To cause pearly pear blossoms
> To burn from within

By presenting the image of the pear blossoms glowing and burning "from within" at the first sunlight from the east, Wright might be subtly suggesting his mind glowing and changing within him.

> Coming from the woods
> A bull has a lilac sprig
> Dangling from a horn

This seemingly pastoral or pagan poem also may be taken as suggestive of the joy of a spiritual rebirth, or, at least, a spiritual change of the poet.

> I am nobody
> A red sinking autumn sun
> Took my name away[14]

Though echoing the novel *Invisible Man* by Wright's friend Ralph Ellison, the poem can be taken as an expression of his realization of the importance of a selfless attitude to life, suggesting also the rejection of his previous way of life.

I am not suggesting that Richard Wright was converted to Budhism, but rather that he deeply understood the teachings of Zen through Blyth's book on haiku, and derived comfort from it. Sick in the hospital, toward the end of his life he was certainly tired of fighting racism. He had been trying to escape it since he left Natchez for Memphis and then for Chicago and New York. Finally, he left the United States in 1948 to live in Paris. Perhaps the last spiritual resting place he discovered there was the world of the haiku.

But still he was unable to cast away all his past.

> The crow flew so fast
> That he left his lonely caw
> Behind in the field.[15]

On the surface, the poet's position in the poem seems close to that of the speaker who watches a lonely crow passing him, leaving a caw behind. But the poet may be identifying with the crow. The poem seems an indirect expression of the poet's awareness of his still being a "Jim Crow," as he used to call himself, as in "The Ethics of Living Jim Crow," who is now fading away into an unknown world, leaving his voice behind. Richard Wright never forgot that he was black, of which he was rightly proud.

His attempts to attain selflessness and his wish for escape and self-denial seem to have been mixed with his sense of loss at the death of his mother in 1960.[16] The image of death haunts his last pieces.

> Out of winter mist
> A funeral comes slowly,
> Then fades into it.
>
> A sick cat seeks out
> A stiff and frozen willow
> Under which to die.
>
> Glittering with frost,
> A dead frog squats livingly
> In the garden path.[17]

However, the more Wright was obsessed by the idea of death and self-denial, the more his imagination would "blaze"[18] again and again till the very last moment:

> Keep straight down this block
> Then turn right where you will find
> A peach tree blooming.[19]

Richard Wilbur's Genie in the Bottle

Richard Wilbur (1921–) is often compared with another major American poet, Robert Lowell. If modern American poetry can be classified, as Lowell has suggested, into two kinds, "cooked" and "raw," Wilbur's poetry is the elaborately cooked, "marvellously expert," elegantly sophisticated, and complicatedly "balanced" kind, while Lowell's later works represent the raw, "blood-dripping gobbets of unseasoned experience."[20] If Wilbur is Apollonian, Lowell is Dionysian. But, however antipodal the two poets may seem, they are both deeply immersed in the Western cultural tradition, basically Europe-oriented.

It was in Europe during World War II that Wilbur began to write poetry seriously for the first time, as he recollects. He translated Molière's *Misanthrope* in 1955, and *Tartuffe* in 1964. With great dexterity he has written poetry about European as well as American scenes, in a variety of traditional Western forms of poetry.

Curiously, however, Wilbur wrote an elegantly "cooked" poem under the obvious influence of Japan: "Thyme Flowering Among Rocks." It was first published in the *New Yorker* (December 14, 1968), and later collected in his *Walking to Sleep: New Poems and Translations* (1969). The poem opens with an allusion to Japanese paintings or wood-block prints.

> This, if Japanese,
> Would represent gray boulders
> Walloped by rough seas
>
> So that, here or there,
> The balked water tossed its froth
> Straight into the air.

The whole poem is written in the form of a series of haiku: each stanza consisting of three lines written in the 5-7-5 syllable count.

The speaker encounters a sea of thyme blossoming in the field, the flowers tossing their heads in the wind among New England rocks. Watching the stems one by one, then, "along prone rachitic / Branches," he finds

> A straight-ascending
>
> Spike, whorled with fine blue
> Or purple trumpets, banked in
> The leaf-axils.

The reader is brought into the "dense fact," which is "blinking at detail / Peppery as this fragrance." He feels as if "lost" in the "un-fathomed thyme." The poem ends with a fitting remark supposedly spoken by the Japanese haiku poet, Matsuo Bashō (1644–94).

> The world's
> A dream, Basho said,
>
> Not because that dream's
> A falsehood, but because it's
> Truer than it seems.

References to Japan are made in the beginning and end of the poem. The first and last lines in each stanza are inconspicuously rhymed as if to affirm the presence of order among the series of gentle but broken rhythms in the rigid form. The poem as a whole achieves a subtle balance between form and rhythm, and between Japanese and American sensibilities.

Why did Wilbur think of using the haiku form and making reference to Japan? One answer may lie in his reference to Bashō. Almost exactly the same reference to Bashō can be found in H. G. Henderson's *Introduction to Haiku*.

> It is, however, worthy of note that whenever Basho uses the word "dream" he seems also to be thinking of human life; and perhaps it is even more noteworthy that to him the "illusion" of the world does not seem to mean that it is in any sense unreal, but rather, as with St. Thomas Aquinas, that it is far more real than it seems.[21]

It is fair to speculate that Wilbur must have read that passage carefully sometime before he wrote the poem. It is likely he had seen some Japanese pictures or wood-block prints depicting the white spray over the rocks. Upon encountering the wild thyme flowering over the field, with rocks scattered around, he must have thought the scene was like the Japanese image of gray rocks "walloped by rough seas." But probably the more direct source of inspiration was Henderson's book on haiku, with his explanations of the 5-7-5 form 1, and discussion of Matsuo Bashō.

Wilbur tried to use the haiku because it was a new challenge. He had been trying various poetical forms that had been used in the Western world. A form for him was an important vehicle to relate realities to poetry. Old forms, according to Wilbur, could and should be made new. "When poets put new wine in old bottles," he wrote in one of his essays, "the bottles become new, too." While most other contemporary American poets had broken away from the use of conventional stanzaic forms, he tried couplets, tercets, quatrains, sonnets, terza rima ("A Dubious Night"), Anglo-Saxon ("Junk"), and rondeau ("Rondeau"), maintaining that "the strength of the genie comes of his being confined in a bottle." He tailored and slightly modified the haiku to fit his poem, possibly because he thought he might insert his "genie" in an Oriental bottle.[22]

He may also have been aware that his poetic sensibility in some way was close to that of the Japanese. As he liked Emily Dickinson, so do many Japanese. He thought her poetry annuls "our sense of past and future, cancelling near and far, converting all time and space to a joyous or grievous here and now."[23] And his own poetry, such as "Thyme Flowering Among Rocks" also annuals our sense of time and space, bringing us into the jungle of microscopic fact, "blinking at detail," where we are

> Lost to proper scale
>
> As, in the motion
> Of striped fins, a bathysphere
> Forgets the ocean.

The kind of poetic world where "all time and space" seem to be converted into "here and now," created by both Dickinson and Wilbur, is similar to the world that haiku poets have tried to create: the world of wild imagination where the hereness suggests universality and now-ness eternity—a small world inhabited by bottled genies.

While reading Henderson's translations, Wilbur may have recognized something in common with the haiku poets, in their sensitive response to nature. While the haiku poets accepted the inconstancy of nature, Wilbur appreciated and caught in his own words the moment when "The Beautiful Changes."[24]

However, Wilbur has not published other poems on Japan or in Japanese form after that sole effort. Although he may write one or two more, that kind of poetry probably will not be his major style, for he feels more at home when he expresses himself in the European-New England tradition, in which he has much deeper affinities. Wilbur's understanding of Japan is limited, as is reflected in the fact that he slightly misrepresents Henderson, who slightly misrepresents Bashō. What Bashō was concerned with was not epistemological observations but attitudes to life. Bashō, as all other Buddhists of his time, shared the view that this world was like a dream or illusion, not because a dream was "truer than it seems," nor truer than reality, but because the life of this world was as ephemeral, uncertain, and unstable as a dream. Though short and inconstant it may be, in contrast to the eternal life in the other world, Bashō loved the ephemeral world because of the beauty he found in all the transient beings that nevertheless were striving to live. For Bashō, this world was as ephemeral as a dream, but was real.

The beauty of Wilbur's poetry lies in his perfect control of the subject matter and the form, and, as Cummins rightly says, in the "difficult balance" in his poetry "between freedom and form, spontaneity and tradition, between the religious aspiration . . . and the secular ecstasy."[25] Wilbur is fully aware that he would not satisfy more sophisticated readers by writing in a form in which he is not well versed, which he has imperfect control of, using anything that breaks the subtle balance in his poetry. Perhaps that explains Wilbur's caution in writing more poems on Oriental subjects or in a Japanese mode. But it is important to note that even such a poet as Wilbur showed his interest in haiku and the Japanese aesthetics. It shows the depth and extent of the Japanese cultural impact on America, especially of haiku.

The American Haiku

Innumerable haiku have been written in America since the early 1960s. Schoolchildren have been taught to write haiku in primary schools, and in many towns haiku clubs have been organized. In 1963, a magazine called *American Haiku* was started by those who were more seriously devoted to haiku in English. Though it ceased publication in 1968, such magazines as *Haiku, Haiku West, Modern Haiku,* and *Dragonfly: A Quarterly of Haiku Highlights* have appeared. The Haiku Society of America was founded in New York in 1968 under the auspices of the Japan Society. According to an article in *Poetry Nippon*, the editor of the *frogpond* recently "announced that the *renga* [linked poem] would pave the way to the future world of western poetry."[26]

The Haiku Anthology (1974), edited with an introduction by Cor van den Heuvel, gives a brief history and a bird's-eye view of the American haiku after World War II. "Haiku in English got its real start in the fifties," van den Heuvel writes, stressing its writers' independence from the imagists.

> The Imagists, and those who followed them, had no real understanding of haiku. Because they had no adequate translations or critical analyses available, they failed to see the spiritual depth haiku embodies, or the unity of man and nature it reveals. English language haiku owes practically nothing to their experiments except in the sense that all modern poetry

owes them a debt for their call for concision and clarity in language.

Certainly some of the works by the American haiku poets show that they "see the spiritual depth haiku embodies."

> Time after time
> caterpillar climbs this broken stem,
> then probes beyond.
> (J. W. Hacket)

The futile motion of the caterpillar seems to reflect the poet's understanding of the Buddhist notion of the "vanity" of human work, which underlies the classical Japanese haiku, especially of Bashō.

> Not a breath of air—
> only a water bug mars
> the pine's reflection.
> (Marjory Bates Pratt)[27]

The delicate image of the reflection of a large pine tree on the pond, shaken not by the wind but by a small water bug, is suggestive of the irony and sensitivity to fragile beauty in Japanese haiku.

But most of the more recent "haiku in the English language" by the Americans show definitely American traits quite different from the Japanese models. When they deal with nature, they explore facets of nature distinctly American. Deserts and canyons as well as yucca, blue jays, plover, killdeers, and wild deer are introduced into their poetry. One of the characteristics of the American haiku seems to be boldness. The Americans are breaking away from traditional Japanese images such as those listed in the Saijiki.

> Glimmering morning
> silence unfolds all
> the yucca
> (Michael McClintock)

> Blue jays in the pines;
> the northern river's ledges
> cased with melting ice
> (Robert Spiess)[28]

Nature in America usually was described as wild, and occasionally hostile to man. But in these haiku it is depicted as gentle and domesticated, as in the Japanese haiku. The Americans continue to seek their own subject matter in American scenes. In 1959, Jack Kerouac, Albert Saijo, and Lew Welch made a cross-continental haiku excursion, and published *Trip Trap: Haiku Along the Road from San Fransicso to New York, 1959.* Their driving trip was in a sense a search for the possibility of American haiku with American subjects, as we see in this verse and revisions.

> Albert
> Grain elevator on
> Saturday lonely as
> Abandoned toys

> Lew's Alternate
> Lonely grain elevators
> on Saturday
> —Abandoned toys

> Jack's Alternate
> Grain elevators on
> Saturday waiting for
> The farmers to come home[29]

Their description of sex also is boldly open, and sometimes straightforward.

> The white of her neck
> as she lifts her hair for me
> to undo her dress.
> (Bernard Lionel Einbond)

> the first melt ...
> her eyes gone
> under their lids
> (Michael McClintock)

Boldness also can be found in their introduction of subject matter that is eerie and ugly to the Japanese eye.

> At the river-bend
> wriggling towards the setting sun
> a lone watersnake.
> (Larry Gates)

dead cat . . .
open-mouthed
to the pouring rain
(Michael McClintock)

The most characteristic and noteworthy of the American haiku, however, probably are the attempts to capture with the modern sensibility the peculiar human situation in highly industrialized society.

an empty elevator
opens
closes
(Jack Cain)

The sense of weird loneliness and alienation of urban life in the heavily mechanized society is excellently expressed in this short poem. Another poem, written in memory of a soldier, is a mild but strongly persuasive expression of the futility of modern war.

Deep in rank grass,
through a bullet-riddled helmet:
an unknown flower.
—In Memory of Corporal
Lawrence J. Virgilio, USMC
(Nicholas Virgilio)[30]

These explorations into the new field of American haiku are characterized by a spectrum of ideas about the nature of that type of poetry. Some of the poets insist on holding to the orthodox 5-7-5 syllable count, while most others count far less strictly, and a few of the most experimental poets attempt "concrete" haiku, or "eye-ku." Some try to express religious depth, and some are overtly a-religious. Some try humorous poems, closer to senryu, a witty, often ironical, verse in the same 5-7-5 form as haiku without particular reference to nature.

Yet there are factors common to those American haiku poets. (1) Though some write in four lines and some in one or two lines, most of them write in three. (2) They present concrete images in utmost concentration. (3) They are likely to be suggestive and pithy. These common factors are not to be wondered at, because, as they confess in their biographical notes, these American haiku poets in *The Haiku Anthology* mostly have been inspired by books such as those by Blyth, Yasuda, and Henderson.[31]

Surely there is a strong lyric impulse among modern American poets toward compact gemlike beauty in poetry, even as they are attracted to the Whitmanesque, all-inclusive poetry. If more Americans continue to produce as many good haiku as they have in recent years, and if they continue to be guided by those books that refer to classical examples of haiku, it is possible that some day the form may become as well-established a genre in the English language as the sonnet.

Allen Ginsberg and Haiku

Allen Ginsberg was another who was inspired by R. H. Blyth's book on haiku. Ginsberg wrote in his notebook in 1955:

> Haiku composed in the backyard cottage at 1624 Milva Street, Berkeley 1955, while reading R. H. Blyth's 4 volumes *Haiku*.

And he jotted down twenty-one examples of haiku he had composed. Most of them are boldly, but not well, written. Compared with those by Richard Wright, they are too trivially personal and lack delicacy and sensitivity.

> Drinking my tea
> Without sugar—
> No difference.

The forcefulness of Ginsberg's poetry comes from his howling language with its release of high-voltage emotions in a long, pounding, Whitmanesque rhythm, rather than in a short form like haiku. Haiku is not a suitable vehicle for Ginsberg to convey his best ideas. "The horrifying experiences" in his spiritual "hell" are, as William Carlos Williams writes, better expressed in "a howl of defeat."[32]

From haiku, however, Ginsberg learned the technique of "bridging" the images without using any connectives. After writing his haiku in his notebook, he makes a few comments on the knack of composing a haiku, and writes that one should give only the images "outside mind," not the "relations" of the images to the mind.

> Haiku=objective images written down outside mind the result is inevitable mind sensation of relations. Never try to write of relations themselves, just the images which are all that can be written down on the subject.

This idea of "bridging" by "ellipsis" is similar to Pound's concept of superposition, also derived from Oriental poetry. And Ginsberg's assimilation of the idea into his longer poems is close to Pound's application of his theory to what he called "a longer one-image poem," *The Cantos*. Ginsberg later admits the importance of "the crucial discovery of haiku and ellipsis in the haiku, which really serves as the base in *Howl*."[33] Compared with his shorter, rhymed, and more conventional "earlier poems," such as "An Asphodel" and "Wild Orphan," his poems written in or after 1955 are full of such "ellipses." Part 2 of *Howl*, for example, is a series of images loosely related without connectives.

> Dreams! adorations! illuminations! religions!
> the whole boatload of sensitive bullshit!
> Breakthroughs! over the river! flips and
> crucifixions! gone down the flood! Highs!
> Epiphanies! Despairs! Ten years' animal
> screams and suicides! Minds! New loves!
> Made generations! down on the rocks of Time!

But Ginsberg, in writing *Howl*, is much more indebted to Whitman, Pound, and Williams than to haiku. The parallelism in parts 1 and 3 of this long poem is more like the cataloging method of Whitman. The tone is closer to that of the two lines quoted from "Song of Myself" in the title page of *Howl and Other Poems*:

> Unscrew the locks from the doors!
> Unscrew the doors themselves from their jambs!

The opening passage of *Howl* heavily echoes Ezra Pound.

> I saw the best minds of my generation destroyed
> by madness, starving hysterical naked,
> dragging themselves through the negro streets
> at dawn looking for an angry fix.

Compare it with the passages Pound has written.

> There died a myriad,
> And of the best, among them,
> For an old bitch gone in the teeth,
> For a botched civilization.
> ("Hugh Selwyn Mauberley,"[5])

O generation of the thoroughly smug
and thoroughly uncomfortable,
I have seen fishermen picnicking in the sun.
("Salutation")

Go, little naked and impudent songs.
("Salutation the Second")

O helpless few in my country,

.   .   .

Astray, lost in the villages,
Mistrusted, spoken against,
Lovers of beauty, starved.
("The Rest")

Another Ginsberg poem written in 1955, "A Supermarket in California," is in a sense homage to the "dear father, graybeard, lonely old courage teacher," Walt Whitman. "Kaddish for Naomi Ginsberg, 1894–1956" (1959), a narrative poem about his "holy mother," who had gone mad in Paterson, N.J., reminds the reader of another narrative poet from the same city, William Carlos Williams.

Deathsheads Around the Green Table—The King
& the Workers—Paterson Press printed
them up in the 30's till she went mad....
O Paterson! I got home late that nite. Louis
was worried....

"Kaddish" also echoes Whitman's "Out of the Cradle Endlessly Rocking" with its haunting images of death and mother. Ginsberg has written a haiku about his mother:

My mother's ghost:
the first thing I found
in the living room.[34]

He has written another haiku about the modern hell of a metropolis:

On the fifteenth floor
the dog chews a bone
Screech of taxicabs.

But in his longer poems in the tradition of Whitman, Pound, and

Williams, the same themes are much more forcefully and successfully developed than in his haiku. He has applied, as he says, the "ellipsis" of haiku to his longer poems. But the device is indistinguishably mingled with that of the traditional American epics by Whitman, Pound, and Williams, and is virtually invisible. Although Ginsberg speaks of being much indebted to Japan, surrounded by the mythical Oriental figures, ideas, and practices, reinforced by his visit to Japan in 1963, he is not so much influenced by Japanese values as he suggests.[35]

Gary Snyder in Japan

One of the striking features of Gary Snyder's poetry is its extremely simple and direct presentation of images, with a greatly curtailed use of words, reminiscent of haiku. Indeed, some critics have stressed such an influence on Snyder. Thomas Lyon, for instance, writes, "Snyder's line is typically very short, and his method correspondingly selective and exclusive rather than expansive. This, I think, might be seen as the Haiku influence ... The easy directness of the genre seems to be the guiding principle of Snyder's poetics, whatever the length of the application." [36] Certainly Snyder was familiar with the classical Japanese haiku, and the "easy directness" also is found in many of his longer poems.

Snyder himself wrote haiku on various occasions. While working as a fire lookout on Crater Mountain in the summer of 1952, Snyder entered a haiku in his journal, commenting,

> First wrote a haiku and painted a haiga for it,
> then repaired the Om Mani Padme Hum prayer
> flag, then constructed a stone platform, then
> shaved down a shake and painted a Zenga
> on it, then studied the lesson.
>> a butterfly
>>> scared up from its flower
>> caught by the wind and swept over the cliffs
>>> SCREE[37]

The poem he calls haiku here is not in the strict form according to the syllable count, but it is sufficiently compact, and in the "form of super-position" in Pound's fashion: the butterfly blown down the mountain like a petal is compared to a "scree," the worn or broken-away rock fragments falling from the cliff, and the scree in turn is made into a butterfly dancing in the wind as if alive. Snyder, by 1952, was familiar with the imagist adaptation of haiku and also, to a certain extent, with the traditional Japanese haiku echoing throughout Zen Buddhism.

Snyder wrote more of the same kind of haiku in loose forms about this time. Eighteen of them are collected under the punning title, "Hitch Haiku," in *The Back Country* in 1968. Some of them, however, seem to have been written much earlier:

> They didn't hire him
> so he ate his lunch alone:
> the noon whistle

The unnecessary "so" in the second line suggests that this piece was written by a neophyte. But others exhibit his efforts to gain more precision and better craftsmanship.

> Cats shut down
> deer thread through
> men all eating lunch

There are three snapshot images in the poem: the caterpillars standing quiet in the mountains, wild deer running freely in the woods, and the loggers eating lunch. They are juxtaposed as if at random, but represent respectively civilization, nature, and mankind. And the well-balanced total scene in nature seems to anticipate Snyder's later concern with ecological imbalances.

The technique of paralleling the snapshot images, however, and of giving them the effect of unity, is quite close to what L. S. Dembo points to as Pound's "motion-picture method" of translating Chinese poetry into English: each discrete "idea or image complex" in the poem is presented as a substitute for a Chinese character so that the lines in English resemble "a flow of such ideograms."[38]

Snyder was familiar with *kanji*, or Chinese characters, when he wrote the "Hitch Haiku" poems, as one of them explicitly shows.[39] It seems most probable that Snyder developed this technique of composition from the "motion-picture method" of Pound, whom he had been reading. The fact that each image is dry, concrete, and objective shows that he also followed Williams's dictum, "No ideas but in things."

Another haiku included in "Hitch Haiku" also is a blend of the imagistic practice with a "realistic" mountain scene in the Far West.

The mountain walks over the water!
Rain down from the mountain!
        high bleat of a
cow elk
      over blackberries.

Certainly, as Bob Steuding writes, haiku was "a convenient poetic form for the young and developing poet Snyder."

It blended his interest in Zen and the Orient. It suggested and re-created a response to a life of freedom beyond discipline which he was working toward in his personal life. It exhibited a strong resemblance to Imagistic theory and practice which fascinated him at that time. And it was a form which was easily adapted to his need to capture wild nature and the life of the common man.[40]

Snyder's short poems are microcosms in which he encapsulated almost all aspects of himself. He further blended various forms of humor in them.

Cats Thinking About What Birds Eat
      the kitten
      sniffs deep
      old droppings

Hiking In the Totsugawa Gorge
      pissing
      watching
      a waterfall[41]

The River Totsu flows into the River Kumano, and eventually into the Pacific. The two poems are more like senryu than haiku. But Snyder also knew more respectable Japanese humor, which comes from contentment of mind.

      Drinking saké
            toasting fish on coals
         the motorcycle
   out   parked in the rain

Time spent with a close friend sharing warm drinks and simple food is so satisfying for the speaker, and makes him feel so at home, that it becomes totally unimportant whether his motorcycle gets wet in the rain or whether he should go home on it. Robert Frost might have run back in the bad weather, murmuring, "And miles to go before I sleep." Frost had something in him that prevented him from committing himself totally to something "lovely, dark, and deep." But Snyder laughs at his motorcycle getting wet, which may represent karma. Happiness for him lies not in making and keeping as many promises as possible, or in doing things as scheduled, or in having an ample supply of food, but in having freedom—free time for "warm" friendship, to meditate, or to do whatever he thinks more valuable to do. Snyder does not make excuses, as Frost does, for having been engaged in an unproductive life. It is true that Frost did "refuse to live fully in the modern world," but he was aware also that many of his contemporary readers refused to pay the cost of rejecting "modern" values. Snyder, on the contrary, more "suspicious" of the values and morals of a too highly developed, affluent, and materialism-oriented society, and "the whole Western Tradition," feels the need to urge his readers to reconsider their civilization, and to search for values outside the Western norms to obtain a new kind of spiritual liberation and contentment by "penetrating to the deepest non-self Self." [42]

Snyder's *Myths & Texts*, written between 1952 and 1956, are interspersed with haikulike short poems. The book as a whole is heavily indebted to T. S. Eliot, Ezra Pound, and Carl Gustav Jung, as Bob Steuding has pointed out. [43] To add only a few to those Steuding has discussed,

> Pines, under pines,
> Seami Motokiyo
>
> .   .   .
>
> (Takasago, Ise) float in a mill pond
> ("Logging, 4")

echoes a passage in Pound's Canto 4:

> The pines at Takasago
> grow with the pines of Ise!

The cry of the crane in Snyder's "Burning" also is an echo of Pound's translation of Li Po's onomatopoeia in "The River Song" in *Cathay*.

"Kwan kwan" goes the crane in the field.

> And high over the willows, the fine birds sing
> to each other, and listen,
> Crying—"Kwan, kuan," for the early bird.
> ("The River Song")

But Snyder is also indebted to haiku in writing his *Myths & Texts*. When the speaker watches the swamp in crouched and meditating, he suddenly observes,

> Dying carp biting air
> in the damp grass,
> River recedes. No matter.

These three lines, superposed against the previous context, could be taken as an independent short poem. "There is a haiku influence in my poetry," Snyder writes. "It runs through *Myths and Texts*, the use of a number of very short precise images within longer poems."[44] There are more of these "very short precise images" in *Myths & Texts*, one of them reminding the reader of the haiku Snyder composed on Crater Mountain discussed earlier.

> Ah, butterflies
> Granite rots and crumbles.

And another at the end of the same section presents a sharp, "Japonistic" image, reminding us of Amy Lowell:

> where the sword is kept sharp
> the VOID
> gnashes its teeth.

More poignant and precise than such short poems in Amy Lowell's *Guns as Keys: And the Great Gate Swings*, these terse images of Snyder function as a sort of compressor, making the long poem "gnash its teeth."

In the following study we shall trace various Japanese influences on Snyder's poetry. Snyder's life in Japan "broadened" him in many ways, as he acknowledges.[45]

Snyder sailed for Japan in 1956. In retrospect he summarizes the motives of his "solitary vision quest."

> I began to perceive that maybe it was all of Western culture that was off the track and not just capitalism—that there were certain self-destructive tendencies in our cultural tradition. To simplify a long tale, I also saw that American Indian spiritual practice is very remote and extremely difficult to enter, even though in one sense right next door, because it is a practice one has to be born into. Its intent is not cosmopolitan. Its content, perhaps, is universal ... I knew that Zen monasteries in Japan would be more open to me than the old Paiute or Shoshone Indians in east Oregon, because they *have* to be open—that's what Mahayana Buddhism is all about.[46]

Soon after he landed in Kobe on May 21, 1956, Snyder went to see Ruth Sasaki at the First Zen Institute of Kyoto, which had given him a scholarship to study Zen in Japan.[47] Snyder was a "white faced youth," Hisao Kanaseki recollects, and "came to Kyoto with a letter of recommendation from Alan Watts."[48]

At the suggestion of Ruth Sasaki, Snyder went to Rinkō-in at Shōkoku-ji, another Zen temple in Kyoto, to study Zen under Isshū Miura. According to Kanaseki, Snyder actually lived there, "like an *unsui*," cleaning the temple and cooking for the other residents of the temple, when he was not sitting in meditation or studying the records of the ancient Zen masters.[49] Actually he was not an *unsui* but a *koji*, staying in one of the rooms at Rinkō-in.[50] But he attended the *sesshin* for a period of special training and meditation, as he wrote in the "Spring Sesshin at Shōkoku-ji," in his *Earth House Hold*. Miura Rōshi once confided smilingly to Kanaseki, "The food Gary cooks is tasty. But occasionally sand is mixed with radish and burdock. I wish he would wash it a little more carefully."[51] Later Snyder was to write his name in Japanese fashion, Suna-i-da, with Chinese characters which means literally "sand-well-field."

In the summer of 1956, Snyder received a letter from Will Petersen, an American lithographer, who expressed his desire to come over to Japan. "That you are coming to Japan is a delight & consolation," Snyder replied. "There's nobody here to talk to, the hakujin are all squares & Japaneezers incommunicable. However: I spend my days studying Japanese & (at the moment) memorizing sutras & waiting on Miura Roshi."[52]

When he had time, Snyder liked to climb Japanese mountains. He went up Mount Hiei a few days after his arrival in Kyoto, and two months later he tried the high peaks in central Japan. "Just got back two days ago from a five day hike in the Northern Japan Alps," he wrote to Petersen, "climbed the two highest peaks there & was impressed by the quantity of young Japanese mountaineers about. No place in this country where people won't find you." Compared with Crater and Sourdough, Japanese mountains must have looked crowded. He was so impressed that he wrote of it again to Petersen in his next letter, mentioning the many Japanese alpinists, especially women. "What a scene all those Japanese kids are out hiking & camping & singing songs. After seeing the way the girls can carry big loads for miles I'm set on getting a Japanese woman."[53] Ten years later, in fact, he was to "get a Japanese woman," Masa, whom he married on an active volcano.

It may seem strange that, though he climbed a number of Japanese mountains, Snyder did not write much poetry on them as he had in America. But he was then more interested in Buddhist life. He wrote some poems on the Buddhist temples around Kyoto, which he visited in his spare time. "Did see sanjusangendo—wild notion—what kind of cats was it made those statues day after day? Went off to Hōryuji 2 weeks ago & was bowled over by wooden bosatsus from long ago," he wrote. ". . . I have gotten an unreasonable passion to learn wood-carving now."[54]

His "unreasonable passion" is reflected in some poems probably written during the summer of 1956.

> Men asleep in their underwear
> Newspapers under their heads
> Under the eaves of Tōji.

In this poem, "Tōji," Snyder tries to recapture the atmosphere of the quiet summer afternoon in the large, peaceful precinct of the temple in Kyoto, ending the poem by contrasting it with the occasional noise outside.

> Nobody bothers you in Tōji;
> The streetcar clanks by outside.

What interested Snyder, according to Bob Steuding, was "the complete lack of religiosity and sanctimoniousness in regard to these Oriental places of worship" in contrast to Christian churches.[55] But note how in the middle of the poem he looks intently into the dark to study the wood carvings.

> Peering through chickenwire grates
> At dusty gold-leaf statues
> A cynical curving round-belly
> Cool Bodhisattva—maybe Avalokita—
> Bisexual and tried it all, weight on
> One leg, haloed in snake-hood gold
> Shines through the shadow
> An ancient hip smile
> Tingling of India and Tibet.

In another poem, "Higashi Hongwanji," about the temple in Kyoto, written about this time and included in his *Riprap*, Snyder also makes a keen observation on the "carved wood panel."

> Up high behind a beam: a small
>   carved wood panel
> Of leaves, twisting tree trunk,
> Ivy, and a sleek fine-haired Doe,
>   a six-point Buck in front
> Head crooked back, watching her.

But what Gary Snyder was interested in was not the sculpture itself, but "a love relationship" and "Bodhisattva relaxation" behind, which he was "beginning to see." He wrote in his journal on June 7, 1956:

> "Enlightenment" is this interior ease and freedom carried not only to persons but to all the universe.[56]

He was discovering in the statues and panels the kind of peace of mind he could not find in the Western world, but found commonly in the Oriental as well as in the "hip" way of life.

This discovery seems to have led him to write another poem, "Kyoto: March," written in March 1957. It presents a flow of early spring images with extremely "crisp language."[57] Every object in the poem is depicted as if it is a sharply focused photograph taken in "the

clear air" in cold winter. "The plum / Buds tight and chill," he writes.
And the moon is as if frozen: "a faint slice west / At nightfall."

> At dawn Mt. Hiei dusted white
> On top; in the clear air
> Folds of all the gullied green
> Hills around the town are sharp,
> Breath stings

But behind the chill, and beneath the "crisp" language, he presents a
kind of warmth, just as behind the old and indifferent wood carvings
in the temples he encountered a peaceful, warm Oriental mind. He
ends the poem:

> Beneath the roofs
> Of frosty houses
> Lovers part, from tangle warm
> Of gentle bodies under quilt
> And crack the icy water to the face
> And wake and feed the children
> And grandchildren that they love.

On August 29, 1957, Snyder left Japan for the United States on
the American tanker *Sappa Creek*. He worked twelve hours a day as
"a Fireman-water-tender in the engine room."[58] But still he had
plenty of time to read, write, and think back on Japan. "American food
is too rich & too much," he wrote to Will Petersen in Kyoto from the
Bay of Bengal. "I'm dying for some bancha and tsukemono & rice."
And he asked Petersen, "If you see Yuiko give her my love." He was
missing Japan.[57]

On the tanker he first went to Bahrain in the Persian Gulf to load
oil, and then to Naples to unload it. While there, he made a short trip
to Pompeii and Mount Vesuvius, and then was back in Iran again.
While shuttling across the Pacific, the Indian Ocean, and the Mediterranean, often not knowing at what port they would unload oil, Snyder
sometimes felt the ship "just goes on & on like a Flying Dutchman,"
never returning "home," but he could stretch his imagination on
"Goddesses" of ancient mythology and the "heroes" in Troy.[60] In his
"Tanker Notes," he speculated on poetry in terms of the Muses:

Poems that spring out fully armed; and those that are the result of artisan care. The contrived poem, workmanship; a sense of achievement and pride of craft; but the pure inspiration flow leaves one with a sense of gratitude and wonder, and no sense of "I did it"—only the Muse.

He goes on to write, "This is just the clear spring," like that on Mount Helicon,"—it reflects all things and feeds all things but is of itself transparent.... The hidden water underground."[61]

All these fragments of speculations, reflections, and memories of Japan are filtered into his poem, "A Stone Garden," which he finished writing while voyaging up the Red Sea for Istanbul in December 1957. The poem opens with an image of Japan crystallized in his mind during his days on the tanker.

> Japan a great stone garden in the sea.
> Echoes of hoe and weeding,
> Centuries of leading hill-creaks down
> To ditch and pool in fragile knee-deep fields.
>
> . . .
>
> I recollect a girl I thought I knew.

In sections 1 and 2 of the poem, Japan is described as a mythic landscape garden with a real girl in it. But in section 3, Snyder writes on poetry and alludes to the ancient Mediterranean mythology. He always seems to come back, however, to the Japanese theme.

> Thinking about a poem I'll never write,
> With gut on wood and hide, and plucking thumb,
> Grope and stutter for the words, invent a tune,
> In any tongue....
> O Muse, a goddess gone astray
> Who warms the cow and makes the wise man sane,
> (& even madness gobbles demons down)
> Then dance through jewelled trees & lotus crowns
> For Narihira's lover, the crying plover....[62]

The last line in the quotation above refers to a well-known episode in *The Tales of Ise*, in which Ariwarano Narihira (825–80), an early Heian poet, sees a white waterfowl on the river on his journey to the eastern part of Japan and thinks of his lover in Kyoto.[63] Toward the end of the section, Snyder alludes to an episode about another Japanese poet:

> The long-lost hawk of Yakamochi and Thoreau
> Flits over yonder hill.

The lines must refer to the *chōka* (long poem) by Ōtomo no Yakamochi (ca. 718–85) on falconry and to that passage in *Walden* on the lost turtledove.[64] Yakamochi had a fine black hawk that used to catch many birds, but one day "a foolish old man" took it out without his permission.

> And he came back coughing, reporting to me,
> "The hawk flew over Mt. Futagami
> And away into the clouds."
> There was no way to recall it.
> I did not know what to say.
> My heart burned in fire.[65]

Yakamochi then prayed for God's help in the shrine, and a maid appeared in his dream telling him not to be worried, for it would return to him. . . . Since Snyder had quoted another poem from the *Manyōshū* in his journal on October 24, 1956,[66] he must have been reading these classical works of Japanese literature in the fall of 1956 in Kyoto.

As the filtered memories "sprang" from the "hidden water underground," Snyder seems to have written the section with "pure inspiration flow," though sometimes "groping and stuttering for the words," like a shaman. Section 4 describes an ideal married life in an idyllic Japanese home, which Snyder "never had." "A Stone Garden" as a whole seems to be the "reflection" of the "hidden water" of the poet's mind, which has been "fed" with "all things" and has distilled all things that he experienced in America, on the ship, and in Japan.

On April 15, 1958, Snyder returned to the United States after an eighteen-month voyage on the *Sappa Creek*. For a while he stayed with his father in Corte Madera, California, and occasionally visited San Francisco, where he found "the scene 'beat gen' around," and felt "I'm all invisible and unknown." He soon went to his "hermitage Marin-An" in Mill Valley, California, where he could see the sun break "over the eucalyptus / grove below the wet pasture," and hear "a soft continuous roar" coming "out of the far valley / of the six-lane highway" to San Francisco. In June, he had a minor operation at Seaman's Hospital. But he soon recovered and was climbing the Sierras in August.[67]

About that time, in the August issue of the *Evergreen Review*, Snyder's translation of twenty-four poems of Han-shan (Kanzan in Japanese) was published as *Cold Mountain Poems*. Snyder wrote in the introduction, "He [Han-shan] and his sidekick Shih-te (Jittoku in Japanese) became great favorites with Zen painters of later days." But Han-shan seems to have been a "great favorite" with Snyder himself. He had first seen the painting of the "robe-tattered, wind-swept long-haired laughing man holding a scroll, standing on a cliff in the mountains" at "the Japanese art exhibit that came to America in 1953."[68] He had tried to translate Han-shan's poems from the Chinese while studying Oriental languages at the University of California in Berkeley. But the translation was not good enough. He reworked them in Japan later, with the help of a Japanese scholar of Chinese literature.[69] And, after he received "a note" from a publisher "asking to see Han-shan," he "redid all that & typed it" on his way back to the United States on the tanker. Han-shan was an important figure for Snyder; Nanrei Kobori goes so far as to say, "Kanzan was Snyder's model" as a man and as a poet.[70]

Model or not, Han-shan's way of life, as depicted, for instance, in the seventh poem in Snyder's translation, closely resembles that of Gary Snyder, who was as "freely drifting" and "watching things themselves" as Han-shan had been. While he was living in the mountains as a lookout, Snyder often must have observed "white clouds gather and billow." When he was "siwashing it,"[71] he must have felt that "thin grass does for a mattress," and "the blue sky makes a good quilt." Snyder was probably as happy to "let heaven and earth go about their changes." Neither Han-shan nor Snyder were monks, but both were closely associated with Zen temples. Snyder's Marin-An has many echoes of Han-shan's poems. However, it should be noted that Snyder has never been an escapist, and later developed a sharp ecological sense.

His translation is simple, precise, and sometimes free. Indeed it is so free on some occasions, and it is spoken in such an easy, conversational tone, that the reader wonders whether the scenes are in T'ang period China or in modern America, as in the second of the *Cold Mountain Poems*.

> In a tangle of cliffs I chose a place—
> Bird-paths, but no trails for men.
>
> . . .
>
> Go tell families with silverware and cars
> "What's the use of all that noise and money?"

重巌我卜居

鳥道絶人迹

. . .

寄語鍾鼎家

虚名定無益

. . .

The first two lines are exactly translated. But the last two are very freely and somewhat humorously rendered: *chung ting* 鍾鼎 literally means "bell" and "three-legged pot," and the "house with *chung ting*," the large wealthy family in which the bell is rung at every meal and the food is served from rows of pots. Snyder changed the phrase into "families with silverware and cars," probably because "wealthy" was too abstract, "bell and pots" needed explanations, but "silverware and cars" was concrete and symbolic enough to suggest the rich bourgeois American homes during the fifties.

The last line of the original poem literally means, "Vacant fame must be useless." But Snyder changed "fame" into "noise and money" and the whole sentence into a rhetorical question, "What's the use of all that noise and money?" Snyder probably thought that criticism of American civilization from the Zen point of view might be more poignant if his American readers were forced to consider whether their toil for material success caused anything except noise.

It is significant to note that the *Cold Mountain Poems*, like Pound's *Cathay* poems, present personae of the poet, through which Snyder questions Western values. But Snyder probably is closer to Han-shan than Pound was to Li Po. While Pound was more cosmopolitan than Snyder, Snyder's understanding of the Oriental mind is deeper, and his skepticism of Western civilization more serious than Pound's.

Meanwhile Snyder began to receive guests at Marin-An. "My shack has been a meeting place of many wandering types the last few weeks," he wrote to Petersen, "sleeping bags on the floor in the other room & guests come bringing little cans of ... Right now two guys from Oregon—one I went to Reed with—are staying here."[72] In the early fall Snyder visited Portland, Oregon, and saw Philip Whalen, who promised to visit him in California at Christmas time. There were "poetry readings & exhibits & openings & parties, the usual scene," which Snyder "enjoyed." But finally he confessed:

> As you can imagine it's actually hard to leave America—for all the anticipation of Japan—but I feel I will be able to get more writing & thinking done over there now; if I stayed longer here I'd have to move and hide to have the time to work.[73]

He gave his farewell poetry reading at the Bread & Wine Mission on January 26, 1959, and left the United States to visit Japan for the second time.

He resumed his writings at his new home in Kyoto, and his studies of Zen at Daitokuji under Sessō Oda. Since Snyder could seldom hear the old master at the temple, he went to talk with some monks in Daitokuji. Once he asked the head monk of Sōdō "how he felt towards life of & in the world." The head monk answered,

> You only climb a mountain to see what's around; only a fool wants to stay up there.

On hearing that, Snyder thought of "many a Head around SF" with "a desire to be ... always high."[74]

Snyder's "Pine River" appears to be a comment on the double meanings of "to be always high." During the late summer of 1959, Snyder traveled through "beaches & islands" in the San-in district along the Sea of Japan coastline,[75] visited Matsue, and wrote the poem. It opens with a description of the country as seen from the top of the castle. The speaker, then, delighted to find a schoolboy looking through "a / home made telescope / over the town," observes that the boy, too, is excited about being in a high room from where feudal lords had viewed the country. After speculating about the labor necessary to build the stone walls and castle, he concludes the poem with a description of the hardships that the owners endured during the severe winters in the ancient feudal age.

> The Matsudaira family
> owned it all,
> sat in this windy
>   lookout spire
> in winter: all their
> little villages
> under the snow.

Snyder's assumption seems to be that being in a high place is exciting, but "to be always high" means to share sufferings and work for the prosperity of the people.

In the same month in 1959, Snyder wrote another poem, "Yase: September." In the poem he presents a hardworking woman, "Old Mrs. Kawabata," who "cuts down the tall spike weeds—/more in two hours/than I can get done in a day." He is impressed not only by her skill and industry, but also by her sense of beauty.

> out of a mountain
> of grass and thistle
> She saved five dusty stalks
>   of ragged wild blue flower
> and puts them in my kitchen

But what strikes Snyder most is that behind her sense of beauty is her kindness and love for neighbors, and that this kind of communal love was common in Japanese daily life, especially in the village of Yase.

Mrs. Kawabata was the landlady of the house he had rented in Yase, in the northeastern suburb of Kyoto.[76] The town lies at the bottom of the valley through which the River Takano flows, and Mount Hiei soars up in the east.

"Mt. Hiei" was most probably written in this house in Yase in late autumn of 1959. "The half gone moon . . . in thick coat" rises late from the high mountain range in the east. The speaker feels like singing out a song played on his guitar, but his fingers are "too numb." He only sits quietly and watches intently.

>   stars rise
> back of the ridge.
> like once when a lookout
> I took Aldebaran
> for fire.

The poem compels the reader to imagine that the stars over the mountains of the northwestern United States are so bright and clear that, especially when an alpha star rises above the ridge, we are likely to think a forest is burning. Snyder suggests that it is a kind of happiness he is seeking in Japan: though he cannot see the stars on Mount Hiei so clearly because of the haze, he can enjoy living in a rustic but sufficiently furnished house, with quiet hours to watch the stars move, to sharpen his memory of experiences in his faraway country.

Memory sharpened by distance, whether bitter or delightful, plays an important part in Snyder's poems written about this time in Japan. His life in Yase, surrounded by the kind, rustic, and lovable people who touched his heart, may have brought back memories of his past at home. All of the "Four Poems for Robin," particularly the third, "An Autumn Morning in Shōkoku-ji," and the fourth, "December at Yase," are focused on his recollection of a love affair with a girl when the two were nineteen years old.

> Last night watching the Pleiades,
> Breath smoking in the moonlight,
> Bitter memory like vomit
> Choked my throat.

He begins "An Autumn Morning in Shōkoku-ji" by presenting the speaker watching the stars (the Pleiades and Aldebaran are the stars in Taurus the Bull, the sign under which Snyder was born), which reminds him of his native country and of his separated lover, Robin. The speaker unrolls his sleeping bag "on mats on the porch" in Shōkoku-ji.[77] Past midnight, Robin appears in his dream, "wild, cold, and accusing." He wakes up "shamed and angry." The poem ends, however, with the suggestion that the distance of time and space has made him feel "closer" to Robin now than when she left him ten years earlier:

> Almost dawn. Venus and Jupiter.
> The first time I have
> Ever seen them close.

Being in Japan seems to have made Snyder remember more vividly his past experiences. In "December at Yase" Snyder even recalls the words that Robin murmured when she "chose to be free"—"Again someday, maybe ten years." And "now ten years and more have / Gone by," he says. And again the dream that follows intensifies his memory and the poem:

> Only in dream, like this dawn,
> Does the grave, awed intensity
> Of our young love
> Return to my mind, and to my flesh.

Snyder may have written such poems under the influence of Kenneth Rexroth, who had been writing poems like "Andrée Rexroth" and "Yūgao," included in *The Signature of All Things* (1949). There Rexroth recollects the days he spent with his first wife, now dead. Rexroth writes in the "Mt. Tamalpais" section of "Andrée Rexroth,"

> The years have gone. It is spring
> Again. Mars and Saturn will
> Soon come on, late in the West.
>   ...   Now
> It is almost ten years since
> You came here to stay.

These poems by Rexroth and Snyder have a similar dramatic situation: in both, the speaker is alone watching the stars or trees in a lonesome place at night, counting the years that have passed, and tracing the memory of the days when their loves were new.

But both Snyder and Rexroth seem to have been influenced by Nō plays in writing this kind of poetry. Before discussing that, however, I must comment briefly on Yūgao, for her "cold body" is repeatedly alluded to by both Rexroth and Snyder.

Yūgao is a woman who appears in Lady Murasaki's *Tale of Genji*. When Genji paid a visit to his nurse on her sickbed, he was told about Yūgao, living alone with her maid next door, to whom he introduced himself by sending her a poem. She returned one. Escorted by Genji's men, Genji, Yūgao, and her maid, Ukon, went to a desolate cottage.

> As the night wore on they began sometimes to doze. Suddenly Genji saw standing over him the figure of a woman, tall and majestic: "you who think yourself so fine, how comes it that you have brought to toy with you here this worthless common creature?" ... and with this she made as though to drag the lady from his side.

Genji sat up and drew his sword. The lamp was out, but he found Yūgao "burst out into a cold sweat," losing consciousness. The ghost was still "hovering beside his pillow." Extremely frightened, Yūgao was "scarcely breathing." Genji groped his way out, brought back his attendants with torches, and ordered them to twang their bows to dispel the demon. But Yūgao now lay motionless.

> Lying down beside her, [Genji] began gently moving her limbs. Already they were growing cold. Her breath had quite stopped. . . . He could contain himself no longer and crying "Come back to me, my own darling, come back to life. Do not look at me so strangely!" he flung his arms about her. But now she was quite cold. Her face was set in a dull, senseless stare.[78]

The story was adopted into a Nō play, *Yūgao*, in which a traveling priest, passing by a deserted cottage near the River Kamo in Kyoto, remembers the story of Yūgao. He recalls her story so intently that he sees the ghost of Yūgao in a vision.

The uncanny intensity in recalling the past and meeting the vision of the dead in the Nō play is ingeniously reproduced in Rexroth's poem, "Yūgao." Rexroth begins the poem by presenting a similar dramatic situation as he tells of "Andrée Rexroth": the speaker goes into his dark garden under "the new half moon" late at night. But he piles on line after line of supersensory experiences: in the "ominous dark" he feels the garden "crowded with / Invisible, impalpable / Movement," and the air "breathless" under the trees.

> I seem to stand in the midst
> Of an imcomprehensible
> Tragedy; as though a world
> Doubled against this were tearing
> Through the thin shell of night.

This is the world of yūgen. Rexroth leads the reader further into the world of the Nō play:

> On such nights as this the young
> Warriors of old time take form
> In the Noh plays.

He is attempting to reproduce the Nō world of yūgen, in which memory of the past floods back vividly and overwhelmingly. He then summons before his "mind's eye" the figure of the deceased wife he had once so much enjoyed watching asleep in her bed.

> I can call, plain to the mind's eye,
> Your bright sleeping head, nested
> In its pillow, and your face, sure
> And peaceful as your moving
> Breath.

The title "Yūgao" suggests that he can also call "plain to the mind's eye" his wife's cold dead body, as if "a world / Doubled against this were tearing / Through the thin shell" of memory.

This same kind of intensity can be seen in Snyder's poetry. As Snyder recalls a girl he once loved, the vivid memory leads him to "feel" her presence in "the old capital." In his "A Spring Night in Shōkoku-ji," probably having seen cherry blossoms in Kyoto, Snyder remembers that he once "walked under cherry blossoms" with Robin "at night in an orchard in Oregon." He writes on:

> All that I wanted then
> Is forgotten now, but you.
> Here in the night
> In a garden of the old capital
> I feel the trembling ghost of Yugao
> I remember your cool body
> Naked under a summer cotton dress.

"The trembling ghost of Yugao" is immediately associated with Robin's "cool body" in her summer dress. According to Snyder,

> I read Waley's *Tale of Genji* and also his book of Nō transla-
> tions which was available many years ago. But the other
> influence on the poem is having seen the play *Yugao* at the
> Kawamura Nō theater on December 12, 1960.[79]

Whether he may admit it or not, Snyder was indebted to Kenneth Rexroth, the Nō play, and to *The Tale of Genji* in Arthur Waley's translation.

While living in Yase, Snyder often met his friends Will and Ami Petersen. Will Petersen was keenly interested in Nō plays, and had been taking lessons at the Kawamura Nō Theater. According to Scott Johnson, a friend of the Petersens', Snyder often observed those lessons and formal performances of Nō plays at the theater, and also read the English translations of Nō by Kokusai Bunka Shinkōkai. Traces of Nō are found not only in the Robin poems but also in his *Myths & Texts* and *Mountains and Rivers Without End*. There seems to have remained in his mind the words of his Roshi, who "once said something about 'walking zazen' & Nō." [80]

About this time, probably in December 1959, he wrote a poem, "The Public Bath," comprising sketches of six scenes in the Japanese public baths. [81] The second of them is a short description of

> *the baby boy*
>> on his back, dashed with scalding water
>> silent, moving eyes
>> inscrutably
>> pees.

Usually mothers take care of their little girls in the women's side of the bath. But sometimes a young father comes in with his little daughter. Snyder has a scene with two girls. [87]

> *the daughters*
>> gripping and scrubbing his two little daughters
>>> they squirm, shriek at
>>> soap-in-the-eye,
>> wring out their own hair
>>> with grave wifely hands,
>> peek at me, point, while he
>> soaps up and washes their
>>> plump little tight-lip pussies
>> peers in their ears,
>>> & dunks them in hot tile tub.
>>> with a brown-burnt farmboy
>>> a shrivelled old man
>>> and a student who sings *silent night*.
>> —we waver and float like seaweed
>> pink flesh in the steamy light.

Snyder, however, seems more interested in the kind of relaxed feeling that the Japanese people have when they share experiences in a community. A variety of people "waver and float like seaweed" in the same big bathtub. On the express train, on another occasion, he is delighted to observe all the passengers "jerk with the speedup and slow," as he writes in his "Asleep on the Train." In "The Levels" he describes the pleasure of living in a house together with animals and birds. Snyder's idea of *oikos* (house) of the earth, which he later develops as identical with his cherished global communalism, must have something to do with his observations of these communal experiences in Japan.

In the meantime, Joanne Kyger, a San Francisco poet whom Gary had known, arrived in Kyoto. The two soon became intimate, and, according to Hisao Kanaseki, they got married by the "counsel" of Ruth Sasaki. In October 1960, they moved to a house closer to town in the back of Daitokuji.[83] In late January 1961, he sent out letters to some of his American friends in Kyoto—Will and Ami Petersen, Philip Yampolsky, Burton Watson, and Walter Nowick—to invite them to his house for their "1st Anniversary" on February 28. According to Susumu Kamaike, a close friend of Cid Corman, they sometimes went for drinks to the bars around Kawaramachi Street. Kamaike remembers that once when they were drinking together Snyder talked about Kenji Miyazawa, who Snyder thought was one of the best modern Japanese poets, and whom he was translating into English.[84] Once when they were all drunk, Snyder lost his hat in one of the bars. He recorded this in the second poem of "The Elwha River," as one of the things he recalled having lost in his life.

> A black beret Joanne had given me for my birthday
> left in some
> Kawaramachi bar.

Among other "lost things" he listed with attachment in the poem was "Theodora, Kitty-chan." (*Chan* is a Japanese suffix attached to a name to denote endearment.) And another, a

> Sewing kit. Blown off the cot beside me
> on the boatdeck by a sudden wind
> South China Sea

just before he arrived in Okinawa.[85] In this poem he listed nine such objects all together, like an "elegant catalogue."[86] But it is worth noticing that many of the things to which he felt strong attachment were related to Japan.

Soon Snyder set out for a trip to India with his wife Joanne, Allen Ginsberg, and Peter Orlovsky. After visiting the holy territory in the lower Himalayas in March and April 1962, he returned with Joanne to their old home in Kyoto. Then they learned that Ami Petersen was expecting a baby. The poem with the odd title, "AMI 24. XII. 62" was written immediately after he had see the Petersens at their home,[87] and found Ami had just given birth while her husband was "out to teach." His surprise is well expressed from the opening lines:

> Hair a wild stroke of black
> on white
> pillow—

Snyder subtly expresses his envy also by quoting Ami's casual remark in the poem. "We never thought he'd be a boy." Snyder was 32 years old, and had had a welter of experiences, but he had never been a father. Actually Snyder's friends in Kyoto were aware and worried that Joanne was not enjoying life with Gary in Japan as much as he was. In any event, she and Gary returned to the United States in 1964, but separated.[88]

In September 1964, Snyder began to teach two freshman composition courses and a poetry-writing course at the University of California in Berkeley. He found teaching "exciting," although "so verbal."[89] However, while teaching he began writing a series of twelve poems on Japan—a poem for each month of the year—later collected under the title, "Six Years." Each of them is an excellently refined piece of poetry, but, after these works, his poetry on Japan began to change in style. He spent the summer of 1965 alone in America, and returned to Japan alone: he had been awarded a Bollingen grant to study Zen life. He did this until 1966.

In Japan he lived alone in the same house as earlier near Daitokuji, continuing his study of Zen under Sessō Oda, and teaching English conversation at the Kyoto YMCA.[90] Finding him lonesome, Hisao Kanaseki invited him to dinner one evening at his home in Takatsuki. Kanaseki recalls he also invited one of his fourth-year students in the English department at Kobe University, Masa Uehara, "only because she was lodging alone near his house," her home being in Okinawa.[91] Snyder fell in love with her.

Next spring she went to the Graduate School of Ochanomizu College in Tokyo, and Snyder went back to America.[92] But he returned to Japan a year later, in March 1967, and resumed his relationship with Uehara. It was his fourth visit to Japan. They were married on August 6, 1967, on the rim of an active volcano on one of the Tokara Islands, and he recorded the event in "Suwa-no-se Island and the Banyan Ashram" in the *Earth House Hold*. They lived in the house near Daitokuji.

Changes in Snyder's poetic style are obvious in "A Bed in the Sky," written on January 16, 1968, while Masa was expecting a baby. The poem presents a man on a motorcycle which "strums" the cold, empty street at 1:00 A.M. He sees "ice slicks shine in the moon," and through the cemetery he "weaves a safe way" home. He slips into bed, and his "stomach against your big belly / feels our baby turn." In the poem, the cold outdoors of the old capital, lying like the dead in their graves, is effectively contrasted with the expectation in their warm bed of the birth.[93]

The poem differs, however, from his earlier works, in that the speaker is now a home-loving husband. That is, although he stays out late, he hurries home, and although he is tempted to "watch the moon all night," he "sinks in the warm." When he was younger, Snyder would have left his "motorcycle / out parked in the rain," and might not have returned home all night. But now the tone and even the rhythm of his poem resemble those of Frost's poem referred to earlier.

> The woods are lovely, dark and deep,
> But I have promises to keep.
> ("Stopping by Woods on a Snowy Evening")

> I ought to stay outside alone
>   and watch the moon all night
> But the bed is full and spread and dark
>   ("The Bed in the Sky")

Snyder is beginning to feel his social responsibility as a father.

"When Kai is born / I quit going out," he writes in "Not Leaving the House" in April 1968. "Hang around the kitchen—make cornbread /

Let nobody in." He is now determined to take as much paternal responsibility as possible,

> making a new world of ourselves
> around this life.

Snyder's realization of his responsibility as a citizen of the world and his serious concern with ecological problems as a member of earth's community, as seen in his later works, may stem from this fatherly awareness of his being responsible for the happiness and welfare of other members of the family. He apparently was determined to safeguard not only his family but all the families of the world, and to make "a new world of ourselves/around this life" on the globe, as in his home.

In "Passage to More than India," Snyder wrote on the "solitary vision quest."

> In many American Indian cultures it is obligatory for every member to get out of the society, out of the human nexus, and "out of his head," at least once in his life. He returns from his solitary vision quest with a secret name, a protective animal spirit, a secret song. It is his "power." [94]

Snyder's "vision quest" in Japan seems to have ended with his discovery of the Mahayana family love of all.

Gary Snyder and his family moved to the United States in December 1968. He had by then published four books of poetry, and, as Thomas Parkinson reports, had "become a legend" in the United States. [95] In 1969, *Earth House Hold* and *Regarding Wave* were published. In 1972, he attended the United Nations Conference on the Human Environment held in Stockholm, and on his way home stopped over in Japan in preparation for a book on the Hokkaido wilderness. In 1973, *The Fudo Trilogy* was published and, in 1974, *Turtle Island*, which won the Pulitzer Prize for poetry in 1975. In those works after he left Japan can be traced not only the Japanese influence but Snyder's maturer fusion of the Buddhist ideas and the Western literary tradition.

According to Hisao Kanaseki, the Buddhist traces in Snyder are obvious on three points: (1) Snyder's idea that the universe is "a vast breathing body," and that poetry is "the vehicle of the mystery of voice" of the universe, is based on Mahayana Buddhism; (2) his idea of "light" that it "warms" the "bones" of the stones and "grows" the trees may have derived from the concept of the light of Tathagata; (3) his ecological ideas and proposals are based on native American animism and also on his Buddhist belief that "mountains, rivers, grass, and trees . . . have life."[96] Indeed all of this seems quite sound. But Snyder's ecological idea in relation to his Buddhist belief calls for closer examination, for it has been Snyder's most serious concern as well as one of his most powerful messages.

Snyder has written a number of poems with strong ecological concern. "Front Lines" describes the ground leveling at the newly "developed" land in America, and warns the people that their avarice has brought the destruction of the forest and the desert. In "Mother Earth: Her Whales," written in Stockholm, Snyder howls in the manner of Ginsberg at the "robots in suits" attending the U.N. Conference on the Human Environment:

> How can the head-heavy power-hungry politic scientist
> Government two-world   Capitalist-Imperialist
> Third-world Communist   paper-shuffling male
>   non-farmer jet-set bureaucrats
> Speak for the green of the leaf? Speak for the soil?

Snyder's vociferous assault on those who cause worldwide pollution and destruction of nature is directed even toward Japan, "a once-great Buddhist nation," for dribbling methyl mercury "like gonorrhea / in the sea." In "LMFBR,"[97] written about 1972, he considers plutonium as the symbol of "Kali yuga," the last dark age of the world. And in "Tomorrow's Song," he regrets that "the USA . . . never gave the mountains and rivers, / trees and animals, / a vote."

In his essays and talks published about this time, Snyder makes his "political" position clear. He thinks "a new definition of democracy" is necessary, and proclaims that "trees and rock should be able to vote in Congress," and also that "whales should be able to vote." It is "legalistically" possible, he continues, if "the court appoints someone to be their representative." But, since his idea of new democracy will meet much resistance, he "wishes," in the meantime, to become "a spokesman" of the nonhuman realm, and "to speak for these things, to carry their voice into the human realm" with "an ecological conscience."[98]

His idea of new democracy, however, is fundamentally based on his mystic "perception" that every thing is "alive." To the question put by Doug Flaherty about *satori* in Zen, Snyder answers:

> I have had a very moving, profound perception a few times that everything was alive (the basic perception of animism) and that on one level there is no hierarchy of qualities in life.

This perception leads him to the Mahayana love of every existence on "this planet." It is "not the humanistic love of the West—but a love that extends to animals, rocks, dirt, all of it," he says. "Without this love, we can end even without war, with an uninhabitable place."[99]

Snyder's idea of global communalism derives from this religious perception. Instead of the traditional concept of the family, based on the formalized marital relationship, he foresees the possibility of a variety of communities of "men, women and children—all of whom together hope to follow the timeless path of love and wisdom, in affectionate company with the sky, wind, clouds, trees, waters, animals and grass." In order to attain the ideal community, the revolution of the mind is necessary, and like Walt Whitman, he advises the reader repeatedly to take "passage to more than India." "The next great step of mankind is to step into the nature of his mind." It is "to uncover the inner structure and actual boundaries of the mind." And the poet's function in the community is to embody his own "rare and powerful states of mind" which are "at deeper levels common to all who listen."[100]

Thomas Lyon places Gary Snyder in the tradition of the "Western" writers, represented by such authors as John Muir, Robinson Jeffers, Walter Van Tilburg Clark, and Frank Waters, who have been "working toward a post-humanist, post-technological world-view in which man fits into natural patterns rather than simply following his greed into the city of ecological imbalance and poisoning." Certainly Snyder is a Western poet in the sense that he embodies the "Western ecological vision."[101] His response to nature resembles that of Natty Bumppo.[102] But all of his ideas cannot be explained fully only in terms of the Western literary tradition and American Indian animism and shamanism. Jean Jacques Rousseau's idea of the "noble savage," William Blake's visionary quest, Karl Marx's communism, Emerson's idea of the vast universe, Thoreau's life in nature, Whitman's prophetic posture and his idea of democracy and freedom, and the modernists' concern with human alienation all are fused in Snyder.[103]

But above all the Buddhist philosophy has enriched much of Snyder's thought. The communalism, for instance, has heavy overtones of Mahayana Buddhism, in the sense that he considers it to be directed "ultimately toward the true community (sangha) of all beings." [104]

Behind Snyder's belief that everything is alive, and that "we not only should but *do* love one another," is the Buddhist doctrine of interrelatedness of all the existence in the universe.

> Every person, animals, forces, all are related via a web of reincarnation—or rather, they are "interborn." . . . It is clear that the empirically observable interconnectedness of nature is but a corner of the vast "jewelled net."

Buddhist derivation is suggested in this passage by the use of such terms as "reincarnation" and "jewelled net." But Snyder explains the same idea of the universe's "interconnectedness" elsewhere more accurately as the Buddhist teaching.

> The Buddhists teach respect for all life, and for wild systems. Man's life is totally dependent on an interpenetrating network of wild systems.

And in "Buddhism and the Coming Revolution," he writes more specifically that "Avatamsaka (Kegon) Buddhist philosophy" is the source of this idea of the "vast interrelated network."

> Avatamsaka (Kegon) Buddhist philosophy sees the world as a vast interrelated network in which all objects and creatures are necessary and illuminated. [105]

The notion Snyder makes repeated reference to is what Buddhists know as "Indra's net," which is described in a passage in the Avatamsaka-sutra. According to the 26th book of the sutra,

> there are in each smallest particle billions of Buddha preaching, and innumerable kingdoms of Buddha, Sumeru, the Seven Peaks of Gold, and the mountains surrounding the world, and still it is not cramped. There are in it the Three Hells, the Heaven, the People's world, and the Asura, where every existence is receiving its retribution accordingly. [106]

The "smallest particle" here refers to the jewel on each of the knots of the large net (hence the "jewelled net") in the palace of Sakradevanam Indra on the summit of Sumeru. The metaphor of the sutra passage then is: just as each jewel on the net reflects the universe and also the reflections of all the other jewels that reflect the universe, so the whole universe is limitless and interrelated.

Snyder is trying to explain his idea of ecology in terms of his understanding of the Buddhist philosophy of the interrelatedness of the universe. He has created his own idea of ecology by fusing Buddhist philosophy with ecological science. He is in the tradition of the Buddhist ecologists, such as Kumakusu Minakata, and the Buddhist poets, such as Kenji Miyazawa.

For Snyder, Buddhist philosophy is not mere embellishment: it is more deeply rooted in his ideas and his way of thinking than has been supposed. Snyder recollects how he studied the Buddhist writings with dictionaries "in a small house" in Kyoto.

> It was really necessary to spend most of the time at the house, because in a monastery you have no access to texts or dictionaries. All of the other monks had already memorized everything, literally. As an outsider-novice-foreigner, you are continually wrestling with problems of translation and terminology—you have to go look things up.[107]

He does not reveal exactly what Buddhist writings he read at that time, though he states *how* he read them. But from his various other writings we can gather that he has read the Lankavatara-sutra (Ryōgakyo in Japanese) with the Avatamsaka-sutra; he has read the writings of and about such Zen masters as Hui Nêng (Enō), Po-chang Huai-hai (Hyakujō Ekai), and Hsiang-yen (Kyōgen); and memorized the Prajna-paramita-sutra (Hannya Haramita Shingyo).[108] He must also have read other Buddhist writings.

The speaker in his "Avocado" has not attained the final enlightenment. "The Dharma is like an Avocado!" begins his poem. Comparing the central idea in Buddhism with a common California fruit, he writes:

> The great big round seed
> In the middle,
> Is your own Original Nature—
> Pure and smooth
>
> . . .
>
> Hard and slippery,
> It looks like

> You should plant it—but then
> It shoots out thru the
> > > fingers—
> Gets away:

Dharma in Buddhism is the truth that Buddha has taught. It is the law of the world that every existence follows. But, as is well known, there have been a variety of interpretations concerning what the "law" is. It is the fundamental principle of Buddhism that existence is the infinite interplay of the infinitely minimal elements of the world. It means the realization of selflessness and the perception of nothingness. And it is also the law of the process of attaining the most esoteric bliss of nirvana through practicing religious asceticism. Snyder writes elsewhere,

> The Buddha-Dharma is a long, gentle, human dialog—2,500 years of quiet conversation—on the nature of human nature and the eternal Dharma—and practical method of realization.[109]

According to him, dharma is (1) the search for the truth, (2) the eternal truth itself, and (3) the practical method of realization of the truth. In the poem "Avocado," however, instead of giving the definitions of the term, he is rather bitterly laughing at the speaker's distance from the true understanding of dharma, by alluding to Hui Nêng's *satori* (enlightenment). According to the sutra of Hui Nêng, the key is the givenness of human nature:

> Hui Nêng was suddenly enlightened and realized that all the laws are not separated from the Original Nature. At last he told his master, "I have not thought that the Original Nature is originally pure; I have not thought that the Original Nature is essentially immortal; I have not thought the Original Nature is self-complete itself; I have not thought the Original Nature is essentially unmoved; I have not thought the Original Nature produces all the laws."
> > Master said to Hui Nêng, "you are now the Sixth Master. ... Listen to my poem: Hui Nêng comes and plants the seed, and the ground will produce the fruits."[110]

The assumption of both the sutra and the avocado poem is that the human "Original Nature" has the nature of the Buddha, which, like the seed, could grow and produce the fruit. Since enlightenment is only achieved by the perceiving self, the search for the truth leads one to the realization that the core of the law of the world lies in our "own Original Nature" which is "pure and smooth," like the seed of an avocado. But Snyder writes in the poem that the speaker has not gone deep enough into the core of this "Original Nature," which is for him still "hard and slippery."

In an interview in 1969, Snyder declared, "I don't lay claim to any great enlightenment experiences or anything like that."[111] This may give the idea that he is not totally committed to Buddhism. But he is an avowed Buddhist, and he is only modest. The "Avocado" should be taken as a playful poem, mildly satirizing the young American Zen students.

However, Snyder's fascination with Buddhism cannot account for all of his ideas and poetry. His readings in Hindu classics, anthropology, mythology, and various religions are fused into his philosophy. Nevertheless, the single deepest and most powerful religious influence on Snyder seems to be the Mahayana Buddhism that he studied in Japan.

The very tendency of Snyder constantly to fuse and synthesize is itself a characteristically Buddhist attitude. According to the Buddhist teaching, "one is all, and all is one," just as "a circle is the fusion of limitless points without obstacles." Snyder tries to fuse Basho's dictum "to learn about the pine, go to the pine," with Zen, with native American animism, and with some of the ideas of Ezra Pound, by saying that "you learn by becoming totally absorbed in that which you wish to learn." And he declares himself "a Buddhist-shamanist." When asked how he "links" the Oriental teachings and the American Indian myths, Snyder answers, "Oh, it's all one teaching."[112]

"Every day I meditate," Snyder says. "I do zazen as a daily practice." When we recall that he once wrote that in meditation "one begins to see the connecting truths hidden in Zen, Avatamsaka and Tantra," we may assume that, in his meditations, he has constantly been trying to find "the connecting truths," and been synthesizing them into new truths.[113] Snyder's continual search for the "connecting truths," the "convergences," and syntheses may be seen as a habit he acquired from the Buddhist practice of zazen.

There may be some who are puzzled when told that everything is alive. But it is a metaphorical expression, and by that Snyder means that everything has Buddha's nature. Those who are interested in animism may wonder why Snyder did not inquire much into Shintoism while in Japan. But he has been interested in its mixture with Buddhism, Honchi Suijaku. Some of us may question whether he can find answers to all our present-day problems. But we are warned, moved, and inspired when we hear him vehemently denounce our civilization, which might be slowly destroying itself by pollution, the unwise use of nuclear energy, and by wholesale squandering of our natural resources. It is significant that his "vision quest" in Japan has led him to his discovery of the Mahayana love of all and his identity as a family member of this precious planet, and by fusing it with his experiences, he has been able to propose one practicable solution to the problems of our civilization and to give a most powerful message to his readers, now living in the post-industrial society.

Conclusion

It is both embarrassing and encouraging to begin this conclusion by saying that there is no end in tracing the history of the Japanese influence on American poets. As I reach this point I discover there are a number of American poets who have shown their interest in Japan but who have not been dealt with here, and there still may be more in the future. Though, as time passes, Japan may lose the fresh fragrance it had for past generations of Americans, American poets always seem to be able to find something new in Japanese culture. Although a list of the American poets who have shown their interest in Japan might continue endlessly, perhaps this is the proper place to summarize that list, to generalize about, to categorize those poets to whose work reference has been made and those who were missed.

There are three types of American poets who have displayed some interest in Japan. The first is the conservative poet, who, having confidence in the traditional Western values, is still liberal enough to be attracted by Japanese "exotic" beauty. Generally speaking, those poets fitting this category cannot read or write Japanese, but have been charmed by Japanese ceramics, lacquerware, paintings, ukiyoe, and other visual *objets d'art*, or by the short forms of Japanese poetry. Many of them have gained considerable knowledge of Japan through translations, letters from Japan, or books about Japan written in English. Most of them are old-line white Anglo-Saxon Protestants, poets like Longfellow, Amy Lowell, and Adelaide Crapsey. Somewhat more recent members of this group include A. D. Ficke, John Gould Fletcher, Carl Sandburg, William Carlos Williams, Yvor Winters, and Richard Wilbur. Probably they all would agree with T. S. Eliot that they could never understand the Oriental philosophy "well enough to make it a mainstay," and share the sentiment with him that their "only hope of really penetrating to the heart of that mystery" may lie "in forgetting how to think as an American or a European."[1]

In contrast to this type, the second category of poet consists of the cosmopolitans, who believe that to be an American is to be a world citizen, and that the world civilization is in a sense an extension of American culture. Their attitude toward different cultures is pluralistic and relativistic in the sense that they juxtapose the cultures of the world as having more or less equal value. Yet they are transcendentalist in the sense that these values would all be included, amalgamated, and unified into one worldwide renaissance. For them, Japan is not a decoration to their poetry, but an essential part of their panoramic poetic scheme. Although their knowledge of each civilization may appear unbalanced, perhaps somewhat sketchy, and though sometimes they may even confound elements of several quite disparate cultures, they have a broad range of knowledge and are more eager to learn the relevant languages than those who belong to the first category. To this group belong Whitman and Pound, and possibly Louis Untermeyer.

Belonging to the third category are those poets who have become genuinely skeptical of traditional values and in seeking new anchorage have attempted to absorb Japanese values. They are likely to be somewhat younger. As American society began to accept a variety of ideas and the tenets of minority groups during the 1970s, conformity was possible without total acceptance of traditional ideologies. Therefore, many recent American poets have not necessarily refuted the traditional American values in order to accept the Japanese. It is also true that as an increasing number of books on Japanese culture have been published in the past three decades these poets have had less need to learn the Japanese language to "appreciate" Japanese verbal culture. However, many of the members of this group have a limited command of the language, through which they have gained a knowledge of Japanese classical literature, religion, or philosophy. To this group belong Kenneth Rexroth, Gary Synder, Philip Whalen, and Cid Corman.

Having set up these less-than-neat categories, however, I find considerable overlapping. That is, cosmopolitan as he was, Pound showed some conservative traits in his earlier years, having been "born in a half savage country out of date." And though skeptical about the traditional values of the establishment, Allen Ginsberg and Richard Wright are deeply rooted in the "American grain."

It should also be noted that it is not only the poets, who have felt love for Japan. The painters are interested in the simple *zenga* (Zen painting) and *sumie* (brush and ink drawing), and the minimalist artists and sculptors, in particular, seem attracted by the kind of simplicity and impersonality they find in Japanese art. The musicians are interested in the sound of a temple bell, and John Cage, for instance, has composed "Seven Haiku" and other short pieces such as "4′ 33," providing an ample "musical sphere" of silence and reverberations. The film and the docudrama makers edit series of short and intense cuts. Naturally those poets who are inclined to accept such minimalist-imagist principles as precision and utmost condensation look to the fresh visions in haiku as well as Dickinson and Plath when they attempt to write on more varied subjects or with new sensibility. The trend toward minimalization may also explain why modern Japanese fiction, which has absorbed the rich tradition of the realistic and naturalistic European novels of the last century, has not had much impact on American fiction. It may be that the fascination with minimalization, a prominent trend in modern American arts, also accounts for the interest in haiku shown by so many American poets who have had an interest in Japan. Even those poets who have had only passing interest in Japan, such as Wilbur, Untermeyer, and Etheridge Knight, are interested in this short form of poetry.

In any event, when Louis Untermeyer visited Kyoto in 1963, he wrote a poem in the form of haiku:

Thunder at Hosokawa

The far-off mountain
And this intimate garden
Speak to each other.

In contrast to the violent Alpine thunderbolts, which Childe Harold observed flung "from hand to hand," the thunder in the old capital in Japan sounded to Untermeyer as if it were gentle 17-syllable murmurings of the mountain and the old garden.

Etheridge Knight wrote several haiku while he was in prison. One sample is:

In the August grass
Struck by the last rays of sun
The cracked teacup screams.

In the manner of Richard Wright, the poet seems to be comparing the speaker in his emotional crisis to "the cracked teacup" thrown away at the corner of the prison and "screaming."

Lindley William Hubbell, who has been living in Japan for more than a quarter of a century, Cid Corman and Edith Shiffert, who have lived in Kyoto for twenty years, have published their poems both in Japan and in the United States on their Japanese experiences and deserve much more attention than they have received. Other old-timers in Japan, such as Amy Horiuchi, Marie Philomene, Philip Williams, and Edith G. Williams, to name a few, have published in *Poetry Nippon* since 1967. Inspired by the idea of *renga* (linked poetry), Thomas Fitzsimmons made an attempt with Makoto Ōoka to co-author the sequence of twenty poems that they called *renshi*, "Linked Poems: Rocking Mirror Daybreak," in the fall of 1981, and published it in *Shinchō* in March 1982.

I venture to say that there may be no country in the world outside of Japan in which the traditional Japanese values have been more appreciated by its artists than the United States. The Chinese, the Koreans, and other Asian neighbors in general seem to have been more interested in modern Japanese technology and economy than in Japan's literature. The French, the British, and other Europeans have tended to ignore Japan, and to be haunted still, to a certain extent, by Orientalism in the old sense, with exoticism and with "the high-handed executive attitude of the nineteenth-century and early twentieth-century European colonialism." [2] In the recent *Oxford Book of Verses in English Translation* are collected 600 pages of French, German, Chinese, Persian, Bengali, Icelandic, Hungarian and other non-English poems but none from the Japanese. [3] Americans, on the contrary, have shown little of this kind of paternalism or "colonialism" toward Japan. Perhaps the British economist and Japanologist, Endymion Wilkinson, was wiser than he knew, in stating, "It was the Europeans after all who 'opened' China, and the Americans who 'opened' Japan." [4] But surely the American poets have so far been far ahead in their studies and understandings of Japan.

In fact, so many American writers have displayed an interest in Japan that it could be said a history of American literature, especially of the twentieth century, should be rewritten with references to its relation to Japanese culture. If we think back to the beginning of this century, we recall that Jack London was in Japan as a war correspondent during the Russo-Japanese war, 1904–5. John Hersey, who wrote about the bombing of Hiroshima, William Faulkner, and John Steinbeck all visited Japan two or three decades ago. J. D. Salinger was seriously interested in Zen and haiku. More recently, Saul Bellow, E. L. Doctorow, the late John Gardner, Adrienne Rich, and Richard Brautigan have visited Japan. And it is expected that a wave of American writers will be visiting in 1984 when the International PEN Conference will be held in Tokyo. The experience of American writers in Japan has had, and will continue to have, an impact on the American world of letters, comparable to that generated by American writers who went to Paris in the 1920s.

As for the reception these Americans may expect, Shunsuke Kamei quite rightly has noted that the Japanese are "inclined either to be worshipful without discrimination or to be repulsive with narrow nationalistic attitude."[5] Thus, some Japanese probably will maintain their rather querulous attitude (especially toward the recent cheap journalism), complaining of the limited understandings of Japan by the Westerners. However, at the same time they will continue to feel respect if not admiration for the Americans' ingenious attempt at translations, adaptations, and interpretations.

This ambivalent attitude partly derives from the fact that the Japanese in general consider their "insular" cultural experiences to be "peculiar," unfathomably rich in meaning, and therefore hardly understood fully by foreigners, although Japanese still want them to be understood. Therefore, when Salinger writes a haiku:

> The little girl on the plane
> Who turned her doll's head around
> To look at me,

we find Tsutomu Fukuda reacting quite typically: "In this haiku-like poem we cannot find any suggestive depth required by haiku, any emotional undertone that invites our re-reading of the poem." Yet toward the end of the same essay, Fukuda expresses his wish that Salinger would write "a true haiku ... with its deep suggestive beauty."[6]

It may seem that we have directed our attention mainly to those aspects of American literature that should be admired. But it is finally my hope that this book may be an encouragement for the further serious creative works of art and studies on the subject, and a better mutual understanding of the two countries.

Notes

Chapter 1

1. Cf. Edmund Morgan, *The Birth of the Republic: 1763–1789* (Chicago: University of Chicago Press, 1956), p. 6. "For the great majority of Americans who still spoke of England as home, even though they had never been there, being English meant having a history that stretched back continually into a golden age of Anglo-Saxon purity and freedom."

2. Father Dominick Bouhours's account of Saint Francis Xavier's voyage to the Far East, including his visits to Cangoxima (Kagoshima), Bungo, Meaco (Kyoto), and other Japanese cities, were later translated into English from French by John Dryden in 1688, see *The Life of St. Francis Xavier: The Works of John Dryden*, vol. 16 (London: William Miller, 1808), pp. 290–379. William Adams (1564–1620) stayed in Japan from 1600 till his death and wrote a number of letters home, eleven of which are known. See Mutsuo Kikuno, ed., *Logs and Letters of William Adams* (Tokyo: Nan'undo, 1977). E. M. Thomson, *The First Englishman in Japan* (1904), and Richard Blaker, *The Needle-Watcher: The Will Adams Story, British Samurai* (London: Heinemann, 1932; reprint Rutland, Vt.: Tuttle, 1973). The diaries of Richard Cocks (1566–1623) during his stay in Japan between 1613 and 1623 suggest there was at least one unidentifiable book on Japan by an Englishman based on letters of Portuguese and Spanish missionaries in Japan. See Saburo Minagawa, *Japan as Seen by the British in the Early Tokugawa Period* (Tokyo: Taibundo, 1979), p. 3.

3. Minagawa, pp. 42–44.

4. William Bradford, *Of Plymouth Plantation* (New York: Capricon, 1962), p. 46.

5. Thomas Wright, ed., *The Travels of Marco Polo* (London: Henry Bohn, 1854; reprint New York: AMS Press, 1968), p. 350.

6. Maurice Johnson, Muneharu Kitagaki, and Philip Williams, *Gulliver's Travels and Japan: A New Reading* Moonlight Series, no. 4 (Kyoto: Doshisha Amherst House, 1977), pp. 2–3.

7. The first American ship that went to China was the *Empress of China*,

which arrived in Canton on August 26, 1784. The *Columbia* was the first American ship to reach China by Cape Horn, Oregon, and Hawaii in 1789. Akinori Sugiura, *The Age of Great Sail Ships* (Tokyo: Chūōkōron, 1979), pp. 30–31.

8. Arthur Walworth, *Black Ships Off Japan* (New York: Alfred A. Knopf, 1946 reprint Hamden Conn.: Archon Books, 1966), p. 7; and Foster Rhee Dulles, *Yankees and Samurai: America's Role in the Emergence of Modern Japan: 1791–1900* (New York: Harper & Row, 1965), pp. 1–2.

9. Hikomitsu Kawai, *The Record of the Japanese Shipwrecked* (Tokyo: Shakai Shisō-sha, 1967), p. 314. The two ships were anchored at Kashinoura of Ōshima at the southern tip of Kii Peninsula between March 26 and April 3, 1791. Hazel Durnell erroneously writes, "at the end of the Izu Peninsula." Hazel Durnell, *Japanese Cultural Influences on American Poetry and Drama* (Tokyo: Hokuseido Press, 1982), p. 1.

10. Tōru Haruna, *The Story of Drifting of Nippon Otokichi* (Tokyo: Shō-bunsha, 1979), pp. 24–33. Haruna points out that the shipwreck attracted the attention of Washington Irving.

11. Akira Nakahama, *The Life of Nakahama Manjiro* (Tokyo: Fuzambō, 1971), pp. 7–70. Nakahama Manjiro became an interpreter for the Tokugawa government after Perry's visit to Uraga. Among other well-known Japanese rescued by American ships are Hamada Hikozo, or "Joseph Hiko"; Osome, a geisha of Edo; and Oharu, daughter of a fisherman in Kagoshima. More than twenty fishermen were recorded to have been rescued all together. See also Kawai, pp. 109–55.

12. Leon Howard, *Herman Melville: A Biography* (Berkeley: University of California Press, 1967), pp. 41–88.

13. Alexander Winston, *No Man Knows My Grave: Privateers and Pirates, 1665–1815* (Boston: Houghton Mifflin, 1969), pp. 224–25.

14. *New York Times*, January 31 and April 14, 1852. The speech was probably made by Joshua Reed Giddings (1795–1864).

15. Hazel Durnell writes that the mission was "made up of twenty-seven envoys." (Durnell, p. 5.) But there were seventy-seven all together. One of them died while in San Francisco. But a shipwrecked Japanese joined the party later.

16. Muragaki Norimasa, "Diary," *The First Japanese Embassy to America*, (Tokyo: Japan-America Society, 1928), p. 54, June 17, 1860. The author did not change the dates when he crossed the international date line. The Japanese delegation of seventy-seven samurai with Shimmi Buzen no Kami Masaoki as chief ambassador, Muragaki Awaji no Kami Norimasa as vice ambassodor, and Oguri Bungo no Kami Tadamasa as chief censor, left Edo on February 9, 1860. They arrived in San Francisco on March 29, 1860, and in Washington, D.C., on May 12. On May 17, they visited the White House and, after the ceremonial three bows, handed the "national letter" to President James Buchanan. On May 22, they exchanged documents of the treaty. After visiting the Capitol, the prison, an elementary school, and a Navy yard, they left for Baltimore by train on June 8, 1860. There they were welcomed with fireworks and a fire-fighters' show. They were also welcomed in Philadelphia, where they were

taken to the orphanage, the balloon show, and the U.S. Mint between June 9 and 16. All the news about the embassy was reported daily in the newspapers of the major cities. Since many of the New Yorkers read the news and were quite excited when the Japanese finally landed in Manhattan and paraded on Broadway, so Whitman most probably read the news and was excited when he wrote, "I too arising, answering, descend to the pavements, merge with the crowd, and gaze with them." The delegation left New York on June 29, and returned to Edo on November 8, 1860.

17. Masuzu Hisatoshi, "Diary During the Voyage to America," *Documents on American Mission, 1860* (Tokyo: Kazama Shobo, 1961), Vol. II, p. 115.

18. Muragaki, p. 164.

19. *New York Herald*, June 17, 1860.

20. Walt Whitman, "Specimen Days," July 23, 1878.

21. Charles A. Longfellow, telegram to Henry W. Longfellow, June 1, 1871. Houghton Library, Harvard University.

22. Henry W. Longfellow, letters to Charles A. Longfellow, August 9, 1871, January 19, 1872, January 18, 1873, and June 20, 1872. *Omedeto*, not *Medeto*, means *I wish you a happy new year* or *Congratulations*.

23. Charles A. Longfellow, letter to Henry W. Longfellow, July 19, 1872.

24. Charles A. Longfellow, letter to Alice Mary Longfellow, March 15, 1872. "Uncle T." is most probably Thomas Gold Appleton (1812–84) who "devoted his life to travel, philanthropy, and cultivation of literature." *The Letters of Henry Wadsworth Longfellow*, ed. Andrew Hilen (Cambridge: Harvard University Press, 1966), vol. 2, p. 10.

25. Charles A. Longfellow, letter to Henry W. Longfellow, February 10, 1873.

26. The entry for May 7 reads: "Trying to write a poem on the Potter's wheel—a poem of Ceramic Art." Samuel Longfellow, ed., *Life of Henry Wadsworth Longfellow* (New York: AMS Press, 1966), p. 274. Longfellow's growing interest in Japan may be reflected in his, and his surviving family's, inclusion of the books on Japan in his library collection. According to Arthur Christy, "The Oriental library of Henry Wadsworth Longfellow" included Bayard Taylor, *A Visit to India, China and Japan*, Edward Greey, *The Golden Lotus and Other Legends of Japan*, and James Ridley, *Tales of the Genji*. Arthur Christy, *The Orient in American Transcendentalism* (New York: Columbia University Press, 1932), pp. 321–23. Longfellow most probably read the first book on the list, for its author, who went to Japan with Perry, had been one of Longfellow's close friends.

27. Imari is originally the name of a seaport north of Nagasaki, from which the ceramics produced in the neighboring villages are exported.

28. The "Oedipus complex" of the Americans toward their European fathers is discussed fully in Tadashi Aruga, "The American Revolution and the American Spirit," in Shōichi Saeki, ed., *America and Europe: Essays on American Culture*, vol. 5. (Tokyo: Nan'undo, 1970), pp. 65–95.

29. *The Journal of Richard Henry Dana, Jr.*, ed. Robert E. Lucid (Cambridge: Harvard University Press, 1968), vol. 3, pp. 1004, 1005, 1008, 1015, and 1020.

30. *The Works of Washington Irving* (New York: AMS Press, 1973), vol. 3, p. 523.

31. Giacomo Puccini, *Madame Butterfly*, Act I.

32. Most of Fenollosa's notebooks are kept in the Beinecke Rare Book and Manuscript Library, Yale University, and in Houghton Library, Harvard University.

33. David Belasco, "Madame Butterfly," *Six Plays by David Belasco* (Boston: Little, Brown, 1928), p. 21; p. 32.

34. John Luther Long, *Madame Butterfly* (New York: Grosset and Dunlap, 1897; reprint 1903), pp. 14–19.

35. Belasco, p. 19.

36. For further discussion of dime novels and popular culture in America, see Henry Nash Smith, *Virgin Land: The American West as Symbol and Myth* (Cambridge: Harvard University Press, 1950), ch. ix, and also Shunsuke Kamei, *The Circus is Coming!—Essays on American Popular Culture* (Tokyo: Tokyo University Press, 1976), pp. 151–201.

37. Pound, *Gaudier-Brzeska: A Memoir* (1916; reprint New York: New Directions, 1960) p. 94.

38. Quoted from Earl Miner, *The Japanese Tradition in British and American Literature* (Princeton: Princeton University Press, 1958) p. 183.

39. See Miner, p. 191.

40. Amy Lowell, *Tendencies in Modern American Poetry* (1917; reprint New York: Octagon Books, 1971), pp. 336–37.

41. Dulles, p. 206.

42. *The Collected Poems of Yvor Winters* (Manchester: Carcanet New Press, 1978), p. 13.

Chapter 2

1. Louis Untermeyer, who was later to edit her *Complete Poetical Works*, said of this book that it could not even "rouse one at all," in the *Chicago Evening Post*. Jean Gould, *Amy: The World of Amy Lowell and the Imagist Movement* (New York: Dodd, Mead & Co., 1975), pp. 108–9.

2. Percy Bysshe Shelley, "Adonais," *The Complete Works of Percy Bysshe Shelley*, eds. Roger Ingpen and Walter E. Peck, vol. 2 (New York: Gordian Press, 1965), p. 404, lines 462–63.

3. F. Cudworth Flint, *Amy Lowell* (Minneapolis: University of Minnesota Press, 1969), pp. 13–14. According to Flint, Lowell came across the book in her father's library. However, Flint writes, "Unfortunately, Miss Lowell's studies were too largely grounded on a model that was nearly eighty years out of date."

4. The source of inspiration for this poem might be a landscape painting by Shōkei (fl. c. 1478) in the Fenollosa-Weld Collection of Boston Museum of Fine Art. His "Sansuizu" (39.2 × 91.4) shows a waterfall in the center, and a little winding path on the cliff on the left, which leads along the stream above the waterfall to the pass between high mountains. Two travellers are walking to-

ward the pass beyond which can be seen the roofs of the palace–like houses.

5. Percival Lowell, *Chosŏn, The Land of the Morning Calm: A Sketch of Korea* (Boston: Tichnor, 1885); *The Soul of the Far East* (Boston: Houghton Mifflin, 1888); *Noto: An Unexplored Corner of Japan* (Boston: Houghton Mifflin, 1891); *Occult Japan, or the Way of Gods: An Esoteric Study of Japanese Personality and Possession* (Boston: Houghton Mifflin, 1894).

6. Percival Lowell, letter to Amy Lowell, August 4, 1883.

7. Amy Lowell, Letter to Tsunejirō Miyaoka, January 13, 1921.

8. The same sentiment is expressed on various other occasions. See for instance her letters to Paul K. Hisada (August 13, 1917), Theodore Maynard (November 16, 1921), Kōchi Doi (1923). As to "a sort of atavism," probably she had in mind the fact that Comdr. Perry, about whom she heard many stories from her friend, August Belmont, was his grandfather. See Gould, pp. 3, 237.

9. Hilda Doolittle, unpublished letter to Amy Lowell, February 1, 1919.

10. Amy Lowell, Preface, *Can Grande's Castle* (New York: Macmillan, 1918), pp. xi, xiv–xv, xv.

11. John La Farge, *An Artist's Letters from Japan* (New York: Century, 1890, reprint 1897), pp. 8–9. La Farge arrived at Yokohama on July 2, 1886, with his friend, Henry Adams. This is an account of their first visit to "Tokio, which is about twenty miles off on July 4." In the copy bequeathed to Harvard University, Amy Lowell's signature is in the book: "Amy Lowell, Boston—1897." The castle moats had been kept deep during the feudal age in Japan. If a man had thrown a stone into the moat, he would have been arrested because its depth could be known by the sound.

12. Seichi Naruse, "Young Japan," *The Seven Arts* (April 1917), pp. 616–26. This is a Japanese version of "Young America," written by Van Wyck Brooks for the same magazine. Naruse traces an intellectual history of modern Japan from the restoration to the early twentieth century. He was a novelist, playwright, translator, and editor of a literary journal, *Shinshichō.* Amy Lowell acknowledges her debts in the preface to her *Can Grande's Castle:* "The inscription on the tree I have copied word for word from Mr. Naruse's translation" (pp. xvi–xvii). One of her poems, "Orange of Midsummer," also appeared in the same issue. *Guns as Keys* appeared in the August issue.

13. Naruse, p. 620.

14. Amy Lowell, Preface, *Can Grande's Castle*, p. xvi.

15. *The Complete Poetical Works of Amy Lowell*, ed. Louis Untermeyer (Boston: Houghton Mifflin, 1955), p. 172.

16. Amy Lowell, Preface, *Pictures of the Floating World*, (New York: Macmillan, 1919) p. viii.

17. According to a version of the story, Yoshimitsu was so "arrogant" that he did not correct the Chinese reference to him as emperor. Having built a gold pavilion, Kinkakuji, in Kyoto, he desired to see snow in the summer. The legend goes that his attendants covered the hill behind the garden with sheets of white silk, and hence it was called Kinukake Yama, or silk-covered mountain, which is today called Kinugasa Yama.

18. Abe no Nakamaro was blown back to China by a storm on his return trip to Japan, and decided to stay. On seeing his friend off to Japan, he wrote:

> I look up the endless sky
> And gaze at the moon—
> Which I used to see
> Above the Hills
> Of Mikasa in Kasuga.
> > (Ama no hara
> > Furisake mireba
> > Kasuga naru
> > Mikasa no yama ni
> > Ideshi tsuki kamo.)

Sōjō Henjō is comparing the court dancers to *tennyo*, the maidens of heaven:

> Blow and stop the cloud
> Oh, heavenly wind
> That I may see awhile
> The dancing maidens returning
> As if upon the cloud.
> > (Amatsu kaze
> > Kumo no kayoiji
> > Fuki toji yo
> > Otome no sugata
> > Shibashi todomen.)

19. Durnell, p. 61; Katsushika Hokusai, "Fuji in a Cup of Sake," *One Hundred Views of Fuji* (n.p., 1835), vol. 2, p. 7.

20. Katsushika Hokusai, "Five Nightingales and Pale Red Plum," *Wood-Block Prints on Flowers and Birds* (Tokyo: Kineido, 1891), pp. 72–73.

21. Amy Lowell, Letter to Arthur Davison Ficke, April 20, 1916, pp. 4–5.

22. Amy Lowell, Letter to Richard Aldington, February 17, 1919. S. Foster Damon, *Amy Lowell: A Chronicle* (Boston: Houghton Mifflin, 1935), p. 505.

23. Arthur Davison Ficke, *Chats on Japanese Prints* (London: Ernest Benn, 1915, reprint 1917), pp. 279, 328.

24. Perciva Lowell, *Soul*, pp. 148–49. According to a biographer, Lafcadio Hearn was greatly influenced by this book, which led him to Japan. See Abbott Lawrence Lowell, *Biography of Percival Lowell* (New York: Macmillan, 1935), p. 37.

25. Van Wyck Brooks, *New England: Indian Summer, 1865–1915* (New York: E. P. Dutton, 1940), p. 531. "The Yankee will" of Amy Lowell is reflected in many passages of her writings. For example: "No one expects a man to make a chair without first learning how, but there is a popular impression that the poet is born, not made, and that his verses burst from his overflowing heart of themselves. As a matter of fact, the poet must learn his trade in the same manner, and with the same painstaking care, as a cabinet-maker." Amy Lowell, *Sword Blades and Poppy Seed* (Boston: Houghton Mifflin, 1914), p. vii. She may have inherited "the Yankee will" from her family but her manner of writing the poetry of will may have been influenced by Ezra Pound. Cf. "Don't imagine

that the art of poetry is any simpler than the art of music, or that you can please the expert before you have spent at least as much effort on the art of verse as the average piano teacher spends on the art of music." Ezra Pound, "A Few Don'ts by an Imagist," *Poetry*, 1, no. 6 (March 1913), p. 202.

26. Adelaide Crapsey, *The Complete Poems and Collected Letters of Adelaide Crapsey*, ed. Susan Sutton Smith (Albany: State University of New York Press, 1977), p. 11.

27. Louis Untermeyer, *Modern American and British Poetry* (New York: Harcourt and Brace, 1920, reprint 1942), p. 255. Untermeyer had selected and published three of her poems in his anthology, *Modern American Poetry* (New York: Harcourt, Brace and Howe, 1919).

28. Crapsey, p. 25. Susan Sutton Smith refers to Mary Elizabeth Osborn in *Adelaide Crapsey* (Boston: Bruce Humphries, 1933).

29. Miner, p. 188.

30. Hideo Kawanami, "Adelaide Crapsey and Michel Revon: Their Connection with Japanese Literature," *Osaka College of Commerce Aniversary Festschrift*, vol. 19–20 (1963), pp. 223–27. He also points out (pp. 229–30) that the source of Crapsey's cinquain,

> Why have
> I thought the dew
> Ephemeral when I
> Shall rest so short a time, myself
> On earth?

is Revon's French translation,

> Comment ai-je pu penser
> Que la rosée
> Était chose éphémère,
> Quand moi-même sur l'herbe
> Je resterai si peu de temps?

the source of which is a tanka in *Kokinshu* by Fujiwara no Koremoto:

> Mimakarinan tote yomeru
> Tsuyu o nado
> Ada naru mono to
> Omoi ken
> Wagami mo kusa ni
> Okanu bakari o.

31. Crapsey, p. 27.

32. Crapsey, p. 33.

33. Crapsey, p. 11.

34. T. S. Eliot, *After Strange Gods: A Primer of Modern Heresy* (London: Faber and Faber, 1934), pp. 40–41.

35. T. S. Eliot, "Ezra Pound," *Poetry*, 68 (September 1946), cited in Walter Sutton, ed., *Ezra Pound: A Collection of Critical Essays* (Englewood Cliffs, N. J.: Prentice-Hall, 1963), p. 19.

Chapter 3

1. Dulles, p. 211; and *Philadelphia Inquirer*, June 14 and 15, 1860.

2. Pound, "A Pact," *Ezra Pound: Selected Poems*, ed. T. S. Eliot (London: Faber and Faber, 1928; reprint 1959).

3. Pound, "What I Feel about Walt Whitman," *Ezra Pound: Selected Prose, 1909–1965*, ed. William Cookson (London: Faber and Faber, 1973), p. 115.

4. Pound, "A Pact."

5. Noel Stock, *The Life of Ezra Pound* (New York: Pantheon Books, 1970), p. 61; and J. B. Harmer, *Victory in Limbo: A History of Imagism, 1908–1917* (New York: St. Martin's Press, 1975), p. 30.

6. This episode is related in the section called "Vorticism" in Pound, *Gaudier-Brzeska*, pp. 81–94, is the revised version of his essay, "Vorticism," *Fortnightly Review*, September 1, 1914. But in both versions Pound writes "three years ago" referring to the experience in question. Miner, pp. 112–15, dates it in 1911, perhaps correctly.

7. See William Pratt, ed., *The Imagist Poem: Modern Poetry in Miniature* (New York: E. P. Dutton, 1963), pp. 30–31. The first to point out the significance of the episode was Earl Miner, "Pound, *Haiku*, and the Image," *Hudson Review*, 9 (Winter 1956–57), pp. 570–84.

8. Pound, *Gaudier-Brzeska*, pp. 87 and 89.

9. According to Kazuo Sato, the naval officer probably was Hiroharu Kato, who was to become admiral of the Japanese navy, but was stationed in London, 1909–11. He was also a haiku poet. Kazuo Sato, *Can Rapeflower be Transplanted?* (Tokyo: Ōfūsha, 1978), p. 19.

10. One of the haiku Pound had in mind was that of Takeari Arakida (not Moritake Arakida as erroneously known, especially abroad): "The fallen blossom flies back to its branch: A Butterfly." Otoo Fujii, "'The Fallen Blossom' is not a Haiku by Moritake," *Studies of Haiku* (May 1941), pp. 163–65. The piece had been translated into German by Karl Florenz (*Dichtergrusse aus dem Osten, Japanische Dichtungen*, 1896); into French by Paul-Louis Couchoud ("Les Haikai: Les Epigrammes poetique du Japon," *Les Lettres*, April 1906); into English by F. S. Flint ("Book of the Week: Recent Verse, *The New Age*, July 11, 1908), and by W. G. Aston (*A History of Japanese Literature*, 1899). Probably Pound read Flint's version, which was a translation from the French doctor's version, and which was, fortunately, in the "form of superposition." See Harmer, pp. 126–36; Yasuo Iwahara, "The Relation between Imagist Poets and Haiku," *Kōgakuin University Kenkyū Ronso* 17 (1979), pp. 1–2.

11. Pound, *Gaudier-Brzeska*, p. 89.

12. Ezra Pound, *The Letters of Ezra Pound, 1907–1941*, ed. D. D. Paige (New York: Harcourt, Brace and World, 1950), p. 10. Letter to Harriet Monroe, September [24], 1912.

13. Pound, "Tagore's Poetry," *Poetry* 1, no. 3 (December 1912), pp. 93–94.

14. Pound, "What I Feel," p. 116.

15. Stock, p. 129. According to Donald Gallup, ed., *A Bibliography of*

Ezra Pound (London: Rupert Hart-Davis, 1963), p. 203, "Certain Poems of Kabir" was published in *Modern Review*, Calcutta, 13, no. 6 (June 1913).

16. T. S. Eliot, "Ezra Pound: His Metric and Poetry," *To Criticize the Critic* (London: Faber and Faber, 1965), p. 177. The essay was first published anonymously in 1917 from Alfred A. Knopf. Kainan Mori (1863–1911), a poet himself, was one of the greatest sinologists of the Meiji period in Japan, and was the author of a number of books, including commentaries of T'ang period poetry.

17. Eliot, "Ezra Pound," p. 177.

18. Lawrence Chisolm, *Fenollosa: The Far East and American Culture* (New Haven: Yale University Press, 1963), p. 222. Based on Mary Fenollosa's unpublished manuscript essay, "Ezra Pound."

19. *Writers at Work: The Paris Review Interviews* (London: Secker & Warburg, 1963), p. 45. Quoted from "Ezra Pound's notes for edition of lecture, 1958–59." Chronologically speaking, Mary Fenollosa probably had read some of Pound's writings, such as his essay on Tagore, before she met Pound at Naidu's in London. When they met, Pound "questioned her at length about her husband's work and their life in Japan." She answered, and might have questioned him about his poetry and poetic principles. After the meeting, Pound sent her some of his works, including those which appeared in the April issue of *Poetry*, "subsequently incorporated in Lustra." After "a couple of weeks," and after she read them, she let him know, probably by writing him a letter, that she wished to meet him again. When they met a second time, and, as Stock writes, "after three weeks' acquaintance," Mary Fenollosa "decided" to give him "a free hand to edit and publish the material." (Stock, p. 148.) She herself might have handed some of the material to Pound while in London. But the bulk of it she mailed from America to Pound and he received it in early December 1913. Of all the accounts available now about the meeting of Pound and Mary Fenollosa, the most dependable source of information seems Pound's response at the interview with D. G. Bridson:

> "I read Giles' history and I wasn't content with the translation. I wanted to know how I could get some Chinese, but I knew if he knew he would keep it to himself! And within a few weeks I was at Sarajini Naidu's and I met Mrs. Fenollosa. Fenollosa had been scrapping with academic fatheads and he'd left his manuscript with her and she'd sat on it. She hadn't turned it over to anybody ... and after a couple of weeks I got a note: would I come to that hotel in Trafalgar Square—is it Moreley's?—at any rate, it is where my grandfather stayed. There she was, gone like a priestess at an altar, and she merely said, 'You're the only person who can finish this stuff the way Ernest wanted it done.' Then she sent me his manuscript—that's the whole story." D. G. Bridson, ed., "An Interview with Ezra Pound," James Laughlin, ed., *New Directions* 17 (New York: New Directions, 1959), p. 177.

20. Pound, *Letters*, p. 27; p. 31. Letter to Harriet Monroe. The Nō play is a classical Japanese theater, existent since the fourteenth century. The players,

wearing masks, act and dance accompanied by chorus, flute and drum. The stage is simple and often symbolic.

21. K. K. Ruthven, *A Guide to Ezra Pound's "Personae" (1926)* (Berkeley: University of California Press, 1969), pp. 31, 68, and 188. The source of "After Ch'u Yuan" is "Mountain Gods" in H. A. Giles's *A History of Chinese Literature* (London: William Heineman, 1901), pp. 52–53; and also Giles's *Chinese Poetry in English Verse* (London: B. Quaritich, 1898), p. 35. The source of "Fan-Piece for Her Imperial Lord" is a ten-line poem by The Lady Pan in Giles, *a History*, p. 101; and that of "Liu Ch'e," a poem by a Han Emperor in Giles, *a History*, p. 100. See also Wai-lim Yip, *Ezra Pound's Cathay* (Princeton: Princeton University Press, 1969), pp. 60–65.

22. T. S. Eliot, Introduction to *Ezra Pound: Selected Poems*, p. 15; F. R. Leavis, *New Bearings in English Poetry* (London: Chatto and Windus, 1959), p. 136; Yvor Winters, *In Defence of Reason* (Denver: University of Denver Press, 1947), pp. 494–95. As for other eulogical criticisms, see Glenn Hughes, *Imagism and the Imagists* (Stanford: Stanford University Press, 1931), pp. 234–35; Hugh Kenner, *The Poetry of Ezra Pound* (Norfolk: New Directions, 1951), p. 137; Babette Deutsch, *Poetry in Our Time* (New York: Columbia University Press, 1958), p. 128.

23. From Ernest Fenollosa's unpublished notebook, file 8, "Early Chinese Poetry / Kutsugen / KA-GI / E. F. F. / translation by Ariga." The following quotation from Fenollosa's notebook is also from file 8.

24. Peter Makin, *Provence and Pound* (Berkeley: University of California Press, 1978), p. 36. Hugh Kenner also thinks that "Song of the Bowmen of Shu," as well as "Lament of the Frontier Guard," "South Folk in Cold Country," and "Exile's Letter" are "among the most durable of all poetic responses to World War I." Hugh Kenner, *The Pound Era* (Berkeley: University of California Press, 1971), p. 202.

25. Ezra Pound, (trans., *Cathay* (London: Elkin Mathews, 1915), [p. 32].

26. Achilles Fang, "Fenollosa and Pound," *Harvard Journal of Asian Studies* 20 (1957), p. 228.

27. Fenollosa, Notebook, file 21, pp. 104 and 103.

28. Fenollosa, Notebook, file 21, p. 102.

29. Concerning Li Po's death, Fenollosa writes:

So he determined to live and end his life among those mts. [Hanan, Yangtsu Valley]. There he died at any age somewhat over 60. But a more commonly accepted version: that he was, as usual, taking pleasure in ferry boat along the Yangtsu, and one night as the moon was so fine, and he was at the very extreme of his poetical hilarity, he wanted to grasp the moon on the water, and lost in balance, and was drowned." (Notebook, file 20, pp. 13–14).

But the source of Pound's "Epitaphs" is more probably Giles's *History*. Giles gives his translation of Fu I (Fu Eki)'s own epitaph:

Fu I loved the green hills and the white clouds ... Alas! he died of drink. (p. 135).

As for Li Po, Giles writes:

> After more wanderings and much adventure, he was drowned on a journey, from leaning one night too far over the edge of a boat in a drunken effort to embrace the reflection of the moon. (p. 153).

Note Pound's use of Giles's way of romanization of the personal names.

Fu I

Fu I loved the high cloud and the hill.
Alas, he died of alcohol.

Li Po

And Li Po also died drunk.
He tried to embrace a moon
In the Yellow River.

30. Ezra Pound, *Patria Mia and the Treatise on Harmony* (London: Peter Owen, 1962), pp. 23–24. Though published late, the manuscript of "Patria Mia" had been "posted" by Pound in 1913 to his publisher in Chicago.

31. Fenollosa, Notebook, file 21, pp. 103–4.

32. Bernetta Quinn, *Ezra Pound: An Introduction to the Poetry* (New York: Columbia University Press, 1972), p. 96.

33. Eric Homberger, ed., *Ezra Pound: The Critical Heritage* (London: Routledge and Kegan Paul, 1972), p. 111. The passage cited is from A. R. Orage, *The Art of Reading* (New York: Farrar and Reinhart, 1930), pp. 143–45.

34. Homberger, p. 221. From Ford Madox Ford, "Ezra," *New York Herald Tribune Books* (January 9, 1927), sec. vii.

35. Ezra Pound, "Chinese Poetry," *Today* 3, No. 4, (April 1918) p. 95.

36. Donald Davie, *Ezra Pound: Poet as Sculptor* (London: Routledge and Kegan Paul, 1965), p. 44.

37. Kokumin Bunko Kankō-kai, eds. *Chinese Classics in Japanese Translation* (in Japanese), 2nd ser., vol. 1 (Tokyo: Kokumin Bunko Kankō-kai, 1928), p. 405. See also Ayscough-Lowell translation, which Achilles Fang fails to mention in his list of translations of the poem into English:

> At fifteen, I stopped frowning.
> I wanted to be with you, as dust with its ashes
> I often thought that you were the faithful man
> who clung to the bridge post,
> That I should never be obliged to ascend
> to the Looking-for-Husband Ledge.

Amy Lowell, *Complete Poetical Works of Amy Lowell*, ed. Louis Untermeyer (Boston: Houghton Mifflin, 1955), p. 335. Florence Ayscough's Chinese teacher was Nung Chu.

38. Shōji Yamana points out the desire of "physical union" in Pound's line, "I desired my dust to be mingled with yours." Shoji Yamana, "The Meaning and the Structure of Ezra Pound's 'The River-Merchant's Wife: A Letter'," *American Literature* (Tokyo Chapter of American Literature As-

sociation of Japan), No. 29. Shiro Tsunoda, however, thinks that there is "no erotic connotation" in the line, and that it simply means that the speaker desired both she and her husband "would be dust and ashes together when they die." Shirō Tsunoda, "'The River-Merchant's Wife: A Letter' Reconsidered," *Journal of Obirin University: English and American Numbers*, vol. 15. Although the erotic overtones are hardly noticeable, Pound's repetition of "forever" in the following line seems to express the presence of eternity rather than the eternity of the future.

39. Yip translates the line as "In the eighth month, butterflies come," (p. 194) based on the text 「八月蝴蝶来」. But the text Kainan Mori and Fenollosa used was a different version with 「八月蝴蝶黄」: "In the eighth month, the butterflies are yellow."

40. Ezra Pound, "Hugh Selwyn Mauberley," second sequence, sec. 2.

41. "Chokanko" is in the manuscript notebook of Ernest Fenollosa, File 20, pp. 128–35.

42. Yip, pp. 148, 157; Kenner, *Pound Era*, p. 204; Peter Brooker, *A Student's Guide to the Selected Poems of Erza Pound* (London: Faber and Faber, 1979), p. 135.

43. Fenollosa, Notebook, File 21, pp. 2–10.

44. Wai-lim Yip, without reading Fenollosa's manuscript, argues that "The River Song" is "The 'howler'," but he notices correctly "a contrast between two forms of life" in the poem set in "superposition." Yip, pp. 157–58.

45. Kokumin Bunko Kankō-Kai, eds., *Chinese Classics*, vol. 25, p. 643.

46. Fenollosa, Notebook, File 21, pp. 2–4.

47. Masaru Aoki, ed., *An Anthology of Chinese Poetry*, vol. 8 (Tokyo: Shūeisha, 1965), pp. 164–65. Cf. Toshio Takebe, ed. and trans., *An Anthology of Chinese Poets*, 2 vols. (Tokyo: Iwanami-shoten, 1957, 1958).

48. Fenollosa, Notebook, File 21, pp. 5–10.

49. T. E. Hulme, *Speculations: Essays on Humanism and the Philosophy of Art*, ed. Herbert Read (London: Routledge and Kegan Paul, 1924, reprint 1954), pp. 113–40. Harmer, pp. 17–44.

50. Hulme, p. 115; and T. S. Eliot, "What is a Classic?" *Essays on Poetry and Criticism*, ed. Kazumi Yano (Tokyo: Shōhaku-sha, 1959; rpt. 1971), p. 68.

51. Charles Norman, *Ezra Pound* (New York: Macmillan, 1960), p. 122; Ezra Pound, "Serious Artist," *Literary Essays of Ezra Pound*, ed. T. S. Eliot (Norfolk, Conn.: New Directions, 1954), p. 50; "How to Read," p. 23; and *Letters*, p. 91.

52. Personal interview with Ezra Pound, September 1, 1968, Rapallo. I asked him, "Aren't you at heart a romanticist?" He answered, "Possibly."

53. Pound, *Literary Essays*, p. 420; *Letters*, p. 36; and *Patria Mia*, pp. 26–27.

54. Pound, *Selected Poems*, p. 19.

55. Pound, *Letters*, p. 82. Pound's letter to Iris Barry, June 1916.

56. Ernest Fenollosa, *The Chinese Written Character as a Medium for Poetry*, ed. by Ezra Pound (San Francisco: City Lights Books, 1964), pp. 9, 16, and 23. Since its first publication in 1919 in the *Little Review*, Fenollosa's essay has been criticized by sinologists. George Kennedy, for instance, writes, regarding this passage, that "only 364 [out of 9,353], or 3.9 per cent of the characters could

at that time [around A.D. 100] be traced to a pictorial origin." George Kennedy, "Fenollosa, Pound and the Chinese Character," *Yale Literary Magazine* 126 (1958), p. 29. But, by "primitive Chinese characters," Fenollosa obviously meant, not the Han period characters, but the hieroglyphs on tortoise shells and animal bones about 1300 B.C. Most of the sinologists' attacks on Fenollosa's theory about Chinese characters are based on valid grounds but miss the point. The important thing in Fenollosa's essay is not his theory but the poetics he developed from it.

57. Fenollosa, *Chinese Written Character*, pp. 17, 9, and 15–16.

58. Fenollosa, *Chinese Written Character*, p. 24. Printed here from Fenollosa's manuscript notebook.

59. Fenollosa, Notebook, File 14.

60. Pound published the poem "Mesmerism" in 1908, which "takes the form of an homage to Robert Browning." Ruthven, p. 170. But in 1916, Pound wrote to Iris Barry, "The hell is that one catches Browning's manner and mannerisms. At least I've suffered the disease." Pound, *Letters*, p. 90. Later Pound was to write, "Hang it all, Robert Browning," in Canto 2.

61. Pound, *Literary Essays*, pp. 4–12. For instance Pound wrote, "Use no superfluous word, no adjective which does not reveal something." (p. 4.) Or "the poetry which I expect to see written during the next decade or so . . . will be harder and saner. . . . It will be as much like granite as it can be." (p. 12.) See also Harmer.

62. Pound, *Gaudier-Brzeska*, pp. 88–90. For instance, Pound wrote, "Vorticism is an art before it has spread itself into flaccidity, into elaboration and second applications." (p. 88.) See also Timothy Materer, *Vortex: Pound, Yeats, and Eliot* (Ithaca: Cornell University Press, 1970), pp. 23–25.

63. After Pound read French poetry with T. S. Eliot in 1917 (though Pound had read it before), he wrote "Hugh Selwyn Mauberley" under the strong influence of Theophile Gautier. See J. J. Espey, *Ezra Pound's Mauberley: A Study of Composition* (Berkeley: University of California Press, 1955), pp. 25–48. Though "Hugh Selwyn Mauberley" is known as Pound's farewell to England, it is also his farewell to the Pound who had lived through the London years, presenting the failure of an artist who much resembles an aspect of Pound himself. "The little poetic renaissance," insofar as Pound was concerned, was not sudden revolution, but a succession of steady absorption and sloughing off.

64. "Ezra Pound," *Writers at Work: The Paris Review Interviews*, p. 45.

65. See Sanehide Kodama, "The Chinese Subject in Ezra Pound's Poetry," *Studies in English Literature* (The English Literary Society of Japan), English Number, 1970, pp. 50–53.

66. Yip, pp. 159–60. L. S. Dembo had found a similar method applied in Pound's later translation of Confucian odes: "Pound had tried to render the so-called motion picture quality of the Chinese, mentioned by Fenollosa, by dividing each line into two idea or image complexes so that each side of the line would resemble, as far as possible in English, an ideogram, and the whole poem appear to be a flow of such ideograms." L. S. Dembo, *The Confucian Odes of Ezra Pound: A Critical Appraisal* (Berkeley: University of California Press, 1963), p. 27.

67. Compare Pound's lines with Fenollosa's:

ko	–jo	ku	tai	baku
desolate	castle	sky	large	desert
		vacant		

"I see a ruined fortress in a vast black desert"
(Fenollosa, "14th Kofu," File 20.)

Sands surprised by wind cover in their turmoil
the desert Sea sun
(Fenollosa, "Another Kofu 6th," File 20.)

hi	sui	gi	ran	cho
red bird	green bird	play	orchid	clover or a kind of pea

a kind of kingfisher to be merry
Red and green kingfishers play among the orchids
and clovers
(Fenollosa, "Yu sen shi," file 17.)

68. See also Fenollosa, *Chinese Written Character*, p. 23, Pound's footnotes; and p. 29.

69. Pound, *Patria Mia*, pp. 26–27; Pound, "The Renaissance," *Literary Essays*, pp. 215, 220, and 224. This essay was first published in *Poetry* 5 (February–May, 1915).

70. See Ezra Pound, "Four Periods," *ABC of Reading* (London: Routledge and Sons, 1934), pp. 118–19.

71. Ezra Pound and Ernest Fenollosa, trans., *The Classic Noh Theatre of Japan* (New York: New Directions, 1959), p. 151.

72. Norman, p. 183; and Helen Caldwell, *Michio Ito, The Dancer and His Dances* (Berkeley: University of California Press, 1977), pp. 37–54. As to the Japanese adaptations of "At the Hawk's Well," see Yukio Ōura, "The Theme of 'At the Hawk's Well'," *Report of Yeats Society of Japan*, no. 5, pp. 10–15.

73. Ezra Pound, Introduction, Pound and Fenollosa, trans., *The Classic Noh*, p. 3.

74. Regarding the influence of Nō on Pound, Earl Miner points out: "This method of unifying diverse materials through meaningful archetypes is another example of Pound's deriving a technique of form from Japanese literature, in this case 'what we call Unity of Image,' the technique which he felt the nō had to offer to make a long Vorticist poem possible. The range of such archetypal, unifying images in the *Cantos* is considerable." And he gives three examples of "such unifying images"—"the heavenly earth-visitor, 'the sacred influence of light,'—and the gold mean." See Earl Miner, *The Japanese Tradition*, pp. 144–52. His argument is quite inspiring. It should be noted, however, that what Pound calls unity of image found in the Nō play is not anything that suggests a unifying function, as an archetype that unifies diverse materials in the Nō, but it is the repeated and intensified single image like the waves in *Suma Genji*, along with which the play proceeds, and with which the atmosphere of the play is created. Regarding the influence of Nō on "Near

Perigord," see Yasuo Iwahara, "The Poetic Structure of 'Near Perigord'," *Kogakuin University Kenkyū Ronsō*, no. 18 (1981), pp. 1–32.

75. Carroll F. Terrell, *A Companion to the Cantos of Ezra Pound*, vol. 1 (Berkeley: University of California Press, 1980), p. 12. The source cited is: Camille Chabaneau, *Le Biographies de Troubadours en Langue Provençale* (Toulouse, 1885).

76. Pound, *Letters*, pp. 3–4. Pound wrote to William Carlos Williams, October 21, 1908, "To me the short so-called dramatic lyric—at any rate the sort of thing I do—is the poetic part of a drama the rest of which (to me the prose part) is left to the reader's imagination or implied or set in a short note. I catch the character I happen to be interested in at the moment he interests me, usually a moment of song or self analysis, or sudden understanding or revelation."

77. George Dekker, "Myth and Metamorphosis," Eva Hesse, ed., *New Approaches to Ezra Pound* (London: Faber and Faber, 1969), p. 281; and Walter Baumann, *The Rose in the Steel Dust: An Examination of the Cantos of Ezra Pound* (Corol Gables: University of Miami Press, 1970), p. 29.

78. The Nō play is also called *Aioi*, or "the hermaphroditic pine tree." A traveling Shinto priest comes to Takasago, and meets an old man and his wife cleaning the beach surrounding an old pine tree. The priest, realizing that it is the famous "hermaphroditic" pine, asks the old couple why it is called a hermaphrodite although its better half grows in Sumiyoshi across the bay. The old man gives the enigmatic reply that it is so called because he is there with her, though he lives in Sumiyoshi. The pines at Takasago and Sumiyoshi had long been the symbols of longevity and marital happiness. The old couple turn out to be the spirits of the pine trees, and disappear in the mist. The god of Sumiyoshi reappears, dances, and declares prosperity and long life for all men. The Nō play is based on several works of the classical Japanese literature with allusions to the legend. One of the sources is a poem in *Ise Monogatari (The Tale of Ise)*, ed. Minoru Watanabe (Tokyo: Shinchō-sha, 1976), Ch. 117.

> I wonder how old
> The female pine should be
> On the beach of Sumiyoshi.
> For many years have passed
> Since I first saw her.
>
> (Ware mitemo
> Hisashiku narinu
> Sumiyoshi no
> Kishi no himematsu
> Ikuyo henuramu.)

And another poem in reply to the above:

> Didn't you know that she and I
> Have loved
> Since we were married
> In the shrine
> Ages ago?

(Mutsumaji to
Kimi wa shiranami
Mizugaki no
Hisashiki yo yori
Iwai someteki.)

Pound mistakenly writes "The pines at Takasago / grows with the pines of Isé!" apparently misled by the title of the source: *The Tale of Ise*.

79. The source of the passage by Sō-Gyoku (Sung Yü in Chinese) is also in Fenollosa's Notebook, File 17.

> Jo King of So went to the palace of Rantai (orchid
>   storied house or villa)
> So Gioku & Keisa waited upon him.
>
>   .   .   .
>
> The king then opened his collar and facing [the
>   wind] said
> How pleasant this wind!
> Is this what I partake of with the common people?
> Sogioku responded and said
> This is the wind of the great king only.
> How can common people get and partake of it [?]
> The King said, "Well, this wind is the breath of
>   heaven and earth
> Universally expanding it comes
> It comes not for noble or poor, high or low but
>   blows on them.
> And now you alone make out that this is a wind of
>   mine.
> Is there any opinion (of you) possible?"
> [So Gioku] answer[ed]
>   "
>   .   .   .
>
> It [the wind] blows on slowly refreshing the passes
>   and valleys, and gets violent in the mouth
>   of the mt. caves [earth bag's mouth]—
> Floating lightly it lifts itself, rises and falls,
> Rides climbing up to [a] high castle,
>
>   .   .   .
>
> and soar up to the tip of the fountain's jet,
>
>   .   .   .
>
> It fords through the gauze curtains and gets through
>   to the inner chamber
> And then for the first time it can become the great
>   king's wind for sure...."

80. Baumann, pp. 20 and 52.
81. Based on the report of Pound's account of his *Cantos* by Yeats.

William Butler Yeats, "A Packet for Ezra Pound," *A Vision* (London: Mac-Millan, 1925, reprint 1974), pp. 4–5.

82. According to Noel Stock, the Pounds visited Toulouse, Nîmes, Arles, and Avignon in May 1919. He writes, "And later [they] went to the Pyrenees. Some of the time they slept in the open." They must have passed through Roussillon, Cabestanh's country and crossed the Garonne, referred to in Canto 4. Stock, p. 224.

83. Pound, *Letters*, p. 4. Pound's letter to William Carlos Williams, October 21, 1908.

84. Hugh Kenner, "More on the Seven Lakes Canto," *Paideuma*, 2, no. 1 (Spring 1972), p. 44.

85. Stock, p. 328.

86. On the excellent analysis and interpretation of Canto 49, see George Dekker, *Sailing after Knowledge* (London: Routledge and Kegan Paul, 1963), pp. 179–81; and D. D. Pearlman, *Barb of Time: On the Unity of Ezra Pound's Cantos* (New York: Oxford University Press, 1969), pp. 193–210. A general description of the manuscript book is in Appendix B in Pearlman, pp. 304–11. When I told Mr. Pearlman about the material in 1968, however, many aspects of it were unknown. But since then, under the guidance of Profs. Kojiro Yoshi-kawa, Takeji Tamamura, Junji Tanaka, and Mr. Megumu Nakamura, I have learned some new facts about the authorship, interpretations of the poems, etc. With gratitude to them and apologies to Mr. Pearlman and his readers, I would like to set the record straight.

87. The photograph copies of the original manuscripts in Pound's posses-sion (after his parents' death) were supplied to me by Mrs. Mary de Rachewiltz in 1968. One of them is a photograph of the cover on which is written "Source of 7 lakes canto." They lack two paintings for the sixth and seventh scenes, a Chinese poem corresponding to the seventh scene, and a Japanese poem corre-sponding to the fifth scene. The original must contain them, for Pound uses some parts of them in the canto. The Chinese poems and black ink paintings are drawn on silk, and the Japanese poems on Japanese rice paper. The Japanese poems might have been written after the poets had seen the paintings and the Chinese poems.

88. Genryū Sasaki, *Poems in Chinese and Japanese on the Eight Famous Scenes by Genryū* (Kyoto: Asami, 1683).
The author and probably the editor of the book, Sasaki, (1650–1723), was reputedly a master of penmanship.

89. The "jewel dust" means snow. The last line alludes to an episode of Wang Hui-Chih (O-Kishi). One night when the snow stopped falling, he saw the moon, started to drink and composed a poem. Then he wanted to see his friend, Tai An-tao (Tai-Ando). He rowed his boat from Shan-yin (San In), walked to the gate of his friend's. But he returned home without seeing him. When asked why, he replied, "I come as I feel interested, and I leave as I lose interest. Why should I necessarily see Antao?"

90. That is, the moon is reflected on the waves.

91. The legend behind the poem is about the two daughters of King Yao (Gyo), E-Huan (Gako), and Nü-Ying (Joei). They were married to Shun, their

father's successor, for whom they used to play pipes and strings. When they were around the Hsiao-Hsiang area, they heard that their husband was dead. They wept and their teardrops dyed the bamboo leaves. Thus there still grow the dappled purple bamboos in the area. Later they killed themselves, and their shrine is said to be near the river. The narrator of the poem is on his way to the shrine, and is filled with sorrow.

92. According to one interpretation, the poem refers to the ruin of a Buddhist temple on top of Mount Chiu-i (Kyūgi) in the Hsiao-Hsiang area, and the bell the narrator hears is from a nearby temple.

93. That is, the fishermen are shouting as they gather in fish and shrimps.

94. Pearlman, pp. 195–96.

95. Atsuo Kurumizawa, "Odysseus-Pound as Outis *The Pisan Cantos*," *Studies in Language and Culture* (Faculty of Language and Culture, Osaka University, 1976), p. 77.

96. Ichisada Miyazaki, *Prosperity of the Empire of Shin* (Tokyo: Jinbutsu Oraisha, 1967); and Shigeki Kaizuka, *A History of China*, 3 vols. (Tokyo: Iwanami, 1971). The emperor is referred to also in Cantos 58–61, 98–99.

97. Ayako Tomii, et al., "Guide to *The Cantos* of Ezra Pound: Glosses of Cantos 3, 4, 5, 13, 16, 23, 30, 33, 37, 38, 49, 50, and 75, prepared by Yale students under the direction of N. H. Pearson" (New Haven: Yale University, 1954). Angela Chih-Ying Jung, "Ezra Pound and China," dissertation presented at University of Washington, 1955. Fang, pp. 231–32.

98. Fenollosa, Notebook, File 11. Fenollosa later gave a series of lectures in the United States on Chinese poetry, based on the notes. The poem appears also in the synopses for the lectures, Pound Center, Yale University.

99. There is no necessity of quoting the "Kei Wun Ka" in the Fenollosa notebook, for the whole poem in his notebook is already printed in Hugh Kenner, "More on the Seven Lakes Canto." But I should correct a minor error in his reading: the first word in the last line on p. 45, *Paideuma* 2, no. 1, should be "tree," not "tsu." Also, on the same page, the name of the successor to the Emperor Shun is not Yu, but Wu.

100. Giles, *A History*, p. 59.

101. Fenollosa, Notebook, file 11.

102. Ezra Pound, "Hugh Selwyn Mauberley," lines 7 and 27–28.

Chapter 4

1. Kenneth Rexroth, "The Influence of Classical Japanese Poetry on Modern American Poetry," *The Elastic Retort: Essays in Literature and Ideas* (New York: The Seaburg Press, 1973), p. 149, p. 157. The essay was originally a speech delivered in Japan, and included in the report of International Conference for Japanologists, *Studies on Japanese Culture*, vol. 1 (Tokyo: Japan PEN Club, 1973), pp. 374–92.

2. Kenneth Rexroth, *The Phoenix and the Tortoise* (Norfolk, Conn. New Directions, 1944), pp. 13 and 14.

3. Rexroth, *Phoenix and Tortoise*, p. 14. According to Rexroth, this passage is based on what he witnessed at Thornton Beach, southwest of San Francisco. At the beginning of World War II from 1941 to 1942, "many Japanese submarines were attacking the American ships" along California's coast. "The Japanese sailors did not seem to have any idea of returning home alive." (Interview on June 16, 1978).

4. Rexroth, *Phoenix and Tortoise*, p. 14. According to Rexroth, this is based on his own experience. To the south of San Pedro Point, southwest of San Francisco, is "a large granite plateau" from which "sand slides down to the Pacific." He went camping once with his wife there with sleeping bags. (In California they camp without tents.) But the area has been "destroyed by the developers." (Interview, June 16, 1978).

5. Morgan Gibson, *Kenneth Rexroth* (New York: Twayne Publishers, 1972), p. 60.

6. Rexroth, *Phoenix and Tortoise*, p. 22.

7. Kenneth Rexroth, trans., *One Hundred Poems from the Japanese* (New York: New Directions, 1964), p. 37. In his notes, Rexroth makes a comment on the poem. "The word translated 'shore birds' is *chidori*, which means sandpipers, plovers, birds like our killdeer and phalaropes." (p. 120).

8. Rexroth, *Phoenix and Tortoise*, p. 29.

9. Rexroth, *One Hundred Poems*, p. 67.

10. Rexroth, *Phoenix and Tortoise*, pp. 34–35.

11. Rexroth, *One Hundred Poems*, pp. 9, 69, 45, and 64.

12. Rexroth, *One Hundred Poems*, p. xix.

13. Rexroth, *One Hundred Poems*, pp. 132–40. Included in the bibliography are: F. V. Dickins, trans., *Japanese Odes, A Translation of the Hyakuninisshiu* (London: Smith Elder, 1866); William N. Porter, *A Hundred Verses from Old Japan: A Translation of the Hyakunin Isshiu* (Oxford: Clarendon, 1909). His wartime memory was told to me at Rakucho Bekkan, Kyoto, June 13, 1978.

14. Yū Suwa, "Tomo Empo yori Kitaru," (A Friend comes from a Distance), p. 128.

15. Kenneth Rexroth, *Beyond the Mountains* (New York: New Directions, 1951), pp. 66, 80, 69–70, and 83.

16. Gibson, p. 74.

17. According to his talk on April 23, 1978, in Kyoto, Rexroth produced "At the Hawk's well" in the studio for painting in his house "off Michigan Avenue" in Chicago. He thought it was "the ideal stage," for it was indicated that the play be acted in the drawing room. The part of the hawk was played by "a student at University of Chicago, Edna," and Rexroth acted the part of Cuchullain. Jun Fujita was "advisor." "Michio Ito came to Chicago, but he didn't know the Nō plays." Rexroth invented the flexible masks with "cortex." He used flute, recorder, drum, and zittern for "orchestra, which served also as chorus."

18. Rexroth, "Nō Plays," *Elastic Retort*, p. 146.

19. Rexroth, *Beyond Mountains*, p. 9.

20. Kenneth Rexroth, Introduction, *The Collected Longer Poems of Kenneth Rexroth* (New York: New Directions, 1968), p. 2.

21. Lawrence Ferlinghetti and Nancy J. Peters, *Literary San Francisco* (San Francisco: City Lights Books, 1980), p. 167.

22. Kenneth Rexroth, "Disengagement: The Art of the Beat Generation," *The Alternative Society: Essays from the Other World* (New York: Herder and Herder, 1972), p. 2.

23. Rexroth did not like to be referred to as the "father" of the beats, as he was sometimes called. As a matter of fact, he "turned against the Beat Generation when he returned from his second sojourn in Europe." William Everson, "Rexroth: Shaker and Maker," *For Rexroth: The Ark 14*, ed. Geoffrey Gardner (New York: The Ark, 1980), p. 25. About 1959 Rexroth wrote, "I will not take those would-be allies which Madison Avenue has carefully manufactured and is now trying to foist on me." Rexroth, Introduction to *Bird in the Bush* (New York: New Directions, 1959), p. ix. According to Morgan Gibson, "You do not 'nonconform,' he [Rexroth] wrote in 'Revolt: True and False,' by 'caricaturing the values of the very civilization that debauched you in the first place.... The essence of revolt is understanding!'" *Nation*, April 26, 1958, p. 378; Gibson, p. 94. But Rexroth gave consent to his wife Carol Tinker, who claimed he was the "librarian" for them.

24. Rexroth, *The Heart's Garden / The Garden's Heart, Collected Longer Poems*, p. 283.

25. Lao-tzu (Rōshi), ch. 6. The images of water in Secs. I–IV of *The Heart's Garden / The Garden's Heart* seem to be the echoes of Ch. 8 in Lao-tzu.

26. Rexroth, *Collected Longer Poems*, p. 284.

27. Rexroth, *Collected Longer Poems*, p. 288.

28. Rexroth, *Collected Longer Poems*, p. 297. Most probably the temple mentioned here is Daitokuji and the noise has come from around Ōmiya Street. Rexroth was staying at that time at Rakucho Bekkan, a Japanese-style inn, Ōmiya-Rokken sagaru Higashiiru, near the famous Zen temple. He had been introduced to the manager of the inn by Gary Snyder.

29. Rexroth, *Collected Longer Poems*, pp. 301, 301–2, 300, and 302.

30. Rexroth, *Collected Longer Poems*, p. 303.

31. Rexroth, *Collected Longer Poems*, p. 306.

32. Rexroth, *Collected Longer Poems*, p. 299. When he was in Japan (1974–75), Rexroth told people he was seriously interested in Shingon Buddhism. When he visited Japan the fourth time in 1978, at a press interview at Kagoshima University on July 6, he repeated, "Tell'm I am a Buddhist" to the interpreter. *The South Japan Press* reported him saying, "The last wish of mine who am a Buddhist is to stay at Daikakuji in Kyoto for about a week," on July 8, 1978.

33. Rexroth, *Collected Longer Poems*, pp. 299–300; and Gibson, p. 134.

34. Rexroth, *Collected Longer Poems*, pp. 293 and 297. The garden of "Dasenji" must be that of Daisen-in in Daitokuji, Kyoto. Devadatta, a cousin of Gautama, studied under him, excelled in magic, and later revolted against Gautama.

35. Rexroth, *Collected Longer Poems*, pp. 292 and ii. The temple in question is Zenkyo-an, one of the smaller temples in Kenninji, Yamato Oji Shijo Sagaru, Kyoto.

36. Kongō, an Indian weapon, represents the highest wisdom. As illustrated in the mandala, Kongo Kai, or the Adamant World, is the world of

phenomena of all the universe in which Dainichi, as the incarnation of the supreme wisdom, is immanent. Taizo Kai signifies the Hoarding World, in which, as in the mother's womb, everything is nourished by Dainichi Nyorai as the incarnation of the supreme grace.

37. Rexroth, *Collected Longer Poems*, p. 305, pp. 306–7.

38. Rexroth, *Collected Longer Poems*, p. 307.

39. Rexroth, *Collected Longer Poems*, p. 295.

40. Rexroth, *One Hundred More Poems from the Japanese* (New York: New Directions, 1976), p. 65.

41. Rexroth, *Collected Longer Poems*, p. 288.

42. Rexroth, *One Hundred More Poems*, p. 71.

43. Rexroth, *Collected Longer Poems*, p. 303.

44. Rexroth, *One Hundred More Poems*, pp. 58 and 69.

45. Rexroth, *Collected Longer Poems*, p. 303.

46. Rexroth, *One Hundred More Poems*, p. 56.

47. During his third visit, Rexroth stayed at Rakucho Bekkan near Daitokuji, where he had stayed before for a while. But in November 1974, he moved to a house near Senyuji, 23 Minami Hiyoshi, Imakumano, Higashiyamaku, Kyoto. The house was owned by Toranosuke Okumura, and had a tea ceremony room, an anteroom, a *zashiki* (parlor) with *tatami* (mat), a bath tub made of cypress, a kitchen, *irori* (hearth), and a *doma* (dirt floor) for the stable. According to the family story of the Okumuras, it was originally a thatched, four-storied, 800-year-old house in Takayama, Hida, but was later remodeled to a one-storied house. It was built with original one-foot-square chestnut pillars smoothed without using a plane. The grandfather of the present owner bought the building, brought it to Kyoto, and roofed it with tiles baked from the clay of Hida. He used it as a tea house in his huge garden with seven ponds. After World War II, Donald Keene and E. G. Seidensticker rented the tea house for a while. Rexroth liked it, and its surroundings, also. He used to walk through the woods and hills and tumuli around Senyūji. It was in this house that most of the poems in *The Morning Star* (New York: New Directions, 1979) were written. The house was donated to Doshisha University in 1978 and is now standing on the Imadegawa campus.

48. In Toyonaka, Rexroth and his wife Carol Tinker stayed with Morgan Gibson, who was then teaching at Osaka University as visiting professor. During his stay in Kyoto, he gave a lecture for the Kansai Comparative Literature Association at Kyoto American Center on Japanese and American poetry on July 1. He gave another lecture at Kagoshima University on July 6 on a similar subject, and another at Fukuoka American Center on July 7 on contemporary American poetry.

49. The Kenneth Rexroth Poetry Award for Women Students was initiated by Rexroth, who entrusted $100 to Yuzuru Katagiri and Sanehide Kodama when he left Kyoto in 1975.

50. Kenneth Rexroth, *New Poems* (New York: New Directions, 1974), p. 22.

51. Morgan Gibson, "Rexroth's Dharma," Gardner, ed., *For Rexroth: The Ark 14*, pp. 27 and 31.

52. For instance, at the "navel" is the center in which "one is conscious

in the physical body 'of all kinds of astral influences, vaguely feeling that some of them are friendly and some hostile without in the least knowing why.'" At the "spleen," one is "enabled to remember 'only partially' vague astral journeys, with sometimes half-remembrance of a blissful sensation of flying through the air." At the "heart," "man is instinctively aware of the joys and sorrows of others, sometimes reproducing in himself their physical aches and pains." Between the eyebrows, "there is a power of magnification by means of an 'etheric' flexible tube which resembles 'the microscopic snake on the head-dress of the Pharaohs.'" Arthur Avalon, *The Serpent Power* (1919; reprint New York: Dover Publications, 1974), p. 9.

53. Avalon, pp. 9–10.

54. Rexroth, *One Hundred Poems*, pp. 12, 52, and x–xi.

55. Rexroth, *New Poems*, pp. 29 and 32. Kimiko Nakazawa was an interpreter for Rexroth while he was attending the International Japanologists' Conference in Kyoto, 1972.

56. Gibson, "Rexroth's Dharma," p. 32; Rexroth, *One Hundred Poems*, p. 118; and Rexroth, *New Poems*, p. 26.

57. Rexroth, *Morning Star*, p. 4.

58. Gibson, "Rexroth's Dharma," p. 32.

59. Sanehide Kodama, "The Poetry of Rexroth—From Beat to Post-Beat Period," *The Rising Generation*, December 1975. One day when I visited him in the spring of 1975 at the tea house, he showed me the manuscript of the poem without a word, painfully smiling, still weak. I read the poem and immediately thought of the song of the swan. But I did not mention it. I looked at him. He only smiled.

60. Rexroth, *Morning Star*, p. 8. When I hesitatingly asked him who the "you" in the poem was, he smilingly replied, "Someone living in Yamashina." And then, as if murmuring to himself, he added, "The poem is a sort of adaptation from *Manyoshu*."

61. Rexroth, *One Hundred More Poems*, p. 68.

62. Rexroth, *Morning Star*, pp. 35 and 36.

63. Rexroth, *One Hundred More Poems*, p. 27, 81, 77, and 82.

64. Rexroth, *Morning Star*, p. 83. Part 5 is a "conflation" of three tankas on pages 79, 45, and 36 of *One Hundred More Poems*. Part 8 contains at least three tankas in fragments.

Chapter 5

1. For instance, while I was a student at Amherst College, 1956–58, I was asked the same question several times. It was a standard joke among Japanese students in the United States at that time. Shūichi Kato recollects in 1964 that he spent a year in Paris ten years before "without finding a line referring to Japan in the daily papers" there. Shūichi Kato, "Japan Seen from Abroad," *What is Japanese?* (Tokyo: Kōdansha, 1976), p. 51. The newspapers in the States did a little better than that.

2. See Yasuhiro Yoshizaki, ed., *Studies in Japanese Literature and Language:*

A Bibliography of English Materials (Tokyo: Nichigai Associates, 1979) for further information on translations and studies of Japanese Literature.

3. Richard Wright, "Haikus," *Richard Wright Reader* eds. Ellen Wright and Michel Fabre (New York: Harper and Row, 1978), pp. 252, 254, and 251.

4. Wright, *Reader*, pp. 875, 252 and 251. The editors of the book (one of whom is the widow of Richard Wright) write that "Wright was able to inject a deeply personal tone to these pieces." (p. 243).

5. Wright, *Reader*, p. 251 and 254.

6. Quoted from Richard Wright's typescript. File 162, "Winter," p. 5.

7. Richard Wright, *Black Boy: A Record of Childhood and Youth* (New York: Harper and Brothers, 1945), Ch. 2.

8. Wright, *Reader*, p. 243. According to Fabre, Wright "borrowed the four volumes by R. H. Blyth on the art of haiku in order to systematically learn the complex rules of its composition." Michel Fabre, *The Unfinished Quest of Richard Wright*, trans. from French by Isabel Barzun (New York: William Morrow, 1973), p. 505.

9. R. H. Blyth, *Haiku*, Vol. 1 (Tokyo: Hokuseido Press, 1949), p. 373.

10. Blyth, vol. 1, p. 382.

11. Blyth, vol. 1, p. 384; and Fabre, p. 505.

12. Blyth, pp. 163, 164, and 172.

13. Richard Wright, "Haiku," Typescript, file 161, pp. 37 and 39; file 162, "Summer," p. 1, and "Winter," p. 4; and file 161, p. 5.

14. Wright, "Haiku," Typescript, file 161, p. 5; and Wright, *Reader*, pp. 252 and 253.

15. Wright, *Reader*, p. 254.

16. David Bakish, *Richard Wright* (New York: Frederick Ungar, 1973), p. 96.

17. Wright, "Haiku," Typescript, file 162, p. 2; file 161a, nos. 12 and 19.

18. "She [Ella] told how Bluebeard had duped and married his seven wives, how he had loved and slain them, how he had hanged them up by their hair in a dark closet. The tale made the world around me be, throb, live. . . . My imagination blazed." Wright, *Black Boy*, Ch. 2.

19. Wright, *Reader*, p. 253.

20. Paul F. Cummins, *Richard Wilbur: A Critical Essay* (Grand Rapids, Mich.: William S. Eerdmans, 1971), p. 5.

21. Harold G. Henderson, *An Introduction to Haiku* (New York: Doubleday, 1958), p. 22. When I met Wilbur in 1969, he confirmed the point that he had once read Henderson's book.

22. Richard Wilbur, "The Bottles Become New Too," *Quarterly Review of Literature* 7 (November 1953), p. 188; and "The Genie in the Bottle," *Mid-Century American Poets*, ed. John Ciardi (New York: Twayne Publishers, 1950), p. 7.

23. Richard Wilbur, "Sumptuous Destitution," *Emily Dickinson: A Collection of Critical Essays*, ed. Richard Sewall (Englewood Cliffs, N.J.: Prentice-Hall, 1963), p. 128.

24. At his drawing room I noticed Wilbur standing and talking to himself, looking at the snow through the window. "I think tea with rum is what it

should be on a day like this," he said. Then he went into the kitchen. I heard him repeat the same words to his wife. In a short while three cups of tea with the strong fragrance of rum were brought out. It tasted good on a snowy day, and I was reminded of the Japanese custom of serving different food with the change of seasons and, sometimes, of weather, too.

25. Cummins, p. 44.

26. Atsuo Nakagawa, "On New Trends in the American Haiku," *Poetry Nippon* 55 and 56 (September 1981), p. 13. Nakagawa thinks that Earl Miner's *Japanese Linked Poetry* (Princeton: Princeton University Press, 1979) and some other recent translations of Japanese renga may have been influential.

27. Cor van den Heuvel, ed., *The Haiku Anthology* (Garden City, N.Y.: Doubleday, 1974), pp. xxvii, 28, and 127.

28. Van den Heuvel, pp. 84 and 136.

29. Jack Kerouac, Albert Saijo, and Lew Welch, *Trip Trap: Haiku along the Road from San Francisco to New York, 1959* (Bolinas, Calif.: Grey Fox Press, 1973), p. 32.

30. Van den Heuvel, pp. 17 and 92, 22 and 83, 9, and 191.

31. Van den Heuvel, pp. 253–78.

32. Allen Ginsberg, *Journals: Early Fifties Early Sixties*, ed. Gordon Ball (New York: Grove Press, 1977), pp. 92–95; and William Carlos Williams, "Introduction: Howl for Carl Solomon," *Howl and Other Poems* by Allen Ginsberg (San Francisco: City Lights Books, 1956), p. 7.

33. Ginsberg, *Journals*, pp. 95 and xx.

34. Allen Ginsberg, *Kaddish and Other Poems, 1958–1960* (San Francisco: City Lights Books, 1961), p. 16; and *Journals*, p. 94.

35. In one of the interviews, Ginsberg says, "I'm not a specialist in Zen; I know some Zen people like Gary Snyder and Watts and Roshi Suzuki." He shows more interest in abdominal breathing, "Om Ah Hūm." *Allen Ginsberg Verbatim: Lectures on Poetry, Politics, Consciousness* ed. Gordon Ball (New York: McGraw-Hill, 1975), p. 9.

36. Thomas Lyon, "Gary Snyder, A Western Poet," *Western American Literature*, 3 (Fall 1968), pp. 209–10.

37. Gary Snyder, "Lookout's Journal," *Earth House Hold* (New York: New Directions, 1969), p. 8. "Om Mani Padme Hum" literally means, "Verily, in the lotus there is pearl (treasure)." "Zenga" is a Zen painting.

38. Dembo, p. 27.

39. See Snyder's poem in "Hitch Haiku." Kanji means Chinese character in Japanese.

> Old kanji hid by dirt
> on skidroad Jap town walls
> down the hill
> to the Wobbly hall

Gary Snyder, "Hitch Haiku," *The Back Country* (New York: New Directions, 1968), p. 24. "Wobbly" refers to the Industrial Workers of the World. The scene is in Seattle.

40. Bob Steuding, *Gary Snyder* (Boston: Twayne Publishers, 1976), p. 62.

41. Gary Snyder, *Regarding Wave* (New York: New Directions, 1970),

pp. 79, 74. Totsugawa, the River Totsu, runs down from the high southern mountains of Nara Prefecture.

42. Roy Harvey Pearce, *The Continuity of American Poetry* (Princeton: Princeton University Press, 1961), p. 274; and Gary Snyder, "Why Tribe," *Earth House Hold*, p. 114.

43. Steuding, pp. 39–45, 66–74.

44. Gary Snyder, Letter to the author, March 10, 1982.

45. Gary Snyder, *The Real Work: Interviews and Talks, 1964–1979*, ed. William Scott McLean (New York: New Directions, 1980), p. 66.

46. p. 94.

47. According to Hisao Kanaseki, Ruth Sasaki had been in Daitokuji since the end of World War II, studying and translating Buddhist writings such as Rinzairoku (Lin-chi Lu) into English with a group of Japanese and American scholars, including Kanaseki. She was a wealthy woman and was determined to restore Ryosenan there by the will of her second husband Shigetsu Sasaki, whom she had met at the First Zen Institute of America in New York before the war.

48. Hisao Kanaseki, "American Literature and Zen," *Gendai Shisō* (Seidosha), 8, no. 14 (1980), p. 46. Alan Watts had been married to Ruth Sasaki's daughter by her first husband, and was then in San Francisco.

49. Kanaseki, "American Literature and Zen," p. 46. *Unsui* is a Zen monk living in a temple in ascetic practice under a master. He is free to leave the Zen community any time in search of the truth like "cloud" and "water."

50. A *koji* is one who, while usually living outside of the temple, participates in Buddhist practices in the temple under a master. According to Mrs. Nakabayashi, who has been working at Rinko-in (with her elder sister, Mrs. Kobayashi, who died in 1981), Snyder did not "live" there, but "stayed" there, while Walter Nowick was living there.

Walter Nowick, now Rōshi at a Zen institute in Surry, Maine, appears as "W" in Snyder's journal in his *Earth House Hold*, climbs Mount Hiei with Snyder (May 25, 1956), and "sits down at black piano" and "plays Haydn" (October 6, 1956).

According to Mrs. Nakabayashi, Snyder had a big bicycle. She recollects that once she saw him on this bicycle, crossing the front yard of the temple on the white gravel, and she cautioned him not to. She remembers him as often wearing simple clothes, carrying a large cloth bag on his shoulder. (Mrs. Nakabayashi to the author in conversation on March 8, 1982).

51. Kanaseki, p. 46. According to Nanrei Kobori Roshi, who knew Gary Snyder at Daitokuji, this remark by Isshū Miura has "deep meaning." It seems to mean to him that Gary Snyder has "savor in his personality," but also has "something to be washed off." (Nanrei Kobori to the author, March 13, 1982). Sand may stand for "words" or "freedom."

52. Quoted from Gary Snyder, letter to Will Petersen, August 9, 1956.

53. Gary Snyder, letters to Will Petersen, August 9 and September 17, 1956.

54. In Sanjūsangendo, there are 1,001 statues of "one thousand-armed" Kannon carved from wood in the eleventh and twelfth centuries. The wooden statues in Hōryūji in Nara date back to the seventh century.

55. Steuding, p. 50.

56. Gary Snyder, "Japan First Time Around," *Earth House Hold*, p. 34.

57. In reply to Will Petersen, Snyder wrote him on January 4, 1957, with his comments on the poem Petersen had sent to him.

> The romantic language—"marked by song" "eternal quiet" etc & emphasis on beauty gives it a feeling of 19 cent. aestheticism which I think is probably far removed from your actual intention. The phrasing & language is far from normal speech, & it is not the crisp language of modern poetry either. Well all this just goes to show how complicated poetry is when you start taking account of the tradition & the audience.

Snyder was by this time well aware that "taking account of the tradition & the audience" led him to believe that the language of modern poetry would be "crisp."

58. Gary Snyder, letter to Will Petersen, from "Just off Singapore," September 6, 1957. He had signed "a thing called ship's article, which means I am supposed to stay on this ship until it goes back to America—which won't be for another five months unless the engine breaks down or the crew goes totally mad, which it may well do."

59. Gary Snyder, letter to Will Petersen, from "Bay of Bengal," September 8, 1957. *Bancha* is common Japanese green tea made of less tender tea leaves, and *tsukemono* are pickles.

60. Gary Snyder, letter to Will Petersen, from "Aegean Sea," December 22, 1957.

61. Gary Snyder, "Tanker Notes," September 12, 1957, *Earth House Hold*, pp. 56–57.

62. Gary Snyder, "A Stone Garden," sec. 3, *Riprap, & Cold Mountain Poems* (San Francisco: Four Seasons Foundation, 1976), p. 22. "Narahito" in some editions should be Narihira.

63. The episode in *The Tales of Ise* is as follows:

> They continued to travel and came to a very large river flowing between Musashi and Shimofusa. It was called the River Sumida. They took a rest by the bank and talked to one another, looking back on how far they had traveled. Then the oarsman of the ferry cried, "Hurry up, and get on the boat. It's getting dark." They got on, but while crossing the river, they were helplessly filled with sorrow. Just then, they saw a white bird with red beak and red legs, about the size of a *shigi* (snipe), floating and feeding on fish in the river. They had not seen such a bird in Miyako, and did not know what it was. So they asked the boatman, and he replied, "This is Miyako-dori." On hearing it, Narihira composed a poem:
>
> > Since you are given that name,
> > Let me ask you,
> > Oh, bird of Miyako,
> > How is my beloved?
>
> And all of them wept on the boat.

From *Ise Monogatari*, p. 23. Translated by the author.

64. Henry David Thoreau, "Economy," *Walden* (New York: Reinhart, 1955), p. 12. "I long ago lost a hound, a bay horse, and a turtledove, and am still on their trail. Many are the travellers I have spoken concerning them ... I have not one or two who had ... even seen the dove disappear behind a cloud."

65. *Manyoshu*, ed. Bummei Tsuchiya with notes (Tokyo: Chikuma-shobō, 1955), vol. 17, p. 162, no. 4011. Translated by the author.

66. Snyder, *Earth House Hold*, p. 38. "My love thoughts these days / Come thick like the summer grass / Which soon as cut and raked / Grows wild again." The poem Snyder translated and attributed to Yakamochi is from the *Manyoshu*, vol. 10, no. 1984.

67. Gary Snyder, letters to Will Petersen, April 22 and May 31, 1958; and Gary Snyder, "Marin-An." See Lok Chua Cheng and N. Sasaki, "Zen and the Title of Gary Snyder's 'Marin-An'," *Notes on Contemporary Literature*, 8, no. 3.

68. Introduction to "Cold Mountain Poems," *Riprap, & Cold Mountain Poems*, p. 33; and *Evergreen Review*, vol. II, no. 6 (August 1958), p. 69.

69. Prof. Hisao Kanaseki recollects that Gary Snyder asked questions of Prof. Yoshitaka Iriya, a Japanese scholar of Chinese literature, about Han-shan's poems at Daitokuji. (Kanaseki to the author, February 17, 1982).

70. Gary Snyder, letter to Will Petersen, September 6, 1957; and Nanrei Kobori Rōshi, conversation with the author, March 13, 1982.

71. "Siwashing it" means "camping or traveling with minimal equipment; roughing it." Richard Ellman and Robert O'Clair, eds., *The Norton Anthology of Modern Poetry* (New York: Norton, 1973), p. 1265, note to Gary Snyder's "Siwashing It Out Once in Siuslaw Forest."

72. Gary Snyder, letter to Will Petersen, July 21, 1958. Among other guests were Nancy Brewer, Albert Saijo, Erika Munk, and Jack Kerouac, the last of whom was to dedicate his *Dharma Bums* to Han-shan. The same story takes Snyder as model for a leading character.

73. Gary Snyder, letter to Will Petersen, January 20, 1959.

74. Cf. Gary Snyder, *The Real Work*, p. 98; and Gary Snyder, letter to Philip Whalen, March 16, 1959, *Origin 2* (July 1961), p. 31.

75. Gary Snyder, letter to Philip Whalen, September 23, year unspecified, *Origin 2* (June 1961), p. 32. The letter probably was written in 1959, since the two preceding letters and the two following poems printed in the June 1961 issue of *Origin 2* were written in 1959. "Pine River" may be a curious hybrid as a literal translation of "Matsue" by Snyder. *Matsu* is "pine," and *e*, "an inlet, gulf, or a lake," in Japanese. But in Chinese, the same character means "a large river."

76. The full address of the house was Konoecho, Yase, Sakyōku, Kyoto. "Yase: September" printed in the June 1961 issue of *Origin 2*, has a second stanza between the first and last stanzas:

> her breasts are tan & leathery
>   but nipples
>   pink and young.

But this passage had better be dropped as Snyder did in later editions. Women of Yase are traditionally known as hard workers, for hundreds of years until the end of World War II, gathering and selling chopped wood for fuel to the citizens of Kyoto. In recent years, dressed in old-fashioned costumes of *oharame*, they have sold rice cakes and pickles.

77. Snyder spent a night then in Rinkō-in in Shōkoku-ji, where the corridors facing the garden are all carpeted.

78. Murasaki Shikibu, *The Tale of Genji*, trans. Arthur Waley (1925; reprint New York: Random House, 1960), pp. 67 and 68.

79. Gary Snyder, letter to the author, March 10, 1982. The interior evidence suggests that "A Spring Night in Shokoku-ji" was written in May 1957. It opens with the lines, "Eight years ago this May / We walked, . . ." and they had "broken up" in 1949. But according to his letter, Snyder wrote after he saw the play *Yūgao* in December 12, 1960. Probably he wrote the first draft of the poem in May 1957, and reworked it after he saw the play in 1960.

80. Scott Johnson to the author in conversation on February 16, 1982; and Gary Snyder, letter to Will Petersen, February 1, 1958.

81. "Generally speaking, foreigners do not like to go to the public baths here, because people often stare at them out of curiosity," recollect the secretaries of the YMCA at which he taught English. "But Snyder did not mind."

> getting dressed, in the mirror,
>   the bath-girl with a pretty mole and a
> red skirt is watching me:
>   am I
>   different?

By "bath-girl" he meant "a young woman who took money from both sides, men and women, as you come in." Gary Snyder, Letter to the author, March 10, 1982.

82. Snyder wrote these sketches of the public baths that he frequented on his way home from town along the River Takano. He wrote in the same letter of March 10, 1982:

> Those were several different public baths that I stopped at on the way home from evening sitting at Daitokuji sōdō, on my way to a little house that I was renting in Yase. I certainly couldn't describe where they are now, except somewhere along the Takano River.

83. According to Snyder, it was "a small house that was ten minutes' walk from the monastery," where he was "continually wrestling with problems of translation and terminology" of the Buddhist writings. Snyder, *The Real Work*, p. 100. The house was at 31 Nishinoyama-cho, Shichiku, Kitaku, Kyoto. It had a cozy Japanese-style garden with a stone lantern. He put out the nameplate made of a *geta*, a wooden clog, on which he wrote *suna-i-da*, in kanji the way his name is pronounced in Japanese. He actually wrote, however, what translates as "sand-well-fields." Close by the house were the stone steps to Shōzenji, a Jōdo sect Buddhist temple, around which, and sometimes into which, Snyder used to walk in his *samue*, working apparel for Zen monks, according to people of the temple. The area has recently been developed; and the house was torn down by the owner, to build a large apartment house called Manshon Takuma.

84. According to Susumu Kamaike, who had translated Basho and Shimpei Kusano into English with Cid Corman, Snyder's Japanese was so excellent that he may well have translated Miyazawa by himself with only a little help. Kamaike recollects that Snyder was always wearing grayish clothes, holding a big cloth bag, and riding on a motorcycle. He did not "overreach" himself, nor "show off." "His simple, natural way of life without affectation always reminded Kamaike of the Zen spirit. Snyder became a great sympathizer of Miyazawa because the 'life style' of the two poets was similar." (Susumu Kamaike, in conversation with the author, February 11, 1982).

85. In his letter to Will Petersen from Okinawa, February 1, 1958, Snyder wrote, "At Naha will buy some bancha [Japanese tea] & a new sewing kit because one I had blew over the side one afternoon while sitting on deck patching dungarees."

86. Robert Kern, "Recipe for Transcendence: Gary Snyder and Archetype West," Typescript of paper read at the MLA meeting, San Francisco, 1975.

87. The Petersens were living at the same house in Yase that the Snyders had rented earlier.

88. After spending the summer of 1964 in New Mexico and Arizona, Snyder wrote to Petersen that he felt "like a man who's got the monkey off his back—freedom and energy to move & work & communicate like I haven't felt in a long time (and she seems to be experiencing the same sense of release)—" Letter to Will Petersen, September 10, 1964.

89. Gary Snyder, letter to Will Petersen, October 29, 1964. In the same letter he writes that they are "now officially divorced."

90. *Annual Report of Kyoto YMCA*, 1965. The "June" section of "Six Years" is based on his experience at the YMCA.

91. Hisao Kanaseki, in conversation with the author, February 17, 1982.

92. While in the United States, Snyder was very busy. Beside reading and writing, he traveled to British Columbia with Allen Ginsberg, "climbing and sightseeing," in May (Letter to Will Petersen, June 5, 1966), and attended the "Human Be-In" in San Francisco in February 1967. Ferlinghetti and Peters, p. 200.

93. See Sanehide Kodama, "Gary Snyder and 'The Bed in the Sky'," *The YMCA*, no. 241 (April 1, 1968), p. 2. According to one neighbor, Masa was a "hard working girl," "friendly with the neighbors." According to another, "Shijinsan," or "Mr. Poet," used to walk down a couple of blocks to the baker's at the corner to buy bread. Their first son, Kai, was born in April 1968.

94. Snyder, *Earth House Hold*, p. 107.

95. Thomas Parkinson, "The Poetry of Gary Snyder," *Southern Review*, 4 (1968), p. 616.

96. Snyder, "Poetry and the Primitive," *Earth House Hold*, p. 118; Gary Snyder, "The Uses of Light," *Turtle Island*, (New York: New Directions, 1974) p. 61; and Hisao Kanaseki, "Gary Snyder, Buddhism, Kenji Miyazawa," *Notes on Modern American Poetry* (Tokyo: Kenkyusha, 1977), pp. 207–12.

97. Liquid Metal Fast Breeder Reactor.

98. Snyder, "The Wilderness," *Turtle Island*, p. 106; and *The Real Work*, p. 74.

99. Snyder, *The Real Work*, pp. 17 and 4.

100. Snyder, "Why Tribe," *Earth House Hold*, p. 116; and "Poetry and the Primitive," *Earth House Hold*, p. 127.

101. Thomas J. Lyon, "The Ecological Vision of Gary Snyder," *Kansas Quarterly*, 2 (1970), p. 118.

102. Eg. *The Pioneers*, Ch. 24.

103. Snyder, "Poetry and the Primitive," *Earth House Hold*, p. 120; *The Real Work*, pp. 56–57, 63, 73–75.

104. Snyder, "Buddhism and the Coming Revolution," *Earth House Hold*, p. 92. "Sangha" is the ideal Buddhist community.

105. Snyder, "Passage to More Than India," *Earth House Hold*, p. 105; "Poetry and the Primitive," *Earth House Hold*, p. 129; "Energy Is Eternal," *Turtle Island*, p. 104; and "Buddhism and the Coming Revolution," pp. 91–92.

106. *Avatamsaka-Sutra*, Book 26. *Shōwa Shinzan Kokuyaku Daizōkyō* (Tokyo: Tōhō Shoin, 1929), vol. 10, pp. 251–52, translated into English by the author. Sumeru (Shumisen in Japanese) is the mythic high mountain in the center of the world, soaring up from the ocean. On top of it is the palace of Sakradevanam Indra (Taishakuten in Japanese), and about it the sun and the moon turn. Around the mountain are seven gold mountains, beyond which spread four continents.

107. Snyder, *The Real Work*, p. 100.

108. As for the sutra of Hui Nêng, the Lankavatara-sutra, and Po-chang Huai-hai, see Snyder, *Earth House Hold*, pp. 2, 34, 69–82, and 109. Regarding Hsiang-yen, see "One Should Not Talk to a Skilled Hunter about What Is Forbidden by the Buddha," *Turtle Island*, p. 66. As to the Prajna-paramita-sutra, Masao Ikeda recalls that Snyder recited the sutra by heart at his farewell party at Kobe. Masao Ikeda, "Jack Kerouac and Gary Snyder—A Phase of the Post-War American Poetry," *Mukogawa Literary Review*, no. 17, 1981, p. 15.

109. Snyder, "Why Tribe," *Earth House Hold*, p. 114.

110. "The Sutra of Hui Nêng," Book I, ed. and trans. with notes by Sōkan Kōno, *Zen: Chinese Classics*, ed. Keiji Nishitani (Tokyo: Chikuma-shobō, 1969), vol. 6, p. 108, translated into English by the author.

111. Snyder, *The Real Work*, p. 17.

112. Snyder, *The Real Work*, pp. 67 and 33. Cf. Ezra Pound, "The Tree."

113. Snyder, *The Real Work*, p. 33; and "Japan First Time Around," *Earth House Hold*, p. 34.

Conclusion

1. T. S. Eliot, *After Strange Gods*, pp. 40–41.

2. Edward W. Said, *Orientalism* (New York: Vintage Books, 1979), p. 2.

3. Charles Tomlinson, ed., *The Oxford Book of Verses in English Translation* (Oxford: Oxford University Press, 1980).

4. Endymion Wilkinson, *Misunderstanding: Europe vs. Japan*, revised edition (Tokyo: Chūōkōron-sha, 1982), pp. 20–21.

5. Shunsuke Kamei, "The Hearts of the Americans Gazing at Japan,"

America in the Books: There Must be a Man behind the Book (Tokyo: Tōjusha, 1982), pp. 174–75.

6. Tsutomu Fukuda, "Salinger's Haiku," *Poetry Nippon*, no. 23 (Summer 1973), p. 27. The similar attitude is found in the essays by other Japanese scholars, though with more emphasis on the ingenuity of the American poets. E.g. Naoko Thornton, "The Poet and the Society: Robert Bly and America during the 1970s," *Studies in English and American Literature* (Nihon Joshi Daigaku), no. 17 (March 1982); Shirō Tsunoda, *Ezra Pound and the Far Eastern Cultures* (Tokyo: Tsunoda, 1982); and Taiken Tanaka, "Gary Snyder and Buddhism: On His Relation to the Temple," *Journal of Zen Institute at Aichi Gakuin University*, no. 11 (March 1982).

Bibliography

Aoki, Masaru, ed. *An Anthology of Chinese Poetry* (in Chinese and Japanese). Vol. 8. Tokyo: Shūeisha, 1965.

Aston, W. G. *A History of Japanese Literature*. 1899; reprint Rutland, Vt.: Charles E. Tuttle, 1972.

Avalon, Arthur. *The Serpent Power*. 1919; reprint New York: Dover Publications, 1964.

Babcock, Winnifred. *A Japanese Blossom*. New York: Harper and Brothers, 1906.

——. *A Japanese Nightingale*. New York: Harper and Brothers, 1901.

Bakish, David. *Richard Wright*. New York: Frederick Ungar, 1973.

Baumann, Walter. *The Rose in the Steel Dust: An Examination of the Cantos of Ezra Pound*. Coral Gables: University of Miami Press, 1970.

Bradford, William. *Of Plymouth Plantation: The Pilgrims in America*. Ed. Harvey Wish. New York: Capricon, 1962.

Belasco, David. *Six Plays by David Belasco*. Boston: Little, Brown, 1928.

Blaker, Richard. *The Needle-Watcher: The Will Adams Story, British Samurai*. 1932; reprint Rutland, Vt.: Charles E. Tuttle, 1973.

Blyth, R. H. *Haiku*, 4 vols. Tokyo: Hokuseido Press, 1949–1952.

Brooker, Peter. *A Student's Guide to the Selected Poems of Ezra Pound*. London: Faber and Faber, 1979.

Brooks, Van Wyck. *New England: Indian Summer, 1865–1915*. New York: E. P. Dutton, 1940.

Bridson, D. G., ed. "An Interview with Ezra Pound." In James Laughlin, ed. *New Directions 17*. New York: New Directions, 1959.

Caldwell, Helen. *Michio Ito: The Dancer and His Dances*. Berkeley: University of California Press, 1977.

Cheng, Lok Chua and N. Sasaki. "Zen and the Title of Gary Snyder's 'Marin-An'." *Notes on Contemporary Literature* 8, no. 3.

Chisolm, Lawrence. *Fenollosa: The Far East and American Culture*. New Haven: Yale University Press, 1963.

Christy, Arthur. *The Orient in American Transcendentalism*. New York: Columbia University Press, 1932.

Crapsey, Adelaide. *The Complete Poems and Collected Letters of Adelaide Crapsey*. Ed. Susan Sutton Smith. Albany: State University of New York Press, 1977.

Cummins, Paul F. *Richard Wilbur: A Critical Essay*. Grand Rapids, Mich.: William S. Eerdmans, 1971.

Damon, S. Foster. *Amy Lowell: A Chronicle*. Boston: Houghton Mifflin, 1935.

Dana, Richard Henry, Jr. *The Journal of Richard Henry Dana, Jr*. Ed. Robert E. Lucid. Cambridge: Harvard University Press, 1968.

Davie, Donald. *Ezra Pound: Poet as Sculptor*. London: Routledge and Kegan Paul, 1965.

Dekker, George. "Myth and Metamorphosis." In *New Approaches to Ezra Pound*. Ed. Eva Hesse. London: Faber and Faber, 1969.

———. *Sailing after Knowledge*. London: Routledge and Kegan Paul, 1963.

Dembo, L. S. *The Confucian Odes of Ezra Pound: A Critical Appraisal*. Berkeley: University of California Press, 1963.

Deutsch, Babette. *Poetry in Our Time*. New York: Columbia University Press, 1958.

Dryden, John, trans. *The Life of St. Francis Xavier*. Vol. 16 of *The Works of John Dryden*. London: William Miller, 1808.

Dulles, Foster Rhee. *Yankees and Samurai: America's Role in the Emergence of Modern Japan, 1791–1900*. New York: Harper & Row, 1965.

Durnell, Hazel. *Japanese Cultural Influences of American Poetry and Drama*. Tokyo: The Hokuseido Press, 1982.

Egashira, Iwao. *William Adams and the English House in Hirado* (in Japanese). Kyoto: Yamaguchi Shoten, 1980.

Eliot, T. S. *After Strange Gods: A Primer of Modern Heresy*. London: Faber and Faber, 1934.

———. *Essays on Poetry and Criticism*. Ed. Kazumi Yano. Tokyo: Shōhaku-sha, 1959; reprint 1971.

———. *To Criticize the Critic*. London: Faber and Faber, 1965.

Espey, J. J. *Ezra Pound's Mauberley: A Study of Composition*. Berkeley: University of California Press, 1955.

Fabre, Michel. *The Unfinished Quest of Richard Wright*. Trans. Isabel Barzun. New York: William Morrow, 1973.

Fang, Achilles. "Fenollosa and Pound." *Harvard Journal of Asian Studies* 20 (1957).

Fenollosa, Ernest. *The Chinese Written Character as a Medium for Poetry*, Ed. Ezra Pound. San Francisco: City Lights Books, 1964.

——. Notebooks. Beinecke Rare Book and Manuscript Library, Yale University.

Fenollosa, Mary McNeil. *The Dragon Painter*. Boston: Little, Brown, 1906.

Ferlinghetti, Lawrence, and Nancy J. Peters. *Literary San Francisco*. San Francisco: City Lights Books, 1980.

Ficke, Arthur Davison, *Chats on Japanese Prints*. London: Ernest Benn, 1915; reprint Rutland, Vt.: Charles E. Tuttle Co., 1958.

Flint, F. Cudworth. *Amy Lowell*. Minneapolis: University of Minnesota Press, 1969.

Fujii, Otoo. "'The Fallen Blossom' is not a Haiku by Moritake" (in Japanese). *Studies of Haiku*. May 1941.

Fukuda, Rikutaro. *In the Shadows of the West: A Comparative Study of Literature* (in Japanese). Tokyo: ELEC, 1972.

Fukuda, Tsutomu. "Salinger's Haiku." *Poetry Nippon* 23 (Summer 1973).

Gallup, Donald, ed. *A Bibliography of Ezra Pound*. London: Rupert Hart-Davis, 1963.

Gardner. Geoffrey, ed. *For Rexroth: The Ark 14*. New York: The Ark, 1980.

Gayn, Mark. *Japan Diary*. 1951; reprint Rutland, Vt.: Charles E. Tuttle, 1981.

Gibney, Frank. *Japan: The Fragile Super Power*, rev. ed. New York: Norton, 1979.

Gibson, Morgan. *Kenneth Rexroth*. New York: Twayne Publishers, 1972.

Giles, H. A. *Chinese Poetry in English Verse*. London: B. Quaritich, 1898.

——. *A History of Chinese Literature*. London: William Heineman, 1901.

Ginsberg, Allen. *Allen Ginsberg Verbatim: Lectures on Poetry, Politics, Consciousness*. Ed. Gordon Ball. New York: McGraw-Hill, 1975.

——. *Howl and Other Poems*. San Francisco: City Lights Books, 1956.

——. *Kaddish and Other Poems, 1958–1960*. San Francisco: City Lights Books, 1961.

——. *Journals: Early Fifties Early Sixties*. Ed. Gordon Ball. New York: Grove Press, 1977.

Gould, Jean. *Amy: The World of Amy Lowell and the Imagist Movement*. New York: Dodd, Mead & Co., 1975.

Greenslet, Ferris. *The Lowells and their Seven Worlds*. Boston: Houghton Mifflin, 1946.

Harmer, J. B. *Victory in Limbo: A History of Imagism, 1908–1917*. New York: St. Martin's Press, 1975.

Haruna, Tōru. *The Story of Drifting of Nippon Otokichi* (in Japanese). Tokyo: Shōbunsha, 1979.

Hata, Hisashi, et al. *Nō: Sources and Adaptations* (in Japanese). Tokyo: Ōfūsha, 1977.

Henderson, Harold G. *An Introduction to Haiku*. New York: Doubleday, 1958.

Hilen, Andrew, ed. *The Letters of Henry Wadsworth Longfellow*. Cambridge: Harvard University Press, 1966.

Hoffman, Yoel, trans. *The Sound of the One Hand: 281 Zen Kōans with Answers*. New York: Basic Books, 1975.

Homberger, Eric, ed. *Ezra Pound: The Critical Heritage*. London: Routledge and Kegan Paul, 1972.

Howard, Leon. *Herman Melville: A Biography*. Berkeley: University of California Press, 1967.

Hughes, Glenn. *Imagism and the Imagists*. Stanford: Stanford University Press, 1931.

Hulme, T. E. *Speculations: Essays on Humanism and the Philosophy of Art*. Ed. Herbert Read. London: Routledge and Kegan Paul, 1924; reprint 1954.

Ikeda, Masao. "Jack Kerouac and Gary Snyder—A Phase of the Post-War American Poetry" (in Japanese). *Mukogawa Literary Review* 17 (1981).

Irving, Washington. *The Works of Washington Irving*. New York: AMS Press, 1973.

Ise Monogatari. (*The Tale of Ise*) Ed. Minoru Watanabe. Tokyo: Shin-chōsha, 1976.

Iwahara, Yasuo. "The Poetic Structure of 'Near Perigord' " (in Japanese). *Kōgakuin University Kenkyū Ronsō* 18 (1981).

——. "The Relation between Imagist Poets and Haiku" (in Japanese). *Kōgakuin University Kenkyū Ronsō* 17 (1979).

Johnson, Maurice, Muneharu Kitagaki, and Philip Williams. *Gulliver's*

Travels and Japan: a New Reading. Kyoto: Doshisha Amherst House, 1977.

Jung, Angela Chih-Ying. "Ezra Pound and China." Ph. D. diss., University of Washington, 1955.

Kamei, Shunsuke. *Afoot and Light-Hearted, I Take the Open Road* (in Japanese). Tokyo: Tōjusha, 1982.

——. *America in the Books: There Must Be a Man Behind the Book* (in Japanese). Tokyo: Tōjusha, 1982.

——. *The Circus Is Coming!—Essays on American Popular Culture* (in Japanese) Tokyo: Tokyo University Press, 1976.

Kaizuka, Shigeki. *A History of China* (in Japanese). 3 vols. Tokyo: Iwanami, 1971.

Kanaseki, Hisao. "American Literature and Zen" (in Japanese). *Gendai Shisō* (Seidosha) 8, no. 14 (1980).

——. *Notes on Modern American Poetry* (in Japanese). Tokyo: Kenkyūsha, 1977.

Kato, Shūichi. *What is Japanese?* (in Japanese). Tokyo: Kōdansha, 1976.

Katsushika, Hokusai. *One Hundred Views of Fuji*. [Japan]: n.p., 1835.

——. *Wood-Block Prints on Flowers and Birds*. Tokyo: Kineido, 1891.

Kawai, Hikomitsu. *The Record of the Japanese Shipwrecked* (in Japanese). Tokyo: Shakai Shisō-sha, 1967.

Kawanami, Hideo. "Adelaide Crapsey and Michel Revon: Their Connection with Japanese Literature" (in Japanese). *Osaka College of Commerce Anniversary Festschrift*. Vols. 19–20. (1963).

Keene, Donald. *Japanese Literature: An Introduction for Western Readers*. New York: Grove Press, 1959.

Kennedy, George. "Fenollosa, Pound and the Chinese Character." *Yale Literary Magazine* 126 (1958).

Kenner, Hugh. "More on the Seven Lakes Canto." *Paideuma* 2, no. 1 (Spring 1972).

——. *The Poetry of Ezra Pound*. Norfolk, Conn.: New Directions, 1951.

——. *The Pound Era*. Berkeley: University of California Press, 1971.

Kern, Robert. "Recipe for Transcendence: Gary Snyder and Archetype West." Paper read at the MLA Conference, San Francisco, 1975.

Kerouac, Jack, *Dharma Bums*. New York: Buccaneer Books, 1976.

——, Albert Saijo, and Lew Welch. *Trip Trap: Haiku along the Road from San Francisco to New York, 1959*. Bolinas, Calif.: Grey Fox Press, 1973.

Kikuno, Mutsuo, ed. *Logs and Letters of William Adams* (in English and Japanese). Tokyo: Nan'undo, 1977.

Kodama, Sanehide. "Cathay and Fenollosa's Notebooks." *Paideuma* 11, no. 2 (Fall 1982).

———. "The Chinese Subject in Ezra Pound's Poetry. "*Studies in English Literature*. The English Literary Society of Japan, English Number, 1970.

———. "The Eight Scenes of Sho-sho." *Paideuma* 6, no. 2 (Fall 1977).

———. "Gary Snyder and 'The Bed in the Sky'" (in Japanese). *The YMCA*. No. 241 (April 1, 1968).

———. "The Poetry of Rexroth—From Beat to Post-Beat Period" (in Japanese). *The Rising Generation*. December 1975.

Kokumin Bunko Kankō-kai, eds. *Chinese Classics in Japanese Translation* (in Japanese) 2nd ser., vols. 1 and 25. Tokyo: Kokumin Bunko kankō-kai, 1928.

Kōno, Sōkan, ed. and trans. "The Sutra of Hui Nêng" (in Japanese). In *Zen: Chinese Classics*. Vol. 6. Ed. Keiji Nishitani. Tokyo: Chikuma-shobō, 1969.

Kurumisawa, Atsuo. "Odysseus-Pound as Outis in *The Pisan Cantos*." *Studies in Language and Culture*. Faculty of Language and Culture, Osaka University, 1976.

La Farge, John. *An Artist's Letters from Japan*. New York: Century, 1890; reprint 1897.

Laughlin, James, ed. *New Directions 17*. New York: New Directions, 1959.

Leavis, F. R. *New Bearings in English Poetry*. London: Chatto and Windus, 1959.

Legge, James, trans. *The Chinese Classics*. 3 vols. London: Trübner, 1867–76.

Little, Frances. *The Lady and Sada San*. New York: The Century, 1912.

———. *The Lady of the Decoration*. New York: The Century, 1907.

Long, John Luther. *Madame Butterfly*. New York: Grosset and Dunlap, 1897; reprint 1903.

Longfellow, Charles A. Letters. Charles A. Longfellow Papers. Longfellow National Historic Site, Cambridge, Mass.

Longfellow, Henry Wadsworth. *The Complete Poetical Works of Henry Wadsworth Longfellow*. Boston: Houghton Mifflin, 1899.

———. Letters. Longfellow Papers. Houghton Library, Harvard University.

Longfellow, Samuel, ed. *Life of Henry Wadsworth Longfellow*. New York: AMS Press, 1966.

Lowell, Abbot Lawrence. *Biography of Percival Lowell*. New York: Macmillan, 1935.

Lowell, Amy. *Can Grande's Castle*. New York: Macmillan, 1918.

———. *The Complete Poetical Works of Amy Lowell*. Ed. Louis Untermeyer. Boston: Houghton Mifflin, 1955.

———. Letters. Amy Lowell Papers. Houghton Library, Harvard University.

———. *Pictures of the Floating World*. New York: Macmillan, 1919.

———. *Sword Blades and Poppy Seed*. Boston: Houghton Mifflin, 1914.

———. *Tendencies in Modern American Poetry*. 1917; reprint New York: Octagon Books, 1971.

Lowell, Percival. *Chosön, The Land of the Morning Calm: A Sketch of Korea*. Boston: Ticknor, 1885.

———. Letters. Percival Lowell Papers. Houghton Library, Harvard University.

———. *Noto: An Unexplored Corner of Japan*. Boston: Houghton Mifflin, 1891.

———. *Occult Japan, or the Way of Gods: An Esoteric Study of Japanese Personality and Possession*. Boston: Houghton Mifflin, 1894.

———. *The Soul of the Far East*. Boston: Houghton Mifflin, 1888.

Lyon, Thomas. "The Ecological Vision of Gary Snyder." *Kansas Quarterly* 2 (1970).

———. Gary Snyder, A Western Poet." *Western American Literature* 3 (Fall 1968).

Makin, Peter. *Provence and Pound*. Berkeley: University of California Press, 1978.

Manyoshū (in Japanese). Ed. Bummei Tsuchiya. Tokyo: Chikuma-shobō, 1955.

Masuzu, Hisatoshi. "Diary During the Voyage to America" (in Japanese). *Documents on American Mission, 1860*. Tokyo: Kazama Shobo, 1961.

Materer, Timothy. *Vortex: Pound, Yeats, and Eliot*. Ithaca, N.Y.: Cornell University Press, 1970.

Minagawa, Saburō. *A History of the English House in Hirado* (in Japanese). Tokyo: Shinozaki Shorin, 1979.

———. *Japan as Seen by the British in the Early Tokugawa Period* (in Japanese). Tokyo: Taibundō, 1979.

Miner, Earl. *Japanese Linked Poetry*. Princeton: Princeton University Press, 1979.

——. *The Japanese Tradition in British and American Literature*. Princeton: Princeton University Press, 1958.

——. "Pound, *Haiku*, and the Image." *Hudson Review*, (Winter 1956–57).

Miura, Isshū, and Ruth Fuller Sasaki. *The Zen Kōan: Its History and Use in Rinzai Zen*. New York: Harcourt, Brace & World, 1965.

Miyazaki, Ichisada. *Prosperity of the Empire of Shin* (in Japanese). Tokyo: Jinbutsu Oraisha, 1967.

Miyoshi, Masao. *As We Saw Them: The First Japanese Embassy to the United States (1860)*. Berkeley: University of California Press, 1979.

Morgan, Edmund. *The Birth of the Republic: 1763–1789*. Chicago: University of Chicago Press, 1956.

Muragaki, Norimasa. "Diary" (in Japanese). In *The First Japanese Embassy to America*. Ed. Japan-America Society. Tokyo: Japan-America Society, 1928.

Murasaki, Shikibu. *The Tale of Genji*. Translated by Arthur Waley. 1925; reprint New York: Random House, 1960.

Nakagawa, Atsuo. "On New Trends in the American Haiku." *Poetry Nippon* 55 and 56 (September 1981).

Nakahama, Akira. *The Life of Nakahama Manjiro* (in Japanese). Tokyo: Fuzambō, 1971.

Naruse, Seichi. "Young Japan." *The Seven Arts* (April 1917).

New York Herald, June 17, 1860.

New York Times, January to June 1852.

Norman, Charles. *Ezra Pound*. New York: Macmillan, 1960.

Okakura, Kakuzo. *The Book of Tea*. Ed. Hiroshi Muraoka. Tokyo: Kenkyūsha, 1939.

Osborn, Mary Elizabeth. *Adelaide Crapsey*. Boston: Bruce Humphries, 1933.

Ōura, Yukio. "The Theme of 'At the Hawk's Well'" (in Japanese). *Report of Yeats Society of Japan*, no. 5.

Parkinson, Thomas. "The Poetry of Gary Snyder." *Southern Review* 4 (1968).

Pearce, Roy Harvey. *The Continuity of American Poetry*. Princeton: Princeton University Press, 1961.

Pearlman, D. D. *Barb of Time: On the Unity of Ezra Pound's Cantos*. New York: Oxford University Press, 1969.

Philadelphia Inquirer, June 14 and 15, 1860.

Porter, William N. *A Hundred Verses from Old Japan, Being a Translation of the Hyaku-nin-isshu.* 1909; reprint Rutland, Vt.: Charles E. Tuttle, 1979.

Pound, Ezra. *ABC of Reading.* London: Routledge and Sons, 1934.

———. "A Few Don'ts by an Imagist." *Poetry* 1, no. 6 (March 1913).

———. *The Cantos of Ezra Pound.* New York: New Directions, 1975.

———. "Chinese Poetry." *Today* 3, no. 4 (April 1918).

———, trans. *Cathay.* London: Elkin Mathews, 1915.

———. *Collected Shorter Poems.* London: Faber and Faber, 1952.

———. *Gaudier-Brzeska: A Memoir.* 1916; reprint New York: New Directions, 1960.

———. *The Letters of Ezra Pound: 1907–1941.* Ed. D. D. Paige. New York: Harcourt, Brace, and World, 1950.

———. *Literary Essays of Ezra Pound.* Ed. T. S. Eliot. Norfolk, Conn.: New Directions, 1954.

———. *Patria Mia and the Treatise on Harmony.* London: Peter Owen, 1962.

———. *Ezra Pound: Selected Poems.* Ed. T. S. Eliot. London: Faber and Faber, 1928; reprint 1959.

———. *Ezra Pound: Selected Prose, 1909–1965.* Ed. William Cookson. London: Faber and Faber, 1973.

———. "Tagore's Poetry." *Poetry* 1, no. 3 (December 1912).

———, trans. *The Translations of Ezra Pound.* New York: New Directions, 1963.

——— and Ernest Fenollosa, trans. *The Classic Noh Theatre of Japan.* New York: New Directions, 1959.

Pratt, William, ed. *The Imagist Poem: Modern Poetry in Miniature.* New York: E. P. Dutton, 1963.

Quinn, Bernetta. *Ezra Pound: An Introduction to the Poetry.* New York: Columbia University Press, 1972.

Rexroth, Kenneth. *The Alternative Society: Essays from the Other World.* New York: Herder and Herder, 1972.

———. *Beyond the Mountains.* New York: New Directions, 1951.

———. *Bird in the Bush.* New York: New Directions, 1959.

———. *The Collected Longer Poems of Kenneth Rexroth.* New York: New Directions, 1968.

———. *The Collected Shorter Poems of Kenneth Rexroth.* New York: New Directions, 1966.

———. *The Elastic Retort: Essays in Literature and Ideas*. New York: The Seaburg Press, 1973.

———. *The Morning Star*. New York: New Directions, 1979.

———. *New Poems*. New York: New Directions, 1974.

———, trans. *One Hundred More Poems from the Japanese*. New York: New Directions, 1976.

———, trans. *One Hundred Poems from the Japanese*. New York: New Directions, 1964.

———. *The Phoenix and the Tortoise*. Norfolk, Conn.: New Directions, 1944.

Rizawa, Yikio, ed. *Literatures Beyond the Border* (in Japanese). Tokyo: Eicho-cha, 1976.

Ruihley, Glenn Richard. *The Thorn of a Rose: Amy Lowell Reconsidered*. Hamden, Conn.: Archon Books, 1975.

Ruthven, K. K. *A Guide to Ezra Pound's "Personae" (1926)*. Berkeley: University of California Press, 1969.

Saeki, Shoichi, ed. *America and Europe: Essays on American Culture* (in Japanese), 5. Tokyo: Nan'undo, 1970.

Said, Edward W. *Orientalism*. New York: Vintage Books, 1979.

Sandburg, Carl. *The Complete Poems of Carl Sandburg*. New York: Harcourt, Brace, Jovanovich, 1976.

Sasaki, Genryū. *Poems in Chinese and Japanese on the Eight Famous Scenes by Genryū* (in Japanese). Kyoto: Asami, 1683.

Sato, Kazuo. *Can Rapeflower Be Transplanted?* (in Japanese). Tokyo: Ōfūsha, 1978.

Shelley, Percy Bysshe. *The Complete Works of Percy Bysshe Shelley*. Ed. Roger Ingpen and Walter E. Peck. Vol. 2. New York: Gordian Press, 1965.

Showa Shinzan Kokuyaku Daizokyo (in Japanese), Book 26. Tokyo: Tōhō-shoin, 1929.

Smith, Henry Nash. *Virgin Land: The American West as Symbol and Myth*. Cambridge: Harvard University Press, 1950.

Smith, Susan Sutton. *Adelaide Crapsey*. Boston: Bruce Humphries, 1933.

Snyder, Gary. *The Back Country*. New York: New Directions, 1968.

———, trans. "Cold Mountain Poems." *Evergreen Review* 2, no. 6.

———. *Earth House Hold*. New York: New Directions, 1969.

———. *The Fudo Trilogy*. Berkeley: Shaman Drum, 1973.

———. Letters to Will Petersen.

——. *Myths & Texts*. New York: Totem Press, 1960.
——. *The Real Work: Interviews and Talks, 1964–1979*. Ed. William Scott McLean. New York: New Directions, 1980.
——. *Regarding Wave*. New York: New Directions, 1970.
——. *Riprap, & Cold Mountain Poems*. San Francisco: Four Seasons Foundation, 1976.
——. *Six Sections from Mountains and Rivers without End*. San Francisco: Four Seasons Foundation, 1978.
——. *Turtle Island*. New York: New Directions, 1974.
Steuding, Bob. *Gary Snyder*. Boston: Twayne Publishers, 1976.
Stock, Noel. *The Life of Ezra Pound*. New York: Pantheon Books, 1970.
Sugiura, Akinori. *The Age of Great Sail Ships* (in Japanese). Tokyo: Chuokoronsha, 1979.
Sutton, Walter, ed. *Ezra Pound: A Collection of Critical Essays*. Englewood Cliffs, N.J.: Prentice-Hall, 1963.
Suzuki, Daisetsu. *What is Zen?* (in Japanese). Tokyo: Kadokawa, 1954.
Takebe, Toshio, ed. and trans. *An Anthology of Chinese Poets* (in Chinese and Japanese). 2 vols. Tokyo: Iwanami-shoten, 1957, 1958.
Tanaka, Taiken. "Gary Snyder and Buddhism: On His Relation to the Temple" (in Japanese). *Journal of Zen Institute at Aichi Gakuin University* 11 (March 1982).
Terrell, Carroll F. *A Companion to the Cantos of Ezra Pound*. Vol. 1. Berkeley: University of California Press, 1980.
Thornton, Naoko. "The Poet and the Society: Robert Bly and America during the 1970s" (in Japanese). *Studies in English and American Literature*, Nihon Joshi Daigaku, 17 (March 1982).
Tomii, Ayako, et al. "Guide to *The Cantos* of Ezra Pound: Glosses of Cantos 3, 4, 5, 13, 16, 23, 30, 33, 37, 38, 49, 50, and 75, prepared by Yale Students under the Direction of N. H. Pearson." New Haven: Yale University, 1954.
Tomlinson, Charles, ed. *The Oxford Book of Verses in English Translation*. Oxford: Oxford University Press, 1980.
"'The River-Merchant's Wife: A Letter' Reconsidered" (in Japanese). *Journal of Obirin University, English and American Numbers*, vol. 15.
Tsunoda, Shirō. *Ezra Pound and the Far Eastern Culture* (in Japanese). Tokyo: Tsunoda, 1982.
Ueda, Makoto. *Jumping Frog: Haiku in World Literature* (in Japanese). Tokyo: Meiji Shoin, 1979.
——. *Zeami, Basho, Yeats, Pound: A Study in Japanese and English Poetics*.

The Hague: Mouton, 1965.

Ungar, Barbara. *Haiku in English*. Palo Alto, Calif.: Stanford University Press, 1978.

Untermeyer, Louis, ed. *Modern American and British Poetry*. New York: Harcourt and Brace, 1920; reprint 1942.

———. *Modern American Poetry*. New York: Harcourt, Brace and Howe, 1919.

Van den Heuvel, Cor, ed. *The Haiku Anthology*. Garden City, N.Y.: Doubleday, 1974.

Waley, Arthur, ed. and trans. *Japanese Poetry: The 'Uta'*. 1919; reprint Honolulu: The University Press of Hawaii, 1976.

Walworth, Arthur. *Black Ships Off Japan*. New York: Alfred A. Knopf, 1946; reprint Hamden, Conn.: Archon Books, 1966.

Watts, Alan. *Beat Zen Square Zen and Zen*. San Francisco: City Lights Books, 1959.

Whitman, Walt. *Complete Poetry and Selected Prose*. Ed. James E. Miller, Jr. Boston: Houghton Mifflin, 1959.

Wilbur, Richard. "The Bottles Become New Too." *Quarterly Review of Literature* 7 (November 1953).

———. "The Genie in the Bottle." *Mid-Century American Poets*. Ed. John Ciardi. New York: Twayne Publishers, 1950.

———. "Sumptuous Destitution." *Emily Dickinson: A Collection of Critical Essays*. Ed. Richard Sewall. Englewood Cliffs, N.J.: Prentice-Hall, 1963.

———. *Walking to Sleep: New Poems and Translations*. New York: Harcourt, Brace and World, 1969.

Wilkinson, Endymion. *Misunderstanding: Europe vs. Japan*. Tokyo: Chūōkōron-sha, 1982.

Williams, William Carlos. *The Selected Poems of William Carlos Williams*. New York: New Directions, 1963.

Winston, Alexander. *No Man Knows My Grave: Privateers and Pirates, 1665–1815*. Boston: Houghton Mifflin, 1969.

Winters, Yvor. *The Collected Poems of Yvor Winters*. Manchester, England: Carcanet New Press, 1978.

———. *In Defence of Reason*. Denver: University of Denver Press, 1947.

Wright, Richard. *Black Boy: A Record of Childhood and Youth*. New York: Harper and Brothers, 1945.

———. Haiku. Beinecke Rare Book and Manuscript Library, Yale University.

———. *Richard Wright Reader*. Ed. Ellen Wright and Michel Fabre. New York: Harper & Row, 1978.

Wright, Thomas, ed. *The Travels of Marco Polo*. 1854; reprint. New York: AMS Press, 1968.

Writers at Work: The Paris Review Interviews. London: Secker & Warburg, 1963.

Yamana, Shoji. "The Meaning and the Structure of Exra Pound's 'The River-Merchant's Wife: A Letter'" (in Japanese). *American Literature* Tokyo Chapter, American Literature Association of Japan, no. 29.

Yasuda, Kenneth. *The Japanese Haiku: Its Essential Nature, History, and Possibilities in English*. Rutland, Vt.: Charles E. Tuttle, 1957, 1981.

Yeats, William Butler. *A Vision*. 1925; reprint London: Macmillan, 1974.

Yip, Wai-lim. *Ezra Pound's Cathay*. Princeton: Princeton University Press, 1969.

Yoshizaki, Yasuhiro, ed. *Studies in Japanese Literature and Language: A Bibliography of English Materials*. Tokyo: Nichigai Associates, 1979.

Index